BLACK POLITICS TODAY

The late 1980s ushered in a new era of black politics, the Socioeconomic Transition Era. Coming on the heels of the Protest Era and the Politics Era, the current stage is characterized by the emergence of a new black middle class that came of age after the civil rights struggle. Although class still isn't a strong factor in the external politics of the black community, it is increasingly a wedge issue in the community's internal politics. Black politics today is increasingly less about the interests of the larger group and more about the interests of smaller subgroups within the community.

Theodore J. Davis Jr. argues that the greatest threat to the social and political cohesiveness of the black community may be the rise of a socially and economically privileged group among the ranks of black America. This rift has affected blacks' ability to organize effectively and influence politics. Davis traces the changes in economic status, public opinion, political power and participation, and leadership over three generations of black politics. The result is an insightful analysis of black politics today.

Theodore J. Davis Jr. is Associate Professor in the Department of Political Science and International Relations at the University of Delaware. He has a joint appointment in the Black American Studies Program.

Identity Politics
Routledge Series on Identity Politics
Series Editor: Alvin B. Tillery, Jr., Rutgers University

Group identities have been an important part of political life in America since the founding of the republic. For most of this long history, the central challenge for activists, politicians, and scholars concerned with the quality of U.S. democracy was the struggle to bring the treatment of ethnic and racial minorities and women in line with the creedal values spelled out in the nation's charters of freedom. We are now several decades from the key moments of the twentieth century when social movements fractured America's system of ascriptive hierarchy. The gains from these movements have been substantial. Women now move freely in all realms of civil society, hold high elective offices, and constitute more than 50 percent of the workforce. Most African Americans have now attained middle-class status, work in integrated job sites, and live in suburbs. Finally, people of color from nations in Latin America, Asia, and the Caribbean now constitute the majority of America's immigration pool.

In the midst of all of these positive changes, however, glaring inequalities between groups persist. Indeed, ethnic and racial minorities remain far more likely to be undereducated, unemployed, and incarcerated than their counterparts who identify as white. Similarly, both violence and workplace discrimination against women remain rampant in U.S. society. The Routledge series on identity politics features works that seek to understand the tension between the great strides our society has made in promoting equality between groups and the residual effects of the ascriptive hierarchies in which the old order was rooted.

Some of the core questions that the series will address are: how meaningful are the traditional ethnic, gender, racial, and sexual identities to our understanding of inequality in the present historical moment? Do these identities remain important bases for group mobilization in American politics? To what extent can we expect the state to continue to work for a more level playing field among groups?

Titles in the Series:

Black Politics Today
Theodore J. Davis Jr.

Forthcoming:

Jim Crow Citizenship: How Southern Progressives Remade Race, Citizenship and Liberalism in America
Marek Steedman

BLACK POLITICS TODAY

The Era of Socioeconomic Transition

Theodore J. Davis Jr.

Routledge
Taylor & Francis Group

NEW YORK AND LONDON

First published 2012
by Routledge
711 Third Avenue, New York, NY 10017

Simultaneously published in the UK
by Routledge
2 Park Square, Milton Park, Abingdon, Oxon OX14 4RN

Routledge is an imprint of the Taylor & Francis Group, an informa business

© 2012 Taylor & Francis

The right of Theodore J. Davis Jr. to be identified as author of this work has been asserted by him/her in accordance with sections 77 and 78 of the Copyright, Designs and Patents Act 1988.

Library of Congress Cataloging-in-Publication Data
  Davis, Theodore James.
  Black politics today: the era of socioeconomic transition / Theodore J. Davis Jr.
    p. cm. — (Routledge series on identity politics)
    Includes bibliographical references and index.
  1. African Americans—Politics and government—20th century.   2. African
  Americans—Politics and government—21st century.   3. African Americans—
  Economic conditions—20th century.   4. African Americans—Economic
  conditions—21st century.   5. Middle class African Americans.   6. Social
  classes—United States.   7. Social mobility—United States.   I. Title.   II. Series.
  E185.615D386 2011
  323.1196'073—dc22

                                                                2011009574

ISBN: 978-0-415-87914-9 (hbk)
ISBN: 978-0-415-87915-6 (pbk)
ISBN: 978-0-203-85225-5 (ebk)

Typeset in Bembo
by RefineCatch Limited, Bungay, Suffolk, UK

Printed and bound in the United States of America on acid-free paper by
Walsworth Publishing Company, Marceline, MO

To my wife Juanda, and children Trey, Morgan, and Garrison.
This book is also dedicated to the memory of Rosa "Dadee" Davis, 1888 to 1988.

CONTENTS

LIST OF FIGURES

LIST OF TABLES

ACKNOWLEDGMENTS

Many people have contributed either directly or indirectly to the development of the ideas presented in this book. In attempting to name them, I will no doubt leave someone out who should have been mentioned. Thus, I would like to extend in advance my apology. I would like to thank those colleagues with whom I work on a daily basis for their contributions to my professional development, but there are several that I would like to acknowledge for different reasons. I would like to thank Marian Palley, who has been kind enough on occasion to offer comments and suggestions as I prepared the manuscript. I would like to extend special thanks to James Magee for the encouragement, support, and understanding that he has given me over the years. Similarly, I would like to thank Francis Kwansa and Wunyabari Maloba for providing a special kind of friendship and support. Many thanks are due to Michael Kern and all the staff at Routledge. I would also like to thank the anonymous reviewers who have offered invaluable comments and suggestions over various versions of the manuscript. Special thanks go out to Alvin Tillery for his comments, reviews, and suggestions. Likewise, I must recognize the contributions of those who have offered extremely helpful comments and suggestions at academic conferences and other forums where several chapter ideas were presented. Finally, my greatest appreciation is reserved for my wife, Juanda, and children Theodore III (Trey), Morgan, and Garrison, and the other members of my family and friends who have loved and supported me over the years.

1

BLACK POLITICS TODAY

The evolution

With the election of the first U. S. president of African heritage in 2008, one could make several claims about black politics today. For one, it could be argued that black politics has matured and become an integral part of American politics. No longer would the statement "not in my life time" be heard when asking about the prospects of a president of African heritage. It could also be argued that the election of the first president of African heritage was a clear indication that black politics was no longer in its infancy or to be considered fringe politics. That black candidates were now acceptable to significant segments of population beyond the black community and that America had become a post-racial society. Likewise, it could be argued that black politics had moved (or was moving) into a new phase, a new era. That President Obama offered black politics a "paradigmatic atmosphere of 'hope,' 'change,' and 'Yes We Can,' which captured, renewed, and revitalized the faith of an intergenerational remix of people both across the nation and around the world."[1] Finally, it could be said that the election of the first president of African heritage represents "the rebirth of black politics" and "resurrection of black consciousness."[2]

At the other end of the spectrum, it could be argued that the election of Barack Obama was the beginning of the end of black politics. That since the 1970s, there has been sufficient evidence of a black political culture that's decaying, and that effective, results-oriented politics was being replaced with rhetoric and symbolism.[3] That Barack Obama's election represented a "generational transition that was reordering black politics" and embracing "the idea that black politics might now be disappearing into American politics in the same way the Irish and Italian machines long ago joined the political mainstream."[4] Regardless of which position one takes, several things are characteristically different about black politics today when compared with black politics in the past.

First, since the 1980s black politics has moved beyond protest politics and seeking mass political participation. Over the years, there has been an evolutionary change in the elected positions that black politicians have sought and whom they pursued as their electoral constituents. Black politicians in the 1960s and 1970s primarily sought local positions and those representing predominantly black constituencies. As a result, there was a large number of blacks elected to city and county councils, followed by school boards and elected law enforcement offices. There were a few blacks holding mayoral positions in municipalities where blacks were a sizeable majority of the population. During the 1970s and late 1980s, black politicians began to successfully seek federal and state legislative offices representing majority black districts. The late 1990s ushered in a new trend in the type of elected office sought by black politicians. More and more black politicians sought statewide executive and legislative (U.S. Senate) positions. In addition, an increasing number of black politicians sought local and state offices in which the electoral districts were not predominately black. Today's black politicians are also no longer wedded exclusively to the Democratic Party. In 2010, there were more than 30 black candidates who ran for Congress as Republicans[5] further removing themselves from black politics as it was once known. Although Obama was not the first person of African heritage to seek the Democratic Party's nomination for president (Shirley Chisholm, Jesse Jackson, Carol Moseley-Braun and Al Sharpton all sought the nomination), he was the first to have significant appeal to groups outside of the black community enabling him to win the nomination.

Second, over the years the link between black politicians and black politics has also changed. In the 1960s and 1970s, there was a strong link between black politicians and black politics. Black politicians today are just as likely to distance themselves from "black politics" as they are to embrace it. The link has manifested itself over three waves: the civil rights wave, the technocratic wave and the transformative wave.[6] Black politicians in the first wave (the civil rights black politicians) were very attached to the black community—attached to the extent that they were often accused of being involved in highly polarized elections and politics that appealed primarily to blacks, and the legacy of the civil rights politicians was described as "intense racial conflict."[7] For the first wave of black politicians, the civil rights movement served as valuable training ground.[8] Furthermore, first-wave black politicians (along with black ministers) were the primary architects of black politics. For first-wave black politicians, black politics was the only path available to political office.

From the late 1970s into the early 1990s, the link between black politicians and black politics weakened somewhat as black politicians sought to expand their electoral base. Black politicians in the second wave were described as "technocrats" who promised to manage government in an effective and efficient manner while attempting to appeal to business owners and middle-class whites.[9] Much of the pro-black political rhetoric of the 1960s and 1970s began to change (to soften) among this wave of black politicians in order to appeal to populations beyond blacks. Thus, this wave of black politicians looked toward broadening their political base by forming coalitions with other minority groups and white liberals. By the start of the millennium, the third wave of black politicians had begun to emerge. Third-wave black politicians were described as "transformative."[10] Third-wave black politicians looked to galvanize cross-racial segments of the population by building coalitions among various groups. Many of today's black politicians have completely abandoned the pro-black political rhetoric of the past and the appeal exclusively to black voters. They have embraced a style of politicking that hardly focuses on race at all. Today's black candidates are less likely to be leaders in the black community or to overtly tie themselves to black politics. Manning Marable wrote of the lack of a connection between black social and political institutions and today's black politician.[11] For a growing minority of today's black politicians the main link to black politics is through Democratic Party politics. Thus, the link between contemporary black politicians and black politics is somewhat weaker.

Finally, the political strategies employed by black politicians also make black politics today different from the past. Today's black politicians tend to minimize the issue of race. Fraser refers to this as the "post-racial" or "post-black" model of black politics.[12] According to Fraser, under this model, candidates like Obama avoid focusing on issues of race and downplay their blackness. That's not to say that race isn't important to them; rather it is to suggest that there has been a shift in how race is dealt with in black politics. Prior to the passage of the civil and voting rights legislation of the 1960s, the electoral political strategy employed by black politicians was more a symbolic act of protest. Most blacks who ran for office did so without the expectation of winning; rather they sought to make a political statement. Many were well known individuals like Paul Robeson and W. E. B. DuBois and others were lesser known black leaders like Ella Baker and James Ford who ran as third-party candidates seeking offices ranging from vice president to U.S. Senator.[13] The political strategy employed by black politicians in the 1960s through the early 1980s was about empowerment and mass direct political action. There was nothing symbolic about their political intentions. Black politicians during the 1970s and early 1980s sought to make the black community a political force to be reckoned with while improving the social and economic quality of life within the black community. During this period, black politicians ran as representatives of the group and they directly appealed to and promoted political interests of the black population.

By the late 1980s, black politicians started to pull back from appealing exclusively to black voters and sought to expand the political base. Although today's black politicians identify with the racial group and understand the issues confronting the black community, their campaigns tend not directly to promote the political interests of the black community. Many of today's black politicians have embraced the idea that the best way to advance the cause of the black population is to advance the cause of all people. Obama, for example, employed an unconventional strategy of building his base among white liberals first and then working to attract black voters.[14] This race-neutral strategy minimizes the fear of white voters who would be turned off by policy positions steered too closely to black interests.[15] The logic was that running a campaign that explicitly addresses the issues facing blacks would derail black candidates' chances of winning primary or general elections. This chapter continues with a brief discussion of the evolution of black politics and changes in the focus of black politics over time. Key to this discussion is the view that black politics has moved into a new era or new phase.

The Evolution of Black Politics

Unlike the politics of other minority groups, the foundations for black politics are the issues associated with historical roots, physical characteristics, and institutional practices of society. More specifically, black politics is a reaction to racism, racial oppression, and the socioeconomic plight of a people in a historical context. Over the years, several definitions of black politics have emerged. Black politics has been defined as the sum of the total actions, ideas, and efforts aimed at creating better conditions for African descended people in the U.S.; thus it is an agenda for raising the psychological, cultural or material quality of life.[16] It has been defined as the purposeful activity of black people to acquire, use, and maintain power, and it reflects the historical tensions and constraints between and among black people and white people.[17] It has been described as an empowerment process that includes holding office, enacting public policy, and raising the socioeconomic status of the black community.[18] The definition used for our purpose augments previous definitions of black politics by describing it as the efforts by the black community to seek and effectively use power to influence the allocation of society's resources and values. Additionally, black politics involves all of those activities engaged in by the black community to influence the political conduct of others: namely the white majority.

There is a uniqueness about black politics that sets it apart from the politics of other racial minorities. Black politics has been described as inextricably linked to the collective aspirations of a people to share in the social and economic security and opportunities allocated to others through a process that has often been undemocratic.[19] The characteristic that most differentiates black politics from the politics of other groups is the idea of "struggle." This struggle has manifested itself in many different ways over the years: 1) a struggle over strategy, 2) a struggle by the dominant group to maintain its power base, 3) a struggle to collaborate between and among black and white factions, and 4) a struggle for authority and participation in policy making.[20] Over the years, as new minority groups have emerged, the nature of majority/minority politics and "the struggle" has changed. In post-civil rights United States, the rules of binary racial politics no longer apply because racial politics is not just a black/white phenomenon anymore.[21]

Nevertheless, there is a uniqueness about black politics that distinguishes it from that of other racial and ethnic minorities and this uniqueness has led to black politics going through several periods of change since the 1950s.

The Protest Era

The first era of black politics coincided with the civil rights movement and was labeled the "Protest Era." The Protest Era began to build momentum after World War II. In the initial phase of the Protest Era (the 1940s to late 1950s) the nature of black politics was legalistic. By this it is meant that the courts served as the platform for addressing the social and political injustices that blacks faced. Initiated by calls for justice by numerous individuals and civil rights organizations, efforts to increase blacks' political influence and social quality of life were pursued within the formal legal structures of the political system (the courts). For the most part, these challenges were centered on two key provisions of the Fourteenth Amendment. The equal protection clause requires states to provide the same protection of the law to all people within their jurisdictions; the due process clause states that the government must respect the legal rights of the individual and give them an opportunity to come before the law. There were numerous court cases that successfully used these provisions of the Fourteenth Amendment to challenge discrimination in education, housing, and public accommodations.

At the same time, there were a number of informal and symbolic events that also moved the issues of political and social justice to the forefront of the nation's agenda. Although there were many, and most occurring on the local front, perhaps key among them was Jackie Robinson's integration of major league baseball and President Truman's decision to desegregate the armed forces. Both events were noteworthy because they allowed blacks to be co-participants in two highly-visible and culturally and politically relevant institutions in society. In post-World War II America, baseball was the premier sporting activity. It was one of the ultimate symbols of American culture, producing many of the day's heroes and it was a pastime shared by Americans of all races, age groups, and income levels. For the longest time baseball symbolically reinforced the ideal of racial segregation with one league for whites and another league for blacks. Jackie Robinson's breaking of "the color line" in baseball was one of many symbolic acts indicating that it was time to move toward the inclusion of blacks into the social mainstream of America. Another important action occurred in 1946 when President Harry S. Truman wrote to the National Urban League saying "that the government has an obligation to see that the civil rights of every citizen are fully and equally protected."[22] In July of 1948, President Truman issued Executive Order 9981 that ended racial segregation within the military. The significance of this order was the expansion of blacks' role in defending the nation and thus symbolically giving blacks a meaningful stake and elevated political importance in society.

In the latter phase of the Protest Era (the late 1950s throughout the 1960s), the nature of blacks' political activity became less legalistic and more about direct mass action. Blacks wanted more than symbolic changes in American social structure and they employed new tactics to bring awareness to their desires. All across America, blacks began to engage in various tactics to challenge discrimination, segregation and to gain access to the political system. There were numerous sit-ins, protest marches, and boycotts among other tactics. Sometimes these new tactics were organized and sometimes they were spontaneous. During the second phase of the Protest Era of black politics, blacks also began to use different methods to bring about change within the political system itself. They began to utilize the courts less and to make the most of the legislative process to change or initiate laws to extend civil and voting rights to blacks. The black community did so with a great deal of success.

Because of blacks' political mobilization, Congress passed key pieces of legislation. The Civil Rights Acts of 1964[23] and 1968[24] had great social and political significance, especially several key titles in the Civil Rights Act of 1964 that set the stage for changes in blacks' social and political development, among them voting rights, injunctive relief against discrimination in places of public accommodation, public facilities, and public education. This 1964 Act also called for nondiscrimination in federally assisted programs and promised equal employment opportunities. The Civil Rights Act of 1964 opened doors to greater educational and employment opportunities for upwardly mobile and middle-class blacks. The Civil Rights Act of 1968 prohibited discrimination in the sale or rental of housing based on race, creed, or color. Also known as the Fair Housing Act, it was especially significant because it gave wealthier blacks an opportunity to reside in neighborhoods other than the predominately segregated ones that they had been forced to live in previously.

The Voting Rights Act of 1965 (renewed and expanded in 1970, 1975, 1982, and 2007) further enhanced opportunities for political development by prohibiting discrimination against blacks and other groups seeking the right to vote.[25] It suspended literacy tests and authorized registration by federal registrars in places where these tests were used. Shortly after passage of the various Acts, blacks' political activity increased. In addition, as a result of the Civil Rights Acts of 1964 and 1968, some blacks began to prosper economically, and major changes occurred in the social composition and development of the black community. The significance of the civil rights legislation was that it provided the black community with an opportunity to move toward social, political, and economic equality in a desegregated environment. Changes in the restrictive legislation brought about changes in the roles blacks played in the political system. For example, in 1940, the voter registration rate among blacks was 3.1 percent.[26] By 1968, it had increased to 66.2 percent.[27] Perhaps even more significant was the level of political cohesion that existed in the black community. The issues that galvanized blacks politically were racial discrimination and segregation and the social and economic inequality they produced between the races.

The Politics Era

In the 1960s, Bayard Rustin predicted that the black protest movement of the 1950s and early 1960s would evolve into formal institutionalized activities such as party politics.[28] Rustin predicted that black politics would move from protesting to working within the political process itself to bring about changes in blacks' social, political, and economic development. In the late 1960s, what Rustin foresaw started to come to fruition and this was the beginning of the second era of black politics. The second era began in the late 1960s and was labeled the "Politics Era."[29] The Politics Era also had two phases. The first phase occurred between the late 1960s and late 1970s, and the second phase was in full effect by the early 1980s.

Dawson characterized the political activity of blacks in the first phase of this era as a transformation from protest politics to electoral politics with high levels of black political activity.[30] In the first phase of the Politics Era, "Black Power" became a dominant ideological concept among the majority of black youth and a signifi-cant portion of the black working and middle classes.[31] Marable noted that blacks began to demonstrate their political potential and they became somewhat rebel-lious in working to create a black political agenda. According to Marable, this was the beginning of the second reconstruction of black politics. Dawson's image of black politics during the Politics Era was one of a profound political unity on one hand with, on the other, growing economic polarization within the black commu-nity that would lead to increasing class conflict.[32] Increasingly, in the second phase of the Politics Era the call for Black Power and black rebellion began to give way to a new era of black politics characterized by increased economic polarization as Dawson had suggested. The political unity that emerged was markedly different from that in the Protest and early Politics Eras. Although blacks remained politically unified, that unity could not be said to be "profound." Marable describes the period between 1976 and 1982 as "the retreat of the second reconstruction."[33] Black elites, according to Marable, were very optimistic and he felt there was no need to continue marching in the streets against governmental policies because blacks now were a part of the administration in most cases.[34]

The black community experienced a measurable degree of social, political, and economic success in the Politics Era. Passage of the Civil Rights Acts of 1957, 1960, and 1964 and the Voting Rights Act of 1965 gave blacks an opportunity to play key roles in the political process both as voters and as public officials. However, efforts to increase their political activity faced many challenges from external political forces. From 1960 and throughout the 1980s, there were numerous attempts to dilute the black vote through a series of structural mechanisms such as at-large elections,[35] and annexation.[36] Despite these obstacles, blacks remained a significant voting bloc with the potential to influence election results.

In the first phase of the Politics Era, there was a great deal of emphasis within the black political community placed on increasing electoral participation and elected representation. One could even argue that the social and economic development fortunes of the community were tied exclusively to their political development. To a large degree this emphasis on increased electoral participation and elected representation was a success. In 1965, there were only 280 elected black officials in the U.S., as shown in Figure 1.1.[37] By 1970, the number of black elected officials had grown by 1,189. Between 1971 and 1975 the number of blacks elected to public office increased by 2,034. However, in the five-year periods between 1976 and 1980 and between 1981 and 1985, growth in the number of blacks elected to public office declined to 1,409 and 1,144 respectively when compared with the initial thrust between 1971 and 1975. The latter part of the 1970s also witnessed a decline in the voter turnout rate and stagnation in voter registration among blacks when compared with that earlier in the decade. In 1968, the voter registration rate among blacks was 66.2 percent and the turnout rate was 57.6 percent. In 1984, the voter registration was 64.5 percent and the turnout rate was 55.8 percent.[38] Charles V. Hamilton suggested that the low voter turnout and low participation in other political activities among blacks during this period does not reflect apathetic behavior, but it does show that personal concerns among blacks were greater.[39]

The primary focus of the black community during the Politics Era was political empowerment. As blacks' political development became stagnant in the latter part of the Politics Era, it had significant consequences for the group's social and economic development. While increased black political representation provided greater benefits for the middle class through government employment, minority contracting, etc., there were many blacks whose quality of life changed little between the early 1960s and mid-1980s.[40] As a result, one of the biggest challenges for black leadership during the Politics Era was keeping an increasingly heterogeneous population (that was dividing by class) together as a homogenous political bloc. Another

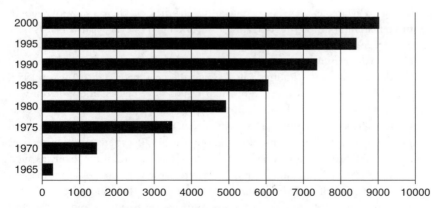

FIGURE 1.1 Number of Black Elected Officials: 1965–2000

Source: Black Elected Officials: Joint Center for Political and Economic Studies

challenge was working to overcome the sense of political alienation and disillusion-
ment that was beginning to emerge among many of the community's subgroups
because of decreasing social and economic opportunities.

So, while the black community's potential for political empowerment was
augmented in the Politics Era, the individual social and economic advances in
society may have marked the beginning of the last real opportunity for sustained
political empowerment efforts at the group level. Class increasingly became an
underlying issue in black politics in the 1980s. In the initial phase of the Politics
Era (the late 1960s and early 1970s) class concerns were not a factor at all because
race, racism, and racial discrimination were more detrimental to blacks' well-
being at the individual and group level. Blacks, regardless of class status in the early
phase, continued to face racial discrimination and viewed race as the greatest
obstacle to their progress as individuals.[41] Although a new black middle class was
beginning to emerge, the political aims of lower and upper socioeconomic status
blacks did not differ much. Blacks' social and political development was tied to
race and to a lesser degree so was their economic development. However, in
the 1980s, economic development in the black community increasingly became
individualized. In a sense, opportunity for economic development at the individual level in the black community began to parallel what was happening in
wider society. As a result, individual economic interests began to compete with
community-based racial interests.

The Socioeconomic Transition Era

It is debatable whether we have moved into a new era of black politics or
just another phase of the Politics Era. However, it is suggested throughout this
book that the mid-to-late 1980s ushered in a new era of black politics. Marable
describes this period in black politics as off "into the wilderness." He referred to
it as such because of a rollback in the liberal reforms on matters of race and an
increasing uncertainty about the role in race in society.[42] Among the many things
that were happening in society during the mid-to-late 1980s was the rise of a
political conservatism that brought the civil rights gains of the Protest Era under
attack. We can add to this the Reagan/Bush administration's benign disengage-
ment from civil rights concerns and the fact that the black community was
dividing from within.[43] Among the defining characteristics of the Socioeconomic
Transition Era of black politics was a rise of a new black middle class. The emergence of class as a key component of black politics and the emergence of a host
of political and structural factors within the black community began to challenge
blacks' political unity.

The 1980s ushered in many changes in the social and economic structure of
the black community. During the late 1960s into the early 1980s, there was significant change in the size of the black middle class due to improved educational and
occupational opportunities. Significant changes in the size and composition of the

black middle class had implications for the rise of a new black political class. Martin Kilson suggests that the rise of a new black political class in the 1960s and early 1970s constituted a social revolution and successful upward mobility of the working-class stratum.[44] This upward and outward mobility of the new social class of the 1960s and late 1970s gave rise to a new black politics in the late 1980s. Unlike the black middle class of the civil rights era, this new black middle class had greater opportunities to pursue the "American dream." Many of them did so by seeking residence outside of their traditional communities. In the late 1960s and throughout the 1970s, many in the first wave of the new black middle class sought residence in white communities that eventually became predominately black. This pattern of migrating to nontraditional black communities continued with the second wave of the new black middle class throughout the 1980s and 1990s. By the end of the 1990s, many middle-class blacks were living in white suburbs or among other middle-class blacks in urban areas. The new black middle class not only moved upward in terms of socioeconomic standing but a large contingent also moved outward away from traditional black communities. Because of these new social and economic arrangements, class inevitably would become important in defining the black community politics and even hampered the establishment of a common black agenda. Furthermore, changes in the socioeconomic dynamics of the black community ushered in a new era of black politics in which there was an inter-racial as well as intra-racial component.

Thus, while protest was the defining characteristic of the first era of black politics and electoral politics the second era, the third era is not to be defined by as much collective action. The third era of black politics is increasingly defined by individual intangibles that would more and more minimize the social, political, and economic issues confronting blacks as a group and maximize the issues confronting individuals and subpopulations within the black community. Thus, in the third era of black politics there has been a gradual decline of shared aspirations, social bonds, and values among blacks and largely along class lines. However, because of the continuing significance of race, divisions in black politics along class lines have not had as much of a dramatic impact on the external politics of the community; rather they have been contained within social and economic behavior among blacks in the internal context of black politics. Thus, in post-civil rights America, politics within the black community will play itself out through the transformation and growing cultural divide within the community based largely on socioeconomic attributes.

So while the intent of the civil rights legislation of the 1950s and 1960s was to improve the socioeconomic quality of life for all blacks, what has occurred is the creation of two black societies: one socioeconomically advantaged and the other socially and economically disadvantaged. The social, political, and economic values of the more affluent black society will be defined by and rooted in their economic prosperity, while the values of the disadvantaged black population are rooted in the struggle for economic survival. As the culture of the advantaged black society focuses on achieving the American dream, the culture of the disadvantaged black community revolves around acquiring the basic necessities of life. In this Socioeconomic Transition Era, race and common experiences associated with racism (whether real or perceived) are the glue that holds blacks together as a political community. This is in spite of the different way in which racism affects the various subgroups within that community. However, with each passing generation the role of race changes in society and the bonds that have traditionally held blacks together will grow weaker and weaker. As a result, the emerging social and economic divides within the black community will become the basis for the emergence of intra-racial politics.

Despite much effort being directed at increasing electoral and political activism during the initial phase of the Politics Era, since the mid-1980s black political activism seems to have reached a plateau. So in spite of a black getting elected president of the United States, black politics in an activist context is stagnant. So, while race today continues to serve as a unifier among blacks when dealing with external political matters, socioeconomic status is increasingly becoming a divider in dealing with matters within the community. As a result, regardless of one's socioeconomic position in society, the political attitudes and behavior of blacks for the most part have remained compatible in an external political context. Consequently, subtle differences in political and social attitudes among blacks will eventually begin to emerge and be the defining characteristics of the internal context of black politics in the Socioeconomic Transition Era.

Changes in the Defining Characteristics of Black Politics

Black politics is essentially about the social, political, and economic development of the black community. Throughout the history of this nation, blacks' social, political, and economic development has been filled with periods of high hopes and major setbacks. By social development we mean all of those things that make a people a community (i.e., culture, sense of identity, traditions, values, beliefs, etc.) and that embrace the variety of cooperative and structural relationships within a group. Economic development includes all those opportunities that would enable blacks to influence the production, distribution, and consumption of goods and services within the black community and society as a whole. Blacks' political development is their ability to influence the allocation of society's resources and values, and it was, for the most part, non-existent prior to World War II.

There is also an interlocking relationship between the black community's social, political, and economic development. As black politics has evolved since the 1940s, the nature of this relationship has changed largely as the result of the political tactics employed to achieve them. In general the political tactics utilized have either been *racialized* (emphasizing racial inequalities and inequities) or *deracialized* (de-emphasizing racial inequalities and inequities). Between 1950 and the late 1960s, the black community's social, political, and economic development were closely connected, and the political tactics employed to facilitate them were highly racialized. This racialization occurred primarily in response to the segregated conditions and nature of the political struggle.

In the immediate post-civil rights America (the first phase of the Politics Era), blacks' social and economic development became largely tied to the success of the group's political development. As a result, the collective behavior and rhetoric of the group was geared toward using the political system to augment their overall social and economic development. Interestingly, while the efforts aimed at social and political development remained highly racialized, the efforts geared toward economic development became less so. After all, the new civil rights legislation had opened the doors to greater educational, employment, and income opportunities in a desegregated environment. By the second half of the Politics Era the efforts geared toward economic development were becoming deracialized and the community's social development efforts now less racialized. The new civil rights legislation had created opportunities for more affluent blacks both to seek residence and explore social opportunities beyond the traditional black community, and this was having an effect on the nature of social interaction among the group. However, the community's efforts toward political development remained highly racialized.

By the Socioeconomic Transition Era, the black community's social, political, and economic development efforts were generally less racialized, but the degree to which they were racialized or deracialized varied across the different socioeconomic strata. Among the less affluent black community, political efforts toward social, political, and economic development remained very racialized, but not to the extent in the previous eras of black politics. Among the more affluent blacks, political efforts geared toward social development were less racialized and those efforts directed at political development were becoming increasingly deracialized. For the most part, political efforts among the more affluent black middle class are becoming more deracialized and are made without regard to the interests of the wider black community, but focus instead on their personal interests. This section continues with a discussion of the changes in the aims, interests, and role of race and class as defining characteristics of black politics over the three eras.

The Aims

The political system has been the principal means used by blacks to influence the conduct of whites and gain access to social and economic opportunities. Because of the significance of race in this society, the aims of black politics over the years have been geared toward achieving (to some degree) either social justice, racial justice (equality), political empowerment, and/or economic empowerment. Social justice demands equality, mutual recognition, and the affirmation of group differences.[45] Social justice includes a sense of collective acceptance that facilitates a sense of individual dignity, self-worth, and respect in a society. Racial justice refers to equal protection, due process of law and other constitutional rights without regards to race. In the past, blacks were often denied constitutional protections and rights, and pursuit of racial justice was an effort to gain these rights. Political empowerment would enable blacks to participate in the decision-making process of the allocation of societal resources. Political empowerment would provide blacks with the ability to influence public policy either directly or indirectly through the vote and political representation in government. The final aim of black politics is economic empowerment. America has always been described as the land of economic opportunity, a place where one could work hard and attain a decent standard of living. However, this has not been the case for blacks. Because of America's system of social and economic segregation, blacks' opportunities for economic development were often denied and beyond their control.

Although these four aims of black politics have remained constant, the emphasis placed on achieving them has changed from era to era. During the Protest Era, the primary aims of black politics were to achieve racial and social justice. Black politics was largely a response to the black community's subordinate status in society. Black politics during the Protest Era was concerned with, among many things, getting white America to uphold the principles and values espoused as the American creed and to get the institutions of society to function likewise. In addition, the politics of black America during the Protest Era was about gaining social acceptance and inclusion (a specific form of social justice). Despite constitutional protections, blacks in America during the Protest Era were treated as second-class citizens and denied the basic political rights of "life, liberty and the pursuit of happiness." The principle of "separate but equal" placed them in a different social category. Achieving economic and political empowerment were secondary aims of black politics during the Protest Era. This does not mean that black politics was not about seeking power to influence the allocation of societal resources or the pursuit of economic opportunity, but it was reasonable at the time to believe that political empowerment would come as the result of achieving racial and social justice. Furthermore, it was reasonable to believe that racial and social justice would pave the way for greater economic development for the black community.

The aims of black politics in the late 1960s and early 1970s gradually moved away from primarily seeking racial and social justice. During the Politics Era, the attention of the civil rights establishment shifted from protesting against social injustices to seeking full participation in the political decision-making process. In fact, increased political participation among blacks and a rise in the number of black elected officials in the early 1970s signaled a shift from protest tactics to electoral politics.[46] This was the era where blacks engaged in the politics of "empowerment." Thus, the late 1960s saw the symbolic end of the Protest Era of black politics and the beginning of the Politics Era. The initial phase of the Politics Era was about getting blacks elected to public office and appointed to key decision-making positions in government. That is, with blacks serving in key governmental and political positions, the black community would get its fair share of the resources allocated by the political process. Furthermore, it was generally surmised that having blacks in important governmental decision-making positions (elected and non-elected) was the key to achieving social justice and social acceptance. In addition, the black community would have a greater role in influencing the political and social values of the larger society. Thus, political empowerment would serve to embolden the black community and give it a sense of equal standing in society.

The Black Power movement of the late 1960s and early 1970s was the ultimate symbol of blacks' efforts to become politically empowered. The Black Power movement and the symbols associated with it emphasized a sense of racial consciousness, racial solidarity, and the development of independent black establishments to complement the existing black organizations.[47] The rhetoric of the Black Power movement implied that black people did not need social acceptance (approval) by others (namely white America); rather they were to be proud of themselves as a people. Racial justice continued to be important to blacks, and the black community felt empowered and were demanding equal treatment from within the political system and other newly accessed arenas. The black community was saying it loud, "I am black and I am proud."[48] The gradual shift away from addressing the indignities of racial and social injustice emphasized in the Protest Era was not to suggest that the black community did not continue to seek racial and social justice during the Politics Era. On the contrary, blacks still sought justice, but they had scored numerous victories in that direction during the Protest Era with passage of the civil rights legislation and it was time to expand the focus. The political activities and behavior of the black community would drive demands for government-sponsored economic empowerment policies. Thus, the general idea was that economic development would occur as a result of political empowerment. After all, the black community, as a result of segregation, had the foundation for economic development in place; what was needed was the infusion of confidence, capital, and expanded opportunities.

As socioeconomic divisions became increasingly more evident within the black community, economic empowerment, racial justice, social justice and political empowerment had different levels of importance to the emerging subgroups within the black community. Thus, in the Socioeconomic Transition Era, the aims of black politics began to differ based on socioeconomic divisions within the community. For one, growing socioeconomic divisions created conditions for the rise of the internal politics among blacks. As a consequence, conditions existed within the black community for the establishment of multiple agendas and dual aims. For example, for the more affluent, social and racial justice (with issues like affirmative action) would become primary concerns. This is not to say that economic justice was not a factor for this group, after all they had experienced some measure of economic success. The problem was that many in this group would continue to feel labeled, stigmatized, and held back economically by the subtle emphasis placed on race in society, and by racism itself. Despite improvements in their educational attainment, they were continuing to hit the employment and income glass ceiling when it came to pursuing opportunities in the higher echelon of the work world. For this group economic justice (at the group level) and political empowerment would become less important.

For the other segments of the black population, access to quality education and health care, the elimination of poverty, the creation of jobs, etc., would be the aim of black politics. In the Socioeconomic Transition Era, calls for political empowerment among the lower socioeconomic segments are being replaced with a desire for "economic empowerment." Blacks in the lower socioeconomic groups are becoming increasingly disillusioned with the outcomes or lack of outcomes generated by politics (and in some instances with the black elected officials). They remain concerned for social justice and the extent to which it affects their economic standard of living. That is, they are aware that their economic position continues to be tied to their race; however it is also increasingly tied to the socioeconomic class. Overall, in the Socioeconomic Transition Era, individualism and the loss of faith in the political system have transformed the aims of black politics away from political empowerment at the group level. Political empowerment during the Socioeconomic Transition Era is sought for the purpose of advancing one's personal or subgroup's social and economic positions.

Collective Versus Individual Interests

The second defining characteristic of black politics is the focal point of political activity or the object of political results. That is, who benefits from black politics? Initially this wasn't an issue because blacks were somewhat politically monolithic in their struggle against racial discrimination and racism. Today, the black community is increasingly a complex population with varying degrees of shared goals and common interests. The political goals and interests of the black community have changed over time, and the focal point has ranged from collectivism to individualism. Hofstede defines collectivism as a situation where "people from birth onward are integrated into a strong, cohesive in-group, which throughout people's lifetime continues to protect them in exchange for unquestioning loyalty." Thus, the individual identifies with group-oriented goals and needs at the expense of their personal interests. Hofstede defines a society or community as individualist if "the ties between individuals are loose: Everyone is expected to look after him/herself and his/her immediate family." Thus, individual interests and needs are more important than the interests and needs of the group.[49] Hofstede regarded American society, in general, as individualist.

In the Protest Era, the focal point of black politics was the augmentation of the community's collective interests. Black politics emphasized the good of the greater community. The basis for the solidarity and unity in blacks' political activity and behavior was a shared social, political, and economic plight. This is not to say that there were no political differences among blacks, rather it is to say that the differences that existed were over the means toward the ends and not the ends themselves. During the Protest Era, the black community had an agenda that was based on collective interests and the common enemies of discrimination, racism, and segregation. Blacks, regardless of socioeconomic standing, religious affiliation, or geographical location, were in the same struggle against racial oppression and social and economic limitations. As a result, black politics in the Protest Era was about advancing the interests and well-being of blacks as a collective entity.

The focal point of black politics during the first phase of the Politics Era (through the late 1970s) continued to be about blacks as a collective group. There was a strong sense of social, political, and economic solidarity fueled by the Black Power and Black Pride movements. The initial emphasis during this phase was on the community helping itself to grow socially, politically, and economically. The second phase of the Politics Era saw a gradual shift away from politics solely to advance the interests of the community. This gradual shift coincided with increased socioeconomic opportunities for blacks. With the increase in the percentage of middle class blacks came changes in blacks' demographic and geographic patterns. No longer were blacks limited in their opportunities and where they could live. Furthermore, there was a shift toward conservatism in the larger society,[50] and it did not exclude blacks (especially those in the new and growing black middle class). In general, politics in America during the 1980s became less about the community and was increasingly driven by the individual or subgroup interests. The focal point of black politics in the Socioeconomic Transition Era has gradually changed. Blacks are increasingly functioning as economic individuals that are drawn together politically by racial circumstances. Improved life chances for blacks have led to the weakening of the sense of common political bond and shared identity. The outcomes of black politics are increasingly less about the political interests of the racial group and more about the interests of the individual and/or subgroups within the community. Thus, the sense of concern and solidarity around the group's social and economic plight in the Protest and early Politics Eras is becoming less of a focal point today. It was the overt violations of blacks' civil and political rights, along with the treatment of blacks as social rejects that galvanized them into a community in the previous eras of black politics. In the Socioeconomic Transition Era, black politics still functions to address many related social and economic conditions of the past; however, increased economic and social opportunities have created an environment that is leading to individuals and subgroups within the black community working together to address their specific needs. On the surface it might appear that the issues confronting blacks are the same; however this isn't always the case. For example, one segment of the black community may be concerned with gaining enhanced job opportunities, while the other is concerned simply with getting any job. As a consequence, an employment issue such as affirmative action has more significance for blacks with higher levels of education than it does for lesser-educated blacks.

The Implications of Race and Class

The role of race and socioeconomic divisions (class) is the third distinguishing characteristic that describes the structural context of black politics. Race and socioeconomic divisions have always played a role in black politics, but their importance has varied from era to era. Race, especially in the binary black/white context, is one of several simple dichotomies and socially constructed definitions that people use to understand and respond to political and social phenomena. Race and racism have always served as the glue that held blacks together as a political unit. However, as Marable notes, "race" within American society is rapidly being redefined with profound consequences for all sectors and classes.[51] Among blacks, socioeconomic divisions are increasingly beginning to matter and their importance is starting to rival that of race. Thus, socioeconomic divisions (along with other factors) are increasingly influencing various aspects of black politics today. While the black community continues to be held politically together by matters of race, it is also being divided by socioeconomic divisions, space, and other factors. Socioeconomic divisions in the black community, among others, are bound to have consequences for black politics in post-civil rights America. One consequence of the increasing socioeconomic divisions within the black community is the paving of the way for the rise in intra-racial politics. Similarly, demographical and geographical changes among blacks are also contributing to the destabilization of a once socially, politically, and economically consolidated group.

During the Protest Era, the black community functioned more as a racially monolithic political unit. Race was extremely important and the consequences of racial discrimination, prejudice, and racism served as a unifier. Race was a major factor in all facets of the blacks' social, political, and economic development. Despite the existence of relatively small socioeconomic divisions within the black community, differences along class lines took a back seat to race when it came to the social and economic quality of life for blacks. Consequently, in the Protest Era, the role of socioeconomic divisions in black politics was truncated by race. Because of the political environment, political tactics employed were highly racialized (meaning race was the center of black political activity). Not only was the tactic to achieve political development highly racialized, but the social and economic development strategies were also racialized. Consequently, the style of black politics was more concerned with influencing conduct of the dominant group's policy-making decisions about matters affecting the racial group than it was about seeking power.

The Politics Era saw a change in black politics and the seeking of political power ruled the day. Marable describes the period of black politics between 1970 and 1976 as including the zenith and decline of black rebellion, and between 1976 and 1982 as the retreat of the reconstruction.[52] During the initial phase of the Politics Era, the importance of race continued to overshadow class. After all, this was the "zenith" of the black consciousness movement and this period witnessed perhaps the high point of black political activity. Blacks registered and voted in record numbers and the period witnesses a record number of blacks elected to local, state, and federal office. In 1972, Shirley Chisholm became the first black American to seek a major political party's nomination for the office of president. Race dominated both the external and internal dynamics of black politics. In the first phase of the Politics Era, socioeconomic divisions within the community seemed not to matter in black politics. However, with the decline of short-lived black "rebellion" and the "retreat of the second reconstruction" the role that race played in black politics began to stabilize and socioeconomic divisions began quietly to emerge as a factor.

The changing dynamics of political and social life in larger society in the late 1970s into the 1980s have contributed to the changing dynamics of black politics today. Race no longer exclusively drives black politics. Race still matters, but the way in which it matters has changed. In the Protest and Politics Eras of black politics, race had implications for the larger group. In the Socioeconomic Transition Era, the impact of race on black quality of life has become individualized or relegated to subgroup concerns. Racism and racial discrimination still exists, but their effects on blacks vary from individual to individual. What also complicates black politics in the Socioeconomic Transition Era is how race and the socioeconomic divisions intersect. The intersection of race and socioeconomic divisions has had little influence on the external nature of (binary black/white) politics, but its influence is felt mostly in the internal politics of the black community. In the Socioeconomic Transition Era, black politics operates on two fronts because of the continuing role of race and the emerging role of class in society: the external front (between blacks and other groups) and the internal front (within the black community). Today, because the individual's social and economic development is less tied to the political development of the larger community, the stage has been set for increased politics within the community along class lines.

The Data and Overview of this Book

In sum, the 1980s ushered in a new era of black politics, and several things distinguish this new era of black politics from the previous eras (the Protest Era and Politics Era). First, in this new era the struggle for social and economic power has become just as important as the struggle for political power. Second, a key development in this new era is the emergence and coming of age of a new black middle class. This new black middle class is better educated and enjoys greater social and economic opportunities than their pre-civil rights counterparts. This new black middle class is not faced with the same limitations and restraints that were faced by the pre-civil rights' era black middle class. The third distinguishing characteristic of this new era of black politics is that it is not only defined by racial politics, but increasingly by class-based politics. Class-based politics and socioeconomic divisions have always been an aspect of life in the black community, whether they manifested themselves during slavery as house slaves versus field slaves or in the post-slavery era by what W. E. B. DuBois referred to as the "better class" versus the "lower class."[53] However, the role of class in black politics was a relatively minor issue until this new era of black politics.

The final characteristic of black politics today is that it has two dimensions. Unlike the politics of the earlier eras, black politics today has both an external as well as an internal dimension. Class-based politics plays a key role in defining the nature of the external and internal politics of the black community. Class remains a non-factor in the external politics of the black community (that is, the binary black/white political paradigm); however, it has increasingly become (and will continue to be) a factor in the internal politics of the community. Consequently, black politics today (in this new era referred to here as the Socioeconomic Transition Era) is becoming increasingly less about the interests of the larger group and more about the interests of smaller subgroups (or individuals) within the community.

The intention of this book is to contribute to the literature on the evolution of black politics. In addition, it considers the implications of growing socioeconomic divisions within the black community on the future of black politics. In the chapters that follow, we will discuss the extent to which improved life circumstances for large segments of the black community have contributed to increased political diversity within the black community. We will consider the degree to which increased socioeconomic divisions and deracialization in black politics have led to what Dawson described as "tension between the racial interests and class interests as factors shaping African American politics."[54] This work will examine the attitudes and patterns of political behavior of blacks to determine how race and socio-economic divisions have influenced black politics in the post-Civil Rights Era. It is suggested that the tensions between racial and class interests that Dawson talks about will play themselves out on two different dimensions of black politics: the internal and external. That is, within the racial group class interests have always been a factor but today they are becoming an even greater force in defining social and political relationships within the population. On the other hand, racial interests continue to drive black politics in the larger societal (majority/minority) context. As a result, the intersection of race and class has less influence on black political behavior in the external political context.

This project relies upon census and national survey data to help draw conclusions. Census data and reports will be used to help plot changes in the socioeconomic status, voter turnout and voter registration patterns of blacks. To explore attitudes and patterns of political behavior, a series of national survey data sets including the General Social Survey (GSS),[55] the American National Election Studies (ANES),[56] the 1996 National Black Election Study (NBES),[57] the CBS News/Black Entertainment Television Monthly Poll,[58] The National Politics Study 2004,[59] and the 2007 Pew Race Survey[60] were utilized.[61]

Chapters 2 and 3 examine the growth of socioeconomic divisions in the black community, and thus the rise of a new black middle class. In this chapter, we consider the implications of growing socioeconomic divisions for black politics in post-civil rights America. In addition, Chapter 2 discusses those issues that cause race to remain a factor in black politics, especially for the emerging black middle class. How the new black middle class resolves these issues will determine the influence of race in future black politics. This chapter considers whether black politics can exist in the absence of racial politics. Furthermore, it ponders if the socioeconomic interests of blacks (at the group level) could replace racial interests as the driving force behind black politics.

Chapter 3 discusses how the socioeconomic transformation of the black community could contribute to the rise of intra-racial politics. This chapter also considers the implications for black politics of the black Baby-Boomer and subsequent generations coming of age, and increasing geographical/residential division amongst blacks today. It discusses the emergence since the end of the Civil Rights Era of a series of political sub-communities in the black community. Consequently, today we can no longer talk about a black political community; rather we must understand the black community as a series of "black political communities." In essence, as the Socioeconomic Transition Era evolves, we have to understand the black political community as a collection of smaller communities with differing social and political agendas developed on socioeconomic interests among other factors.

Chapters 4 and 5 consider the implications of race and class for black politics in the Socioeconomic Transition Era. These chapters explore blacks' political attitudes in the Socioeconomic Transition Era and what they suggest about the future of black politics. Chapter 4 examines the public opinion of blacks and whites in the Socioeconomic Transition Era and discusses the relevance to the future of black politics. It considers the extent to which blacks' and whites' public opinion has converged or diverged in the Socioeconomic Transition Era. This chapter puts into context the nature of the political divide between blacks and whites today. In the process, this chapter considers the extent to which race remains a significant factor in the external politics of black America. Chapter 5 examines the conception that blacks are politically monolithic as it focuses on the electoral and partisan behavior of black Americans in the Socioeconomic Transition Era. On the surface it appears that blacks are politically monolithic, but despite voting patterns and partisanship there is evidence of weakening solidarity among blacks.

Because of the continuing significance of race, contemporary politics leave blacks with few political options when it comes to electoral and partisan politics. The final three chapters discuss some of the political and structural factors within the community itself that are threatening to black politics in the Socioeconomic Transition Era. Chapter 6 examines the perception of blacks as a unified political group. It discusses why blacks (regardless of socioeconomic status) continue to have limited political options when it comes to electoral and partisan politics. It examines why blacks have not reached their fullest potential as a political community, and questions if the black community (based on the social and economic changes in the community) will reach its fullest political potential. Chapter 7 uses the leadership problems in the black community as evidence of a community divided by class and weakening in terms of shared social and political interest. This chapter attributes much of the leadership crisis in the black community to the changing social and economic dynamics of the community. This chapter considers the implications of leadership on black politics in the Socioeconomic Transition Era. Chapter 8 concludes by discussing other factors that will influence black politics as the Socioeconomic Transition Era evolves. It begins by discussing the changing nature of minority group politics in the U.S. It follows with a discussion about how black organizations struggle for influence within the black community and the political arena in general. It concludes with a discussion of the future of black politics.

2

A COMMUNITY IN TRANSITION AND DIVIDING BY CLASS

Since the end of the Civil Rights Era, an upwardly mobile socioeconomic group or middle class has emerged within the black community. The black middle class that has emerged is now a significant part of the nation's social and economic fabric. The existence of a black middle class did not start with the end of the civil rights movement; rather a black middle class began to emerge well before the movement got started. E. Franklin Frazier wrote of post–World War II black society:

> Since the Second World War, Negroes have continued to receive a larger share of the national income than they did before the War. Moreover, the racial barriers in the North, where nearly a third of the Negroes now live, have tended to be lower in all phases of public life. Even in the South, the segregation of the Negro has been less rigid in public transportation, and Negro students have been admitted to some of the public universities. As the result of the changes in the economic status of the Negro, the Negro middle-class, or the "black bourgeoisie" has grown in size and acquired a dominant position among Negroes.[1]

The black middle class today is very different from the black middle class that Frazier wrote about in the 1950s. Blacks today have numerous social and economic opportunities available to them that were denied to blacks in the Protest and Politics Eras. According to Frazier, most middle-class blacks in the pre–Civil Rights Era (Protest Era) earned their livings as businesspeople, clergy, doctors, lawyers, teachers, and other professionals who served the black community. By the 1990s, there were more black businesspeople, doctors, lawyers, and other professionals than ever before in the history of this nation.[2] Despite their educational attainments and occupational standing, members of the black middle class in the Protest

Era were limited (by written and unwritten law) in terms of where they could live, which schools they could attend, and what occupations they could pursue. Today there are no laws to limit where blacks can go to school, work, or live.

The aims of this chapter are twofold. The first aim is to plot the emergence of an upwardly mobile socioeconomic group in the black community (or the "new black middle class"). The second aim of this chapter is to discuss the issues that continue to make "race" important to blacks regardless of the socioeconomic status. This discussion is particularly important to understanding black politics today because current patterns of socioeconomic development within the black community are leading to the emergence of several distinct black communities. At the extremes, there is "one of achievement and another of self-destruction."[3] Consequently, the socioeconomic divisions within the black community have increasingly become as important as race in black politics.

The Rise of the New Black Middle Class (or Upper Socioeconomic Status Group)[4]

Determining who is the new middle class (or upper socioeconomic status group) has never been easy for social scientists. Given the disparities in blacks' and whites' levels of education, income, and occupation, applying a generic definition of stratification to the black population can be even more complicated. German sociologist Max Weber postulated two levels of stratification: class and status.[5] Weber defined class as the grouping of people according to economic position. Thus, class is the economic measure of stratification. According to Weber, class is determined by life chances and based on economic factors such as income, labor, assets, and credit. One's class consists of all of those individuals with similar socioeconomic background and is determined by factors such as income or occupation. Weber defined status as an earned position in the community based on honor or prestige. Status is the "to be" component of stratification, while class is the "to do" component. Status is based on any number of factors ranging from a group's social and economic development to personal social and economic achievements. Landry noted that "class is an objective position in an economic hierarchy, while status is a subjective position in a hierarchy of honor and reputation." As Landry points out, "Class is a slippery concept accompanied by much confusion ... and it is frequently confused with status."[6] It is not the intention here to help settle this confusion; however it is imperative that some effort is made to conceptualize and operationalize who is this new black middle class and how it has increased in size in the post-Civil Rights Era.

Definitions and criteria for measuring the size of the black middle class have varied over the years. Over the years, scholars have used occupation,[7] education,[8] income[9] or home ownership as the primary measure of stratification.[10] Some have used a combination of these measures to determine the size of the middle class or the system of stratification within the black community.[11] Further complicating matters, using characteristics that focus on the black "family's" status can be problematic because of the large number of divorced or never-married blacks who are part of the rapidly growing segment of the black middle class.[12] This author feels that education is a better measure of socioeconomic status than income and thus it will be the primary characteristic used to determine the potential size of the black middle class.

The black middle class was conceptualized in two ways: as the economic-based middle class and as the status-based middle class. The economic-based middle class is determined by an individual's ability "to do." In effect, an individual's inclusion in the economic-based black middle class is determined by their ability to take care of their basic needs and wants using their assets, earning power and/or wealth. The economic-based middle class is consistent with Weber's class stratification. The status-based black middle class is determined by the individual's ability "to be"; that is, the ability to be influential and have power because of some virtue or achievement. For purposes of the study, it was felt that income (despite the concerns with using family income as a measure of socio-economic status for blacks) was the most appropriate measure of the size of the economic-based black middle class and education the appropriate measure of the status-based group. The status-based black middle class is the focus of this book; however, this is not an attempt to ignore or minimize the importance of the economic-based black middle class.

Advances in Occupational Status

Although education and income (respectively) are the representative measures of the status- and economic-based middle classes used in this study, occupation as a defining socioeconomic characteristic is worthy of discussion. Since the 1960s, the changing labor market and expanded employment opportunities have contributed to a significant shift in the nature of the jobs blacks do. For our purposes, blacks were divided into white- and blue-collar occupational groups based on the Standard Occupational Classification System used to organize workers into occupational categories.[13] White-collar occupations included managerial, professional, technical, sales, clerical and other administrative support positions. White-collar occupations are those jobs that involve mental rather than manual labor (the office workers if you would). In 1972, only 34.8 percent of black workers were employed in white-collar occupations as shown in Figure 2.1.[14] By 2006, the percentage of blacks employed in white-collar positions had increased to 49.5 percent. This was a 14.7 percent increase over the 34-year period. Since 1976, the percentage of blacks employed in white-collar occupations has increased steadily. The greatest increase in the percentage of blacks employed in white-collar positions occurred during the 1980s. During the 1970s, the percentage of blacks in white-collar positions grew by only 3.8 percent. However, during the 1980s the percentage of blacks employed in white-collar positions grew by 7.3 percent. The largest increase in the percentage of blacks

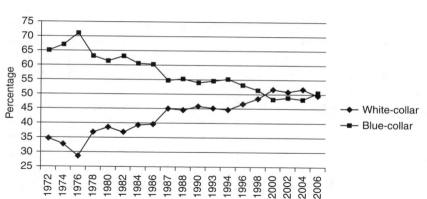

FIGURE 2.1 Blacks' Occupational Classification: 1972–2006
Source: General Social Surveys 1972–2006

employed in white-collar positions occurred in the mid-to-late 1980s. Between 1984 and 1990, the percentage of blacks employed in white-collar occupations grew from 39.4 percent to 45.9 percent. The growth rate for blacks in white-collar positions declined slightly during the early 1990s (after continuous growth since 1972), and between 2000 and 2006 there was no growth at all. Thus despite the large increase in blacks working in white-collar positions during the 1980s, since 1990, the rate of growth in the percentage of blacks employed in these types of jobs has been minimal.

Changes in blacks' occupational characteristics could be further put in perspective by dividing occupations into upper and lower white-collar categories.[15] In 2006, slightly more than one-fifth (26 percent) of black workers were employed in upper white-collar occupations. Between 1972 and 2006, the percentage of blacks in upper white-collar occupations increased by 4.2 percent. The percentage of blacks employed in lower white-collar occupations increased between 1972 and 2006 by 10.5 percent moving from 13 percent in 1972 to 23.5 percent. Interestingly enough, the percentage of blacks in upper and lower white-collar occupations has been unstable since 2000. The percentage of blacks in lower white-collar occupations actually declined from a high of 28.2 percent in 2002 to 23.5 percent in 2006. The percentage of blacks in upper white-collar occupations declined from a high of 29.4 percent in 2000 to 23.5 percent in 2006.

The common perception is that white-collar workers work with their minds and blue-collar workers work with their hands. However, many blue-collar occupations require the ability to work with both the hands and the mind. Some blue-collar workers are very skilled individuals who, depending on their expertise, can command very high wages. Among this group of blue-collar occupations are craftspeople and precision, production, and repair workers. Other blue-collar occupations require fewer skills and usually include jobs such as operators, fabricators, private household and service workers, fishermen, foresters, agricultural and other types of laborer. Blue-collar positions are less prestigious than white-collar positions even though many of these workers have higher skill levels and have higher incomes than some white-collar workers (especially lower white-collar workers) have. Blue-collar positions were once a plentiful, vital part of the labor force and a major source of employment for blacks. In recent years, however, machines and technology have replaced many of these jobs.

The percentage of blacks employed in blue-collar positions has steadily decreased since 1972 as shown in Figure 2.1. In 1972, roughly 65.1 percent of all black workers were employed in blue-collar occupations. By 2006 the percentage of blacks employed in blue-collar occupations had decreased to 50.5 percent. By 2006, the percentage of blacks employed in white-collar and blue-collar positions was almost fifty/fifty. Although many blacks have risen in occupational classification, they still lag behind whites in the percentage employed in white-collar occupations.[16] According to the *General Social Surveys*, the difference in percentage of blacks and whites employed in white-collar occupations has declined significantly. In 1972, the difference in the percentage of blacks and whites employed in white-collar occupations was 22.5 percent. By 2006, the difference was down to 12.9 percent. The percentage of whites employed in white-collar occupations increased only slightly from 57.3 percent in 1972 to 62.4 percent in 2006. In sum, the data show significant changes in blacks' occupational classification since the early 1970s. In the mid-2000s, roughly half of all blacks were employed in white-collar occupations and about 50 percent of those were in upper white-collar occupations.

Determining the Size of the Economic-Based Black Middle Class

The economic-based middle class ("to do" middle class) included those whose income afforded them a moderate or greater standard of living. The economic-based middle class is significant to the black community's political development because of its financial resources and size. This group is the foundation on which the black community will develop and prosper socially, politically, and economically. If this group is unstable and detached, then blacks as a political community will be unstable and politically ineffective. The economic-based black middle class is also relevant to the political effectiveness of the black community because it often serves as the bridge between blacks in the lower and higher socioeconomic strata.

In his discussion of the rise of the black middle class in the 1950s, E. Franklin Frazier wrote:

> In 1949, the median income of Negro families in the United States was $1,665, or 51 percent of the median income of white families, which was $3,232. Only 16 percent of the Negro families as compared to 55 percent

of the white families had incomes of $3,000 or more. .... For the country as a whole, the incomes of members of the black bourgeoisie range from between $2,000 and $2,500 and upward. The majority of their incomes do not amount to as much as $4,000. In fact, scarcely more than one percent of all the Negroes in the country have an income amounting to $4,000 and only one-half of one percent of them has an income of $5,000 or more.[17]

In 2008, the median income for all families in the United States was $61,521.[18] The 2008 median income for black families (alone) was $39,879, and that was only 57 percent of white families' median income, which was $70,070. In 2008, 60 percent of the black families had incomes that placed them in the lower-income group as shown in Figure 2.2.[19] The percentage of black families in the lower-income group was nearly twice that of white families. In 2008, while close to two-thirds of all black families had an income that was less than $50,000 a year only 33 percent of the white families fell into this category. Since 1970, the percentage of black families in the lower-income group has declined by an average of 5 percent a decade. In 1970, the percentage of blacks in the lower-income group was 75.5 percent; this figure had declined to 60 percent by 2008. Interestingly, in the 2000s (through 2008) there was no significant change in the percentage of blacks in the lower-income group.

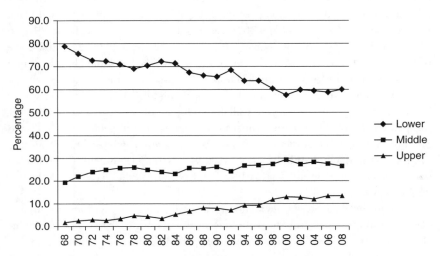

FIGURE 2.2 Black Families Income Groupings: 1972–2008

Source: Table F-23. Families by Total Money Income, Race, and Hispanic Origin of Householder: 1967 to 2008 U.S. Census Bureau Current Population Reports, Annual Social and Economic Supplements and Internet site http://www.census.gov/hhes/www/income/histinc/f23.html. Total family income figures based on 2008 dollars

The change in the percentage of black families in the moderate-income (or middle-income) group between 1972 and 2008 was small, as shown in Figure 2.2. In 1970, only 22.1 percent of the black families had incomes that placed them in the moderate-income group. By 2008, the percentage of families in the moderate-income group had increased to 26.6. During this 38-year period, the percentage of black families in the moderate-income group was never higher than 29.3 (in 2000). Since 1970, the percentage of black families in the middle-income group increased by roughly three percent a decade. However, since 2000 the percentage of blacks in the moderate-income group has actually declined from 29.3 percent to 26.6 percent. In 1970, only 2.5 percent of the black families were in the higher-income group. By 2008, the percentage of black families in this income group had increased to 13.4. Thus, between 1970 and 2008 there was a significant increase in the percentage of black families in the higher-income group and an almost comparable decline in the percentage of black families in the lower-income group. The largest increase in the percentage of blacks in the upper-income group was in the 1980s and 1990s. Between 1980 and 1988, the percentage of black families in the upper-income category rose from 4.5 to 8.4, and between 1990 and 1998, the percentage rose from 8.2 to 12. During the 2000s, the percentage of blacks in the upper-income group increased by only 0.4 percent.

The middle- and upper-income groups were combined to approximate the size of the economic-based black middle class. Since 1972, the percentage of black families in the economic-based middle class has increased significantly. During the 1970s, the percentage of black families in the economic-based black middle class rose from 24.6 to 30.9. During the 1980s, it rose from 29.4 to 33.9 and from 34.5 to 39.5 during the 1990s. Between 2000 and 2008, the percentage of black families in the economic-based black middle class decreased from 42.3 in 2000 to 40 in 2008. Despite a significant rise in the percentage of black families in the economic-based black middle class, the percentage of blacks in this group still lagged well behind that of white families. In 2008, the percentage of white families in the moderate-income group was 36.2 and 30.1 in the upper-income group. The percentage of white families in the economic-based white middle class in 2008 was 66.3. Thus, the difference in size between the economic-based black and white middle classes in 2008 was 26.3 percent.

In sum, the data provide evidence of growing income divisions within the black community and growth in the size of the economic-based black middle-class since the 1970s. The data show there has been a steady increase in the percentage of black families in the upper-income group, while there was a measurable decrease in the percentage of black families in the lower-income group. Despite a significant decline in the percentage of black families in the lower-income group, a sizeable proportion (well over half) of the black families remained in this category. There has not been much change in the percentage of black families in the middle-income category. Finally, between the mid-1980s and through the 1990s the percentage of blacks in the economic-based black middle class steadily increased, but it appears that the percentage has leveled off since 2000. Since the late 1960s, the black community has been slowly dividing into three income groups: one that continues to struggle financially, one with modest means, and a growing segment that is very affluent.

The Expansion of the Status-Based Black Middle Class

The status-based black middle class (or the "to be" group) have levels of education that afford them influence both in the black community and beyond. Honor and prestige are bestowed upon these individuals often because of their educational (and many times their occupational) achievements. The middle class that Frazier focused on in his classic study of the 1950s was the status-based middle-class.[20] Frazier noted that the black middle class that slowly emerged in the post-WWII era was defined by social distinctions such as education and conventional behavior rather than upon occupation and income. Prior to the civil rights movement, the size of the status-based middle class in the black community was very small. Since then, a viable status-based middle class has emerged in the black community and the economic-based middle class has expanded.

Members of this status-based group play a significant role in the politics of the black community because of their leadership potential and organizational skills. If the black community is to prosper and develop socially, politically, and economically, this group must provide solid leadership. The status-based black middle class must coordinate and oversee the effective and efficient use of the black community's resources if blacks are to be socially, politically, and economically viable as a community. The actions of the status-based black middle class are as important (perhaps more so) as those of the economic-based black middle class to the political development of the black community. As mentioned earlier, education was the measure used to determine the size of the status-based black middle class in this study. For purposes of this study, the black population was further divided into three educational categories: lower-educated (less than 12 years of school), moderately educated (12 to 15 years of school, including high school graduates and those with some college including a two-year college degree), and higher educated (those with 16 years or more or college graduates).

In 1940, only 1.3 percent of the black population had completed four or more years of college. The vast majority of blacks (92.3 percent) had completed less than 4 years of high school.[21] By 1972, the percentage of the black population 25 years and older with less than 12 years of school had declined to 63.4.[22] Of the black high school graduates in 1972, only 5.1 percent had 16 or more years of school as shown in Figure 2.3. By 1980, the percentage of blacks with 16 or more years of school had increased to 7.9. Many blacks during the 1970s took advantage of governmental grants, low-interest education loans, increased

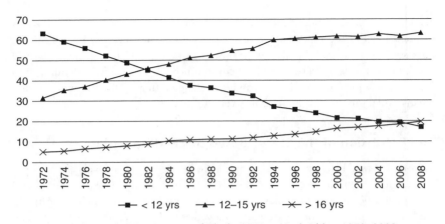

FIGURE 2.3 Educational Attainment of Blacks 25 Years and Older: 1972–2008

Source: Table A-2. Percent of People 25 Years and Over Who Have Completed High School or College, by Race, Hispanic Origin and Sex: Selected Years 1940 to 2008

scholarship opportunities from institutions of higher learning anxious to recruit black students determined to increase their educational credentials.[23] The decade of the 1970s was the first time one could clearly identify a significant status-based black middle class. Between 1980 and 1990, there was an even greater increase in the percentage of blacks with 16 or more years of school. In 1980, 8.8 percent of blacks over the age of 25 had 16 or more years of school and this figure increased to 11.3 percent by 1990. The percentage of blacks with 16 or more years of college continued to grow during the 1990s increasing to a high of 16.5 by 2000. Although the percentage of black college graduates continued to increase during the 2000s, the rate of growth (slightly more than 3 percent) through 2008 was slightly less than that of earlier decades.

The percentage of blacks (25 years of age or over) with less than a high school education declined from 63.4 in 1972 to 33.8 in 1990, as shown in Figure 2.3. By 2008, the percentage of blacks with less than a high school education had declined to 17.0 percent. The percentage of blacks in the moderate educational group rose from 31.5 in 1972 to 63.4 in 2008. Perhaps what is most impressive is that the percentage of blacks with 12 or more years of school (including college graduates) increased from 36.6 percent in 1972 to 82.3 percent in 2008. Overall, blacks have experienced a significant increase in their educational attainment during this 36-year period between 1972 and 2008. As a result, it is important to note that since the mid-1980s there has been significant growth in the size of the status-based black middle class based on the increases in educational attainment.

The New Black Middle Class

Regardless of how one chooses to define the black middle class (or higher socio-economic status group), since the 1960s, the proportion of blacks in the moderate to upper education and income categories has increased significantly. The majority of the individuals in this group are the first generation in their families to be in the middle class. Relative to the old black middle class, the new black middle class is better educated and has greater human capital skills and resources that could be used to augment the black community's political influence. In addition, the new black middle class has greater disposable income, which means that it has economic power, something that the old black middle class never had.

For purposes of this chapter, the middle class (or upper socioeconomic group) was defined as those individuals having access to the financial resources and/or skill sets that would afford them a decent standard of living or comfortable quality of life. The middle class is operationalized by blending the size of the appropriate economic-based middle class group with the appropriate status-based black middle class group. Figure 2.4 charts the rise of the black middle and upper socio-economic (class) groups. The middle (or moderate) socioeconomic group was determined by taking the average of the percentage of blacks in the moderate

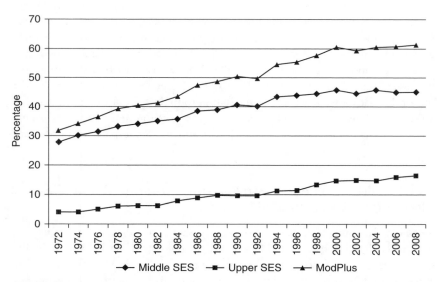

FIGURE 2.4 Projected Growth in the Sizes of the Black Middle and Upper Socioeconomic Status Groups: 1972–2008

The projected size of the "middle class" was calculated by averaging the percentage of blacks with 12 or more years of education with the percentage of black families in the moderate-income bracket. The projected size of the "upper class" was calculated by averaging the percentage of blacks with 16 or more years of education with the percentage of black families in the upper-income bracket

status-based (education) group and the percentage of blacks in the moderate economic-based (income) group.[24] In 1972, based on this measure, 27.8 percent of the black population was in the moderate socioeconomic group. By 2008, the percentage of blacks in this group had increased to 45 percent, representing a 17.2 percent increase in the size of the black moderate socioeconomic group since 1972. In the 36-year period between 1972 and 2008, the greatest increase in the percentage of blacks in the moderate socioeconomic status group came between 1972 and 1990. During this 18-year period, the percentage of blacks in this group rose from 27.8 percent to 40.6. This amounted to a 12.8 percent jump in the size of the number of blacks in the moderate socioeconomic group. On the other hand, the increase in the percentage of blacks in the moderate socioeconomic status group only increased by 4.4 percent between 1990 and 2008.

The growth in the percentage of blacks in the upper socioeconomic status group has been steady and more consistent since 1972. The upper socioeconomic group was determined by taking the average of the percentage of blacks in the upper status-based (education) group and the percentage of blacks in the upper economic-based (income) group.[25] Between 1972 and 1990, the percentage of blacks in the upper socioeconomic status group grew by 5.6. During the 18-year period between 1990 and 2008, the percentage of blacks in the upper socio-economic status group grew by 6.7.[26] Overall, between 1972 and 2008, the size of the black upper socioeconomic group grew from 4.1 percent to 16.5 percent. Combining the percentage of blacks in the moderate and upper socioeconomic groups to gauge the size of what we will refer to as the moderate-plus socio-economic status group (the black middle class), we can see that this group has increased in size from 31.9 percent in 1972 to 61.5 percent in 2008. Likewise, the size of the black lower socioeconomic status group declined from 68.1 percent in 1972 to 38.5 percent in 2008. In addition, it is worth noting that it was around 1988 that the projected size of the lower and moderate-plus socioeconomic groups was comparable in size.

Issues that Continue to Make Race Important to Middle-Class Blacks in the Socioeconomic Transition Era

The new black middle class does not face the same limitations and restraints that the pre-civil rights black middle class faced. Along with fewer economic and social restraints today come greater opportunities for blacks to create individual and subgroup identities around the intersection of their racial and socioeconomic statuses. Although race is the one factor that all blacks must address when fashioning an identity, some blacks have more flexibility in fashioning their overall identity than others. For example, lower-class blacks do not have as many positive options in fashioning alternate identities since they are often trapped by the intersection of their lower racial and lower-class statuses. This is not always the case for blacks in the upper socioeconomic status group, who have the option of fashioning their identity around some combination of their race and class. That is, members of the black middle class have the option of establishing their identity exclusively around their positive socioeconomic status and trying to downplay their negative racial status, or they may choose to play up their racial status because of their socioeconomic status. This is significant to black politics for two reasons. First, intersecting race and class allows for consideration of the similarities and differences in the challenges facing blacks at the different class levels.[27] Second, how the new black middle class as a group or individually shape its identity will determine the future of the black politics of America. The future of black politics will be determined by the emerging black middle class choosing to put their racial interests ahead of their class interests. The degree to which this happens depends on four issues that continue to galvanize blacks as a political unit and especially makes race an issue for the emerging black middle class: 1) differing perceptions of blacks' progress in society between blacks and whites, 2) the continuing significance of race in society, 3) the issue of assimilation, and 4) affirmative action.

Perceptions of Blacks' Progress and Equal Opportunity

The U.S. has been described as two nations, one black and one white, and which are separate, hostile, unequal.[28] Although many would agree with different aspects of this characterization of the relationship between blacks and whites, most would question if the relationship continues to be "hostile." Nevertheless and despite the start of a new era of black politics, there continue to be significant differences in blacks' and whites' perceptions of progress in blacks' quality of life. At the start of the Socioeconomic Transition Era, whites saw substantial progress in race relations and improvements in the quality of life for blacks but blacks saw it differently.[29] Stephan and Abigail Thernstrom summed up the feelings of many whites when they stated that blacks have made significant social, political, and economic progress since the 1940s.[30] They noted a positive change in whites' attitudes towards blacks, and that white America has expressed an impressive commitment to an integrated society. Furthermore, they added that many whites believe that the impact of the civil rights movement on society has been positive. Thernstrom and Thernstrom offered as evidence of progress the crumbling of the taboo on sexual relations between the two races. They noted that although blacks and whites still largely live separate and unequal lives, America is moving away from the racial segregation of the past. It was pointed out that many blacks are moving into predominantly white neighborhoods, more blacks attend integrated college campuses than ever before, and interracial dating and marrying has increased significantly.[31]

Many would question if blacks are still disadvantaged because of their race. Many whites quietly agree that, for example, the real problems are low skills, bad test scores, teenage pregnancy, the disproportionate number of black males in the criminal justice system, and the lure of drug money and addictions among the black underclass.[32] On the other hand, many blacks feel that the existence of the large number of social problems in the black community is the direct result of the continuation of racism in society. Loury summed up the difference in perceptions by suggesting that blacks (especially middle-class blacks) have a tendency to see race as fundamentally important, while whites think blacks are too obsessed with race.[33]

Many whites think of racial progress in terms of "traditional racial integration."[34] That is, for many whites things such as increased racial interaction and the absence of overt racism measure progress. Despite increased interracial contact and decreases in overt racism, the majority of blacks say they continue to experience discrimination in education, employment opportunities, and wages.[35] As a result, well into the start of Socioeconomic Transition Era "a huge racial chasm remained" in our society over the perception of progress.[36] Table 2.1 shows the difference in blacks' and whites' perceptions of progress, and what contributes

TABLE 2.1 Blacks' and Whites' Perceptions of Progress in the Socioeconomic Transition Era

	Whites	Blacks	[a]Coefficient
[b]Conditions for blacks have improved	68.8	58.4	.052★ (.035)
[c]Economic position of respondent's race has gotten worse	35.5	47.8	−.095★★★ (.026)
[c]Blacks have gotten less than deserved	38.1	70.6	−.413★★★ (.025)
[c]Respondent's race fate has a lot of effect on respondent's fate	27.5	48.7	−.197★★★ (.029)
[c]Agree society hasn't dealt fairly with my (racial) group	15.3	80.8	−.630★★★ (.014)
[c]A lot of discrimination against blacks	27.6	54.9	−.284★★★ (.024)
[b]Agree blacks should work their way up to overcome prejudice without favors	75.7	54.0	.141★★★ (.015)
[b]Differences between blacks' and whites' socioeconomic status is due to discrimination	30.8	57.9	−.205★★★ (.018)
[b]Differences between blacks' and whites' socioeconomic status is due to lack of education	42.8	50.7	−.057★
[b]Differences between blacks' and whites' socioeconomic status is due to lack of will	49.8	46.0	.028 (.018)

[a]Kendall's Tau Coefficient, [b]General Social Survey (combined 2002–2006), [c]National Politics Study, 2004 ★$p < .05$ ★★$p < .01$ ★★★$p < .001$

to differences in the two groups' socioeconomic quality of life. The first four questions examine the extent to which there are differences in perceptions of improvement in blacks' quality of life.[37] The latter five questions ascertain attitudes about the factors contributing to the continuing differences in blacks' and whites' socioeconomic status.

When asked whether the conditions for blacks have improved, got worse, or remained about the same in the last five years, the response difference between blacks and whites was significant. Roughly 28 percent of the white respondents and 34.3 percent of the black respondents said economic conditions have remained about the same. On a positive note, well over half of both the black and white respondents felt that conditions for blacks had improved. However, the difference between the percentage of blacks and whites stating that conditions had improved was slightly more than 10 percent. Only 35.5 percent of the whites and 47.8 percent of the black respondents felt that conditions had got worse. When asked if blacks had got less than they deserved in society, there were major differences in the perceptions of blacks and whites. Only 38.1 percent of the white respondents agreed compared to 70.6 percent of the black respondents. Blacks were significantly more likely to say that the economic position of their race has gotten worse. About 47.8 percent of the black respondents felt their race's economic position had got worse when compared with 35.5 percent of the white respondents. When asked if society had dealt fairly with their racial group, the difference in blacks' and whites' positions constituted a chasm. The overwhelming majority of the black respondents (80.8 percent) compared with only 15.3 percent of the white respondents agreed that society had not dealt fairly with their racial group.

Table 2.1 also shows black and white respondents' perceptions of the factors that contributes to the differences in the two groups' socioeconomic status. More than a majority of the black respondents felt that discrimination continued to be a factor influencing their quality of life. About 54.9 percent of the black respondents felt there was a lot of discrimination against blacks. Only 7.3 percent of the black respondents said there was little or no discrimination against blacks. Among whites, only 27.6 percent felt there was a lot of discrimination against blacks and a majority of whites (57.8 percent) felt there was only some discrimination against blacks. When asked directly about the cause of differences in blacks' and whites' socioeconomic status, 57.9 percent of the black respondents felt it was due to discrimination compared with only 30.8 percent of the white respondents. When asked if differences between blacks' and whites' socioeconomic status was due to lack of education, black respondents were equally divided. Among whites, 42.8 percent attributed differences in the races' socioeconomic status to lack of education. There was no significant difference in the two groups' feelings that the differences were due to lack of will. Both racial groups were also evenly divided in the perception of whether the differences were do to a lack of will.

Significance of Race

William Julius Wilson, several years ago, suggested that the relationship between blacks and whites was moving away from one of racial oppression to one of economic class subordination.[38] Wilson believed that since the end of the civil rights movement, life chances for individual blacks have more to do with their economic class position than their day-to-day encounters with whites. According to Wilson, prior to the civil rights movement, blacks were denied access to valued and scarce resources through discrimination, segregation, and other schemes designed to enforce ideologies of racism. This was especially the case in the labor market; however, new sets of obstacles have emerged because of basic shifts in the economy. Wilson felt that the new barriers to improving a person's life chances create even greater hardships for the lower and underclass segments of the black community. This is significant because of the large number of blacks in the lower and under classes. Wilson acknowledged the continued existence of racial prejudice, discrimination, segregation, and racism in society. However, as Wilson writes, "in the economic sphere, class has become more important than race in determining black access to privilege and powers."[39]

As empirical support for his argument concerning the declining significance of race, Wilson referred to the findings of several studies showing that the post-Civil Rights Era socioeconomic attainment process for blacks had become similar to that of whites and that class had become an important factor affecting the occupational attainment of blacks. Wilson suggested that middle-class blacks in the U.S. would eventually reach parity with middle-class whites in their lifestyles and life chances. Over the years, a number of studies have been conducted based on Wilson's "declining significance of race thesis." Many of these studies have suggested that race continues to be a significant factor in American society and refuted Wilson's idea that the significance of race is declining. Hughes and Thomas found that quality of life continues to be worse for blacks than for whites and this did not vary, nor was it explained by socioeconomic status.[40] Wilson and Sakura-Lemessy examined differences in the income gap between two cohorts of males and determined that the racial gap was structured in a manner that was contrary to William Wilson's thesis.[41] In a separate research study, George Wilson found that the negative influence of minority racial status on income actually increased during the 1980s.[42] In the area of employment, D'Amico and Maxwell found a pervasive black disadvantage that did not vary greatly by region of the country or between central city, suburban, or rural areas.[43] In the area of criminal justice, the fact that race and ethnicity has a small-to-moderate effect on sentencing outcomes—favoring whites and penalizing minorities—has been offered as evidence of the continuing significance of race.[44]

A counter hypothesis suggested that the significance of race was increasing, especially for middle-class blacks confronted with issues of desegregation, affirmative action, and the experience of coming into direct contact with whites for the first time.[45] It was argued that black families, because of moving into integrated neighborhoods and work situations, tend to become more consumed with race. To what degree the significance of race has declined, increased or remained constant, the fact remains that race still matters according to Cornel West.[46] West suggests that as long as black people are seen as a "problem people," and as "long as black people are viewed as a 'them,' the burden falls on blacks to do all the 'cultural' and 'moral' work necessary for healthy race relations."[47] Table 2.1 puts the significance of race (for both blacks and whites) in perspective. When asked if their race's fate had any effect on their own personal fate, a clear majority of both the blacks and whites said either some effect or a large effect. Among the black respondents, 48.7 percent felt that their race's fate had a lot of effect on their own fate and 41.1 percent some effect. Among whites, only 27.5 percent felt their race had a lot of effect on their fate, but 57.5 percent of the white respondents felt it had some effect on their fate. Well over two-thirds of the black and white respondents felt that their race's fate had an effect on their own fate.

Race continues to matter in this society according to Andrew Hacker, because "white America continues to ask of its black citizens to have an extra patience and a perspective that whites have never required of themselves."[48] As a result, blacks and whites have different realities and different perspectives on the role of race in society. Perhaps the greatest reason why race matters in the American society is the presence of ideological beliefs and activities that produce the social, political, and economic subordination of a group because of racial heritage. James Jones distinguishes between three levels of racism—individual, institutional, and cultural. Individual racism suggests a belief in the superiority of one's own race over another, for which an individual engages in behaviors to maintain that superior position. Institutional racism is the byproduct of certain institutional practices that operate to maintain a racist advantage over others. Cultural racism generally relates to individual and institutional expressions of the superiority of one race's cultural heritage over that of another race.[49]

Over the last 30 years, there is evidence that suggests racism at the individual level has declined in significance. Robert Smith pointed out that many surveys and studies of racial attitudes in the post-Civil Rights Era have shown a sharp decline in both white racist attitudes and negative stereotypes toward blacks.[50] Smith, nevertheless, questioned if there has really been a decline in the significance of race or a decline in whites' willingness to express such attitudes in public forums such as surveys. Perhaps one could make the argument that in a multicultural society where there are numerous cross-cultural encounters, significance of cultural racism is also in decline. However, regardless of individual social status, black individuals are more likely to be victims of institutional racism. Smith, for example, presented numerous examples of patterns and practices of institutional racism in education, employment, housing, health care, and consumer services that pose a dilemma for blacks regardless of class.[51] Tate puts this issue in perspective when she writes, "Although the issue of racial discrimination may no longer be a political priority among blacks, most still feel that racial discrimination remains a substantial problem in the United States."[52]

Race and racism are key issues in black politics because they are the primary reasons blacks continue to function as a political unit. Race serves as the glue that holds blacks together as a community in a social context. It is the common cultural and social experiences of blacks that mold shared aspirations, beliefs, values, and a sense of oneness. Race and racism also serve as a force that holds blacks together as an economic unit, because huge gaps continue to persist between the economic well-being of blacks and whites today. Therefore, the degree to which race and racism remain significant in this society determines the degree to which blacks will continue to function as a social, political, and economic unit.

The Issue of Assimilation

Park and Burgess, in the 1920s, conceptualized what they regarded as the ultimate resolution for racial and ethnic conflict: assimilation.[53] Park defined assimilation as "a process of interaction and fusion in which persons and groups acquire the memories, sentiments, and attitudes of other persons or groups, and by sharing their experience and history, are incorporated with them in a common cultural life." [54]Thus, assimilation implies that one group adopts the general behavioral and social characteristics of another. The act of assimilating assumes that there is an imbalance of power existing between two distinct groups (one entity is socially, politically, and economically weak and the other is strong) and it suggests a merger of two diverse entities: the weaker of the two adopts the general behavioral and social characteristics of the stronger. This adoption indicates an acceptance of the stronger group's control of the allocation of social, political, and economic resources as legitimate. When assimilation occurs, it usually occurs because the weaker group lacks either an alternative course of action or a position of strength to challenge the majority group's control and influence.

E. Franklin Frazier was convinced that blacks would make every effort to assimilate and become integrated into American life as their socioeconomic status increased, and that "white collar status" would have a positive effect on how assimilated a black became.[55] Frazier in later studies pulled back from his optimism about blacks' assimilation, noting that the black middle class suffered from "feelings of insecurity, frustration, and guilt."[56] The combination of history and race has made it hard for blacks to assimilate. Despite recent changes in the social dynamics of the American society, this reality continues to pose a serious dilemma for the emerging black middle class in the Socioeconomic Transition Era of black politics.

In America, no ethnic or racial minority has controlled outright or dominated the decision making about the allocation of the nation's social, political, and economic resources. Although ethnic and racial minorities have found themselves participating in decision making about the allocation of societal resources, their influence was at the individual level and not the group level. America has always initially reacted harshly to "out-groups"; ethnic and racial minorities. Groups in America who look or behave differently from the dominant group have often faced social pressure to "act American" (to conform to the dominant group's way of life) and failure to do so can result in social, political, and economic hardships. There is a tendency in this nation's social, political, and economic institutions and processes to promote homogeneity by stripping groups of their individual identities. The best examples of how this assimilative process has worked in the United States is through an examination of the plight of early European immigrants (among them the Italians, Irish, Germans, and Polish). Many of the first-generation European immigrants lived in urban enclaves where they spoke their native languages and maintained their cultural traditions. They often faced discrimination and intimidation. They soon learned that their pursuit of the "American dream" required them to conform and integrate into the dominant culture's social, political, and economic way of life. For the dominant group, this pressure also served to stabilize any social, political, and economic opposition. That is, the fewer competitive groups in society, the fewer challenges to the political, social, and economic status quo.

Blacks have never rejected (challenged yes) Americanism (or the American social, political, or economic culture), it was Americanism that has rejected blacks. When asked if it was better for America if the different racial and ethnic groups maintain their distinct culture or blend into the larger society, a clear majority of blacks favored the blending of cultures. In general, 56.2 percent felt blacks should blend into the culture of the larger society, 37.5 percent of all black respondents felt that blacks should maintain a distinct culture, and 6.3 percent said blacks should do both. Figure 2.5 shows blacks' responses differing significantly, however, on this question based on level of education. College-educated blacks were far more likely than the lesser educated to embrace the idea of maintaining a distinct black culture. Approximately 45 percent of the college-educated blacks compared with 35.7 percent of the blacks with a high school degree or some college and 31 percent of the black respondents with less than 12 years of school felt blacks should maintain a distinct culture. A larger percentage of the blacks with 12 years or less than any of the other two educational categories supported the blending of the black culture into the larger culture. There was a 20 percent gap between the proportion of higher- and lower-educated blacks advocating blending cultures and a 13.6 percent gap between the proportion of moderately and higher-educated blacks supporting the blending in of cultures.

Black America (especially the black middle class) has been very reluctant to assimilate for several reasons. First, whites' dominance of the social, political, and economic institutions has had a profoundly negative impact on blacks' social, political, and economic development as a community. Throughout U.S. history,

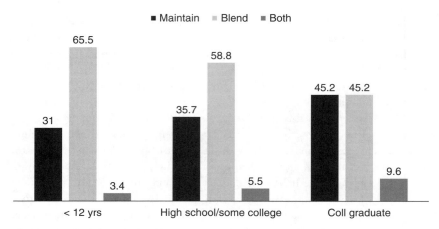

FIGURE 2.5 Blacks' Attitudes About Maintaining a Distinct Culture or Blending into Larger Society Based on Level of Education

Source: National Politics Study, 2004

blacks have had to challenge or question whites' dominance of the allocation of resources and values in society (which has had a profoundly negative social, political, and economic consequence for blacks). In essence, blacks have not fared very well under social, political, and economic systems dominated by whites. Furthermore, it is difficult for any group to embrace a culture and its institutions when that culture has a history of not acting in its interests and, in many instances, has prevented that group from achieving social, political, and economic parity. Furthermore, black Americans (like the immigrant Europeans before them) have always maintained a desire to hold on to their unique cultural attributes, not only to retain them, but also to have them accepted as defining characteristics of American society.

Another reason why blacks have been reluctant to embrace any movement toward total assimilation is what Derrick Bell refers to as the "permanency of racism."[57] Black politics is a response to institutional racism as well as cultural racism. The social, political, and economic institutions in America promote the interests of white America, even when their intention is not to be detrimental to other racial and minority groups. Much of the skepticism of the collective black population about moving toward assimilation is reinforced by the inability of the dominant political group to acknowledge the presence of this cultural and institutional racism and deal effectively with it. The other factor that has prevented the black population (especially the black middle-class) from enthusiastically assimilating into mainstream society is the evolution of different political mindsets or worldviews around the notion of "race." Because of their racial past in America, the political worldview of most blacks has been formulated within a social context. That is, civil and human rights issues (e.g., slavery, discrimination, racism) have driven much of black politics and the formation of blacks' worldview. On the other hand, the political worldview of whites have been molded within an economic context and culture centers on issues such as the allocation of resources, the distribution of goods and services, and building economic security. For the dominant American political culture, social considerations are secondary to economic considerations, while for blacks economic considerations have traditionally been secondary to social considerations. The question arises as to what happens as various subpopulations within the black community (especially the black middle class) become increasingly exposed to a worldview molded by concerns other than their racial group's social plight. In other words, as more and more blacks move into the middle class, will their economic concerns overshadow their social concerns about race? Furthermore, as economic interests increase among blacks will they become less reluctant to assimilate?

Affirmative Action

The fourth issue for the new black middle class is the "problem" of affirmative action. Affirmative action was intended to be a program to remedy the effects of past discrimination, primarily in the areas of employment and education, and was expected not only to redress the problems of the past but also to prevent them from reoccurring. Because of inequity and lack of opportunity based on race and gender in the U.S., affirmative action was intended to overcome these problems by permitting race and gender to become a factor in hiring, contracting, and admissions. Currently, law and various regulations for all governmental agencies require affirmative action for recipients of public funds, such as contractors and universities. Proponents of affirmative action argue that some form of preferential treatment is essential to break down long-standing patterns of discrimination against racial minorities and women in education and employment. They argue that affirmative action is mainly an attempt to level the playing field for disadvantaged people who are trying to compete in a society that has openly discriminated against racial minorities and women for centuries. Proponents also believe that granting modest advantages to minorities and women is necessary to overcome hundreds of years of discrimination. Opponents of affirmative action, on the other hand, claim that affirmative action constitutes "reverse discrimination," and opponents argue that affirmative action denies equality of opportunity based on merit and incompetent minorities and women are displacing white male workers. They maintain that affirmative action favors members of one group over another.

Carol Swain wrote:

> Affirmative action is a complicated national issue, and there are no easy answers. The issue has historically been, and continues to be, plagued by ambiguity surrounding the concept and by the ways in which the various

policies have been implemented. Confusion also stems from factors including the self-serving interpretations of politicians and inaccurate media portrayals. Government officials who rely on public-opinion polls to guide them in their decisions about affirmative action programs need to exercise caution in how they interpret survey results. It is grossly inaccurate to conclude that racial polarization characterizes the opinions of most Americans on affirmative action and related issues.[58]

Clearly, affirmative action is a complicated issue in part because we live in a society that is stratified by race and class. Currently, race and class contribute equally to a social structure of inequality. However, increased social mobility among blacks, along with other factors, such as a reduction in racial prejudice and discrimination, has led to a greater increase in class-consciousness than in race consciousness.[59]

Affirmative action is one of the issues where blacks and whites appear to be hopelessly divided.[60] Blacks tend to favor affirmative action and whites tend to oppose it. There are some blacks (often identified as conservative) who also oppose affirmative action. Blacks who oppose affirmative action often do so because they feel it encourages a feeling of inferiority in blacks based on the assumptions of many whites that blacks are being hired or admitted only due to a policy of racial preference. Blacks who oppose affirmative action often emphasize the personal responsibility of individuals to improve their lives, and they tend to downplay the impact of the racism and discrimination that hold racial minorities and women back. Despite opposition to affirmative action by some blacks, the majority of blacks favor increasing or maintaining affirmative action programs. In one survey, 89 percent of the black respondents indicated that to overcome past discrimination and help blacks get better jobs/education they favored affirmative action programs. Only 52 percent of the white respondents favored the initiative. When asked whether they favored affirmative action programs that give special preference to qualified blacks in hiring/education, 78 percent of the black respondents answered positively compared to 39 percent of the white respondents.[61] Whites' resistance to affirmative action (or preferential treatment) tends to be grounded on the principles of fairness or qualification. Fraser and Kick found that the majority of whites opposed to race-targeting policies framed racial discrimination as a problem of the past, defined race targeting as a subversion of meritocracy, or gave no value to programs that sought to provide opportunities to those groups who have been structurally disadvantaged.[62]

Kluegel and Smith's study reveals that stratification beliefs are a stronger predictor than racial attitudes of whites' support or opposition for race-targeted policies.[63] However, there is evidence that racial prejudice is "alive and well and strongly associated with whites' support against societal policies to assist African Americans" according to Williams and others.[64] Tuch and Hughes found that whites who acknowledge a structural basis for inequality are more likely to support race targeting.[65] Whites' opposition to affirmative action serves to heighten middle-class blacks' sense of racial consciousness. It is worth noting that affirmative action has greater significance for the black middle class than it does for the black lower class. Affirmative action programs have created many of the educational and employment opportunities that otherwise would have been denied to racial minorities and women had such a program not been in existence. Thus, an increasingly assertive opposition movement makes affirmative action a powerful political issue and a divider of the races. Furthermore, blacks continue to be over-represented in lower-paying jobs and they face active discrimination in many sectors of society. Ironically, a small but growing number of racial minorities and women are becoming less supportive of affirmative action because they feel the benefits are no longer worth the side effects.

Conclusion

Because of the changing socioeconomic structure in the black community, one must ask what impact the emergence of a new black middle class will have on black politics as we know it. Prior to the civil rights movement, matters of race dominated black politics. Regardless of an individual's socioeconomic status, racism, racial prejudice, and discrimination affected the lives of all blacks equally. In the post-Civil Rights Era, with the rise of class divisions, race remains a significant factor; however, the impact of race on life chances is different for those in the black middle class than it is for those in the black lower class. The issues confronting middle-class blacks are often very different from those affecting lower-class blacks. Many middle-class blacks are moving to the white suburbs or, in some cases, moving into exclusively middle-class black communities.

In summary, since the end of the Civil Rights Era blacks have made substantial socioeconomic gains. Today, blacks are evenly distributed across occupational categories (upper white-collar, lower white-collar, upper blue-collar and lower blue-collar). There has been a major decline in the percentage of blacks that have less than a high school diploma and a major increase in the percentage of college graduates. The percentage in the upper-income strata is four times larger than the percentage in 1970, and nearly three-fourths of the population is in either the moderate or the upper socioeconomic stratum. Despite significant improvements on the socioeconomic front, major issues regarding race and racism continue to exist for blacks. Although pleased with their progress, they are not as optimistic as whites are about the pace of their progress. They still feel the pressures of race and racism in society and this makes them (especially the more economically prosperous among them) reluctant to assimilate socially, politically, and economically. Finally, the issue of affirmative action serves as a litmus test for many blacks. The fact that affirmative action continues to be an issue serves to reinforce blacks' suspicions about the pace of progress. The next chapter attempts to put in perspective the role of race in the Socioeconomic Transition Era among blacks as a community. It will discuss the changes in black politics that are emerging as the results of the changing socioeconomic dynamics of the black community. Because of the changing dynamics it advances the notion that black politics in the Socioeconomic Transition Era is developing (or has developed) an internal dimension while the external dimension continues to influence black politics.

3

THE FOUNDATIONS FOR A POLITICAL DIVIDE

The foundation for black politics is blacks' reaction to racism, racial oppression, and quality of life issues. Race was a major factor influencing black politics in the Protest and Politics Eras, and it continues to be a factor today. What has changed over the years is the role that class or socioeconomic divisions play in black politics. More specifically, race continues to be a defining characteristic of black politics as it relates to the external political relationship between blacks (as a minority) and whites (as a majority). However, since the end of the Protest Era, class has increasingly become a factor defining the internal aspects of black politics. With the increasing importance of class in black politics today, the intersectionality of race and class has given rise to intra-group politics within the black community. The objectives of this chapter are twofold: first, to discuss the changing dynamics of the black population that serve as the foundation for the rise of intra-racial politics in the Socioeconomic Transition Era; and second, to discuss the emergence of a series of black political communities in the wake of the increased role that socioeconomic divisions now play in the internal politics of the black community.

Events and Changing Dynamics That Contributed to the Rise of Intra-Racial Politics

Growing socioeconomic divisions within the black community are the foundation for the rise of intra-racial politics in the Socioeconomic Transition Era. Although racial concerns remain the basis for interracial (external) politics, class issues are becoming the basis for intra-racial (internal) politics. While the black community's external political activity continues to be about having a voice in the allocation of society's resources, the internal politics is about determining the socialcultural dynamics of the community and defining the path toward communal political and economic development. Among the many issues that serve as the basis for intra-racial politics is the question of who will define and shape black culture. Should the group embrace social and political assimilation or should it move toward self-determination? Should the focus of the black political community be about advancing the collective good of the community or should it be on improving the quality of life at the individual level? The rise of intra-racial politics in the Socioeconomic Transition Era can be attributed to several interrelated events. Our focus here is on the black Baby-Boomer generation coming of age; the rise of a new middle class and economic bifurcation within the population; increased diversity in blacks' lifestyles; and changes in the geographic structure of the community.

Baby-Boomers Come of Age

During the 1980s, the Baby-Boomer generation came of age.[1] This is significant for several reasons. First, the black Baby-Boomers (especially the older ones born between 1945 and 1954) were old enough to have experienced the direct and indirect effects of America's system of apartheid or Jim Crowism. Second, the black Baby-Boomers came of age when the black resistance and social movements of the 1960s challenged the existing social and political order of the day. Third, the Baby-Boomers were the first beneficiaries of those civil and voting rights policies aimed at increasing opportunities and improving blacks' quality of life. Finally, the beginning of the Socioeconomic Transition Era of black politics coincided with Baby-Boomers moving into middle adulthood. By 1990, Baby-Boomers ranged in age from 26 to 44 and made up 30 percent of the total black population. Baby-Boomers were 43 percent of the black adult population (those over 18 years of age) and they were 56 percent of the "stable adult" population (those over 24 years of age).[2] By 2004, Baby-Boomers ranged in age from 40 to 58. Black Baby-Boomers were 11.7 percent of the total Boomer population. They were 25.3 percent of the total black population,[3] and they were roughly 34.1 percent of the black adult population (those over the age of 18) as shown in Table 3.1. In 2004, black Baby-Boomers were 43.1 percent of the black population over the age of 24.[4]

The Baby-Boomers were children and young adults during the Protest Era of black politics. Very few were directly involved in the civil rights struggle of the late 1950s and early 1960s. They were, instead, the symbolic reason for the struggle. Their parents and grandparents engaged in the struggle for civil rights on their behalf. Many Baby-Boomers experienced first-hand racial discrimination and prejudice. Some even witnessed the violence their parents and grandparents endured in the quest for civil and voting rights. For many in this generation their personal experiences growing up and the witnessing of major social changes played a key role in the formation of their social, political, and economic beliefs and values. On the one hand, black Baby-Boomers' closeness to the civil rights

TABLE 3.1 Socioeconomic Characteristics of the Baby-Boomer and Pre-Baby-Boomer Cohorts in the Socioeconomic Transition Era: 2004/2006

	Greatest and the Silent Cohorts	Baby-Boomer Cohort (1946–1964)	Baby-Boomer Older Cohort (1946–1954)	Baby-Boomer Younger Cohort (1955–1964)
Distribution	15.9	34.1	13.8	20.3
Education				
High school diploma	39.8	55.4	53.6	56.6
Associate degree or higher	13.6	29.3	28.5	29.8
Occupational prestige score				
Moderate	46.6	47.8	49.3	46.8
High	22.4	36.5	33.6	38.5
Income				
Moderate	23.9	31.9	32.4	31.6
High	3.4	13.0	16.9	10.5
Socioeconomic index score				
Moderate	13.7	26.4	27.1	25.9
High	11.2	12.5	10.0	14.1

Source: Combined 2004/2006 General Social Surveys. A high occupational prestige score was 45 or greater and a moderate was between 25 and 44. The moderate income category included those with a total family income between $40,000 and $89,000, and a moderate socioeconomic index score ranged from 43.9 to 70.7 and a high SEI was above 70.8.

struggle as youth helped to define their attitudes and behaviors as adults. On the other hand, black Baby-Boomers were not immune to the changes that were influencing the beliefs and values of larger society. Compared with previous generations of blacks, black Baby-Boomers had a greater sense of freedom and independence. This increased sense of freedom and independence also contributed to a greater sense of individualism. This is not to say that black Baby-Boomers and subsequent generations were not committed to advancing the good of the greater black community; however it is to say that the sense of commitment to the larger black community is weaker today. Black Baby-Boomers and subsequent generations have come to value individual economic prosperity as the key to improving quality of life. Furthermore, black Baby-Boomers accepted or embraced the idea that an improved quality of life and a decent standard of living are difficult to achieve without functioning in "the white man's world."

As the direct beneficiaries of the political gains won during the struggles of the Civil Rights Era, there were numerous "firsts" among black Baby-Boomers. In the late 1960s and throughout the 1970s, they were no longer indirect participants in the struggle for social and political equality. In the Politics Era struggle, they were the emerging leaders. This generation often found aspects of their beliefs and values in conflict with the preceding generations, but they also found conflict among themselves. They were more demanding and less patient with the pace of social, political, and economic progress than previous generations. They demanded change in many ways that differed from previous generations. However, black Baby-Boomers were more likely to accept individualized outcomes. Thus, they were more individualistic in what they felt should be the aims of black politics. They disagreed among themselves about how best to achieve racial and social justice, political empowerment, and economic empowerment. Some supported independence, self-sufficiency, and self-containment, while others wanted assimilation, independence, and to become part of the mainstream. Some felt that the quality of life for blacks would best be achieved through economic means, while others preferred the political route. From the very beginning there were divisions among black Baby-Boomers over the route the community should pursue in the post-Civil Rights Era. By the mid-1980s, America as a nation had become more focused on personal interests and less focused on the interests of the larger community and the black Baby-Boomers were not immune. Although race and racism continued to be an issue for blacks, its role (especially for the Baby-Boomers and subsequent generations) became increasingly individualized. This growing self-interest and sense of individualism in part gave birth to the Socioeconomic Transition Era of black politics.

The socioeconomic characteristics of the Baby-Boomer cohort differed from those of previous cohorts in the Socioeconomic Transition Era as shown in Table 3.1. As a group, the socioeconomic characteristics of the Baby-Boomer cohort differed significantly from the Greatest (born between 1907 and 1925) and Silent generations (also referred to as the Depression Babies and born between 1926 and 1944). The data show that the socioeconomic life chances were progressively better for black Baby-Boomers than for the previous generations. In the Socioeconomic Transition Era (in the mid-2000s), over 84 percent of the black Baby-Boomers had at least a high school diploma compared with just under 54 percent of those in the Greatest or Silent generation cohorts. Approximately 29.3 percent of the black Baby-Boomers had at least an associate of arts degree compared with slightly less than 14.0 percent of the blacks born in previous generations. Only 22.4 percent of the blacks born before 1946 had high-prestige occupations to this point in the Socioeconomic Transition Era compared with 36.5 percent of the Baby-Boomers.

Black Baby-Boomers were more likely to have moderate or high socioeconomic index (SEI) scores than the previous generations.[5] Nearly 40 percent of the black Baby-Boomers had a SEI score in the moderate or high range compared to only 24.9 percent of those in the Greatest and Silent generation cohorts. Black Baby-Boomers were more likely to have family incomes in the moderate or high category.[6] Of the Baby-Boomers, 12.5 percent had a family income in the high category. On the other hand, only 3.4 percent in the Greatest and Silent generation cohorts had a family income in the high category. Younger blacks' (in Generation X) socioeconomic life chances were much improved relative to older blacks. This provides some evidence that blacks' socioeconomic status has improved with each generation.

When the Baby-Boomers were divided into two groups, older (born between 1946 and 1954) and younger (between 1955 and 1964), this pattern became even more evident. According to the data presented in Table 3.1 the percentage of the younger Baby-Boomers was, not surprisingly, larger than the older Boomers. The younger black Baby-Boomers were better educated than their older counterparts. Younger black Baby-Boomers were more likely to have an occupation with greater prestige than older black Baby-Boomers. Although the data in Table 3.1 indicate that older black Baby-Boomers have higher family incomes as a group when compared to younger black Baby-Boomers, this could be partly explained by them being in the labor force (and on their jobs) longer than younger Baby-Boomers. The fact that younger black Baby-Boomers as a group have higher SEI scores (combining the moderate and higher categories) than the older black Baby-Boomers gives some support for this assertion. Overall, it appears that each succeeding generation of blacks has benefited from the social and political changes that have occurred in society since the Protest Era of black politics.

Economic Bifurcation and the Black Community

Although blacks as a group have prospered from the civil legislation of the 1960s, at the individual level prosperity has been unequal. Some blacks are much better off economically than the group as a whole. Consequently, the black community is becoming increasingly bifurcated by class.[7] Economic bifurcation among blacks also creates conditions favorable for the rise of intra-racial politics. The blacks (in particular the black Baby-Boomers) that prospered as a result of civil rights legislation are socially and economically different from previous generations. As shown in Table 3.1, they are better educated, advantaged by greater occupational opportunities, and they have a higher standard of living. They are more likely to interact socially with whites than previous generations of blacks, and they were relatively young when they achieved their middle-class status. This section briefly revisits two questions raised by Dawson regarding the structure of the black political economy: 1) what evidence is there of economic polarization or bifurcation within the black community? and 2) if there is economic polarization in the black community, how permanent and stable is it?[8] Dawson felt there was growing economic polarization within the black community, while there was also a continuing economic polarization between blacks and whites.

In the previous chapter it was estimated that the percentage of black families in the higher-income group[9] grew from 3.1 percent in 1972 to 13.4 percent by 2008 (see Figure 2.2). The percentage of blacks in the higher-income group increased by 4.8 percent during the 20-year period between 1972 and 1992, and it grew by another 6.1 percent in the 16-year period between 1992 and 2008. While a significant proportion of blacks have experienced upward socioeconomic mobility, a large proportion remained poor as illustrated in Figure 3.1. Overall, the percentage of black families living in poverty has decreased significantly since the early 1960s. The percentage of black families living in poverty was down from 32.4 percent in 1972 to 23.1 percent in 2006; however it was still high relative to white families. In 1972, the percentage of black families living in poverty was more than four times greater than the percentage of whites living in poverty (7.4 percent). By 2006, the percentage of black families in poverty was three times greater than the percentage of white families (8.5 percent).[10]

While the rate of poverty among black families was gradually decreasing between 1972 and 2006, the percentage of black families in the higher-income group was gradually increasing as shown in Figure 3.1. In 1972, there was a 29.3 percentage-point difference in the number of black families living in poverty and those in the higher-income category. By 2006, the difference between the percentage of black families living in poverty and those in the higher-income category had declined to 9.6 percentage points. In the five-year period between 2000 and 2006 the poverty rate for black families averaged 22.6 percent and the percentage of black families in the higher-income group averaged 12.8 percent. Since the end of the 1990s, the growth in percentage of black families in the higher-income group and the decline in the percentage of black families living in poverty have started to level off.

Figure 3.2 examines the share of aggregate income over time as another indicator of economic polarization and to ascertain its level of permanency. Figure 3.2 shows an uneven distribution of income among blacks. In 2008, the top 20 percent of black households were the recipients of half of the income received by all black households that year. In 1968, the top 20 percent of black households received

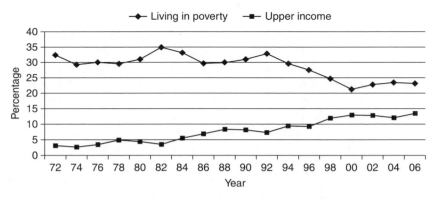

FIGURE 3.1 Changes in the Percentage of Black Families Living in Poverty versus Black Families in the Upper-Income Bracket

Source for Poverty Data: U.S. Census Bureau, Current Population Survey, Annual Social and Economic Supplements. Table 2. Poverty Status of People by Family Relationship, Race, and Hispanic Origin: 1959 to 2006

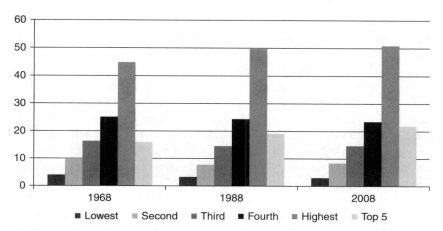

FIGURE 3.2 Share of Aggregate Income Received by Each Fifth and the Top Five Percent of Black Households in Select Years

Source: U.S. Census Bureau, Current Population Survey, Annual Social and Economic Supplements. For information on confidentiality protection, sampling error, nonsampling error, and definitions, see www.census.gov/apsd/techdoc/cps/cpsmar09.pdf[PDF]. Table H-2. Share of Aggregate Income Received by Each Fifth and Top 5 Percent of Households, Black 1967 to 2008

only 44.8 percent of the income received by all black households during that year and 49.7 percent in 1988. Among black households, the top 20 percent was the only group to have an increase in the share of income received by any of the quintiles. When examining the amount of income received by the top 5 percent of black households, in 1968 this group received 15.9 percent of all the income received by black households. By 2008, the percentage of income received by this group had increased to 22 percent. To put this into perspective, the bottom 20 percent of black households earned less than $12,138, the top 20 percent earned more than $67,600 and the top 5 percent earned more than $123,460 that year.[11]

While the average proportion of income received by the top 20 percent of black families increased steadily since 1968, the average amount received by the bottom fifth has declined ever so slightly. In the four-year period between 1968 and 1972, the average share of income received by the bottom fifth of black income earners was 4 percent. By 2008, the average share of income received by the bottom fifth of the income earners had declined to 3 percent. Since 1968, the four-year average of the share of income received by the bottom, second, third and fourth quintiles has actually declined by 1 to 2 percentage points. Unfortunately, 65 percent of blacks who start in the bottom half of the income distribution will not see an increase in their relative position.[12]

Although there is evidence of a growing economic bifurcation within the black community, there is also an uneasiness and economic reality that defines the nature of the relationship between blacks' prosperity and black politics. For example, the new black middle class is particularly vulnerable to falling back into a lower class because they lag behind whites in income, wealth, home ownership, and educational attainment.[13] Relative to white workers, black workers, in general, are more likely to experience a higher incidence of downward occupational mobility.[14] At the same time, because blacks have much poorer occupational status backgrounds than whites, they are less likely to experience upward mobility.[15] Some of the class disparities between blacks and whites can be attributed to the percentage of blacks being clustered into lower middle-class occupations (such as sales and clerical), while whites in the middle class tend to be split between upper-class occupations (professional and managerial) and lower middle-class.[16]

Another socioeconomic reality that tends to impede the financial development of middle-class blacks relative to middle-class whites is their relationship with family and friends. A larger proportion of the new black middle class is first or second generation middle-class.[17] Middle-class blacks are more likely to have grown up poor and have siblings and/or other family members and friends who are poor.[18] As a result, middle-class blacks are more likely to provide financial assistance to their relatives and this interferes with them building wealth.[19] So in conclusion, there is evidence of economic polarization within the black community. The evidence suggests that the divisions are becoming larger between the black "haves" and "have-nots." Furthermore, there is evidence of the continuing economic divisions between blacks and whites.

Increasing Suburbanization of Black America

Another factor that is leading to the rise of intra-racial politics in the Socioeconomic Transition Era is the increasing suburbanization of blacks. The urbanization of blacks began in the early twentieth century when a large number of Southern blacks migrated in search of a better life from rural areas to Northern cities or to urban areas in the South. As blacks moved into the cities, whites began to move to the suburbs and racial segregation in housing escalated. The suburbanization of whites gathered speed with the rise of the civil rights movement and calls for school desegregation. Ironically, after passage of the civil rights legislation in the 1960s, blacks with economic means also began to leave the urban areas for suburbia. Oddly enough, it was the "isms" that drove both whites and affluent blacks to the suburbs: it was "racism" for whites and "classism" for blacks. The movement to the suburbs of blacks in the upper socioeconomic status group has had major social and economic ramifications for the black community. Foremost among them is that it has contributed to cultural and spatial divisions within the population. As a result, geographical separation could become a political factor for blacks by influencing the formation of differing (and sometimes competing) attitudes and values.

Through the mid-1970s, as shown in Figure 3.3, more than 60 percent of blacks lived in a city where the population size was greater than 50,000. In 1972,

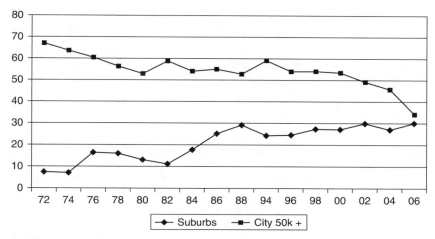

FIGURE 3.3 Residential Patterns of Blacks: 1972–2006
Source: General Social Survey, 1972–2006

only 7.3 percent of the black population lived in the suburbs. Into the new millennium the majority of the blacks still live in large or medium-sized cities or in an unincorporated area near large metropolitan areas, but the percentage of blacks living in cities with 50,000 or more residents had declined to around 50 percent. Between the 1970s and late-1990s there was a significant shift in where blacks resided. There was a large jump in the percentage of blacks living in the suburbs in the mid-1970s. By the mid-2000s, the proportion of blacks living in the suburbs had increased to nearly 30 percent.

The increasing suburbanization and general housing patterns of blacks are evidence of increasing class segregation among the population.[20] Housing patterns show blacks with economic means are moving away from the once segregated black neighborhoods of the 1950s and 1960s into newly established black neighborhoods or racially mixed neighborhoods. Since WWII, the growth of the black middle class has contributed to the forming of larger black middle-class enclaves that increased the distance between them and the black poor.[21] As a result, middle-class blacks often live between urban inner-city neighborhoods that have high areas of crime and poverty and the suburbs.[22] Many of the areas they reside in were once established white communities from which whites moved away in the 1960s, 1970s, and 1980s.

According to Pattillo-McCoy, even with increased socioeconomic opportunities and open housing laws, there is a great deal of neighborhood socioeconomic segregation between whites and blacks. She noted that middle-class blacks and whites remain segregated from each other in terms of where they live.[23] When middle-class blacks do live in racially mixed neighborhoods, their level of education and income is greater than the characteristics of the neighborhood in which they reside.[24] Higher socioeconomic status blacks (those in the top fifth) were more integrated with whites than with low socioeconomic status blacks.[25] Furthermore, higher socioeconomic status blacks have more white neighbors, fewer poor neighbors, and live in neighborhoods with greater housing values.[26] The current housing patterns suggest that not only is there an increase in the suburbanization of blacks, but where and near whom blacks choose to live is driven by their socioeconomic status.

The Emergence of Political Sub-Communities

The changing demographic, geographic, and socioeconomic composition of the black community in the Socioeconomic Transition Era increases the potential for the rise in intra-group politics. Despite the perception of blacks as a unified political entity, the reality is that the political environment today is ripe for the rise of intra-group politics. Today we can no longer speak of a black political community, because increased socioeconomic diversity among blacks has set the stage for the rise of a series of political sub-communities. These emerging political sub-communities differ from each other in terms of their demographic, geographic, and socioeconomic characteristics. Furthermore, they differ in terms of how they choose to pursue the American dream. That is, the internal dynamics of black politics today are just as much about assimilating as they are about resisting assimilation. Park defined assimilation as "a process of interpenetration and fusion in which persons and groups acquire the memories, sentiments, and attitudes of other persons or groups, and by sharing their experience and history, are incorporated with them in a common cultural life."[27] Milton Gordon is noted for devising a theory of assimilation in which he suggests that the outcomes of encounters between racial and ethnic groups are part of a process that include several possible assimilation outcomes or stages.[28] Park and Gordon were very prominent among the theorists who advocated what is now referred to as the traditional or straight-line assimilation theories.

In recent years, a new theory of assimilation has emerged that argues that there are different paths that groups take to becoming submerged into dominant society. According to Portes and Zhou, some groups may follow the traditional or straight-line path to assimilation into the dominant society through acculturation and economic adaptation (the upward mobility path). Other groups adapt to society by voluntarily or involuntarily taking other paths such as straight-lining in the opposite direction to permanent poverty and assimilation into the underclass (the downward mobility path). Still other immigrants experience rapid economic advancement with deliberate preservation of their community's values and tight solitary (upward mobility with lagged acculturation).[29]

Although assimilation theory is most often applied to new immigrant groups who have settled in a foreign land, given the history of blacks in America it is not inconceivable to think of blacks in the context of a newly arrived immigrant group. Despite being in the Americas for more than 400 years, blacks have never rejected the notion of being totally merged (assimilated) into the larger American society. Blacks as a group have long desired to become a part of mainstream America, only to be denied by slavery, a policy of separate but equal, and discrimination and racism. In reality it was not until the post-*Brown versus Board of Education* and the beginning of the Civil Rights Era that blacks were legally allowed to pursue the American dream in the same context as whites. Thus, it is America's racial past that has made (and continues to make) the process of assimilation for blacks an issue that differs in origin from that of other racial and ethnic groups.

Despite recent changes in the social dynamics of the American society, this reality continues to pose a serious dilemma for the emerging black middle class in the Socioeconomic Transition Era of black politics.

Among the other factors that have contributed to the rise of political sub-communities and set the stage for intra-group politics is the evolution of political mindsets or worldviews that are no longer driven purely by racial concerns. Because of their historical past, the political worldview of blacks as a group was primarily formulated within a social (racialized) context. That is, civil and human rights issues (e.g., slavery, discrimination, racism) serve to galvanize blacks around the issue of race. While the political worldview of the dominant society has been molded within an economic context around issues such as building economic security and living the American dream, for blacks economic considerations were secondary to social considerations. As subgroups of blacks (especially the black middle class) become more willing to adopt worldviews that are molded by economic and other non-racial concerns and less by racial and social concerns, we can no longer talk exclusively of a black political community. Thus, it is suggested that the emergence of a set of political sub-communities among blacks is part of the assimilation process and it is becoming an issue for black politics today. Below is an overview of the black political sub-communities that are beginning to emerge.

The Assimilating Political Community

The assimilating political community is the smallest of the four black political communities. The size of this subgroup is estimated to be no larger than 10 percent. Although growing in size, its growth has been slow. As the name suggests, this group is most receptive to the general concept of assimilating. They tend to be on the upward mobility path. They have embraced the economic worldview of the dominant group and they are willing to forgo their cultural identity for that of the dominant group in society. The blacks that make up the assimilating political community are more likely to be from the Baby-Boomer or post Baby-Boomer cohorts. Blacks in this political community tend to have a moderate-to-high socioeconomic standing. They tend to have higher levels of education, income, occupations, and other human capital resources that afford them an opportunity to interact with and function within the larger white community. Blacks in this sub-community usually have minimal interaction with the larger black community. They are more likely to reside in the suburbs or in largely white urban communities. Some criticize this group for having little or no cultural and/or social connection to the larger black community. In addition, they are frequently criticized for having no sense of appreciation and under-standing of blacks' historical struggle for civil rights. Members of the community respond that they do appreciate the significance of the struggle for civil rights, but feel it is time to move on and take advantage of current social and economic opportunities.

Members of the assimilating political community usually see themselves as different from other blacks, and what enables them to distance themselves in this way is their socioeconomic status.[32] These individuals are most comfortable func-tioning in a predominately white environment. Despite their socioeconomic standing, they still encounter racial prejudice and discrimination, and most have developed coping skills that enable them to downplay the impact of such encoun-ters. Many support public policies that neutralize the importance of race in society and that embrace the notion of a "color-blind society." Most have done well for themselves despite society's racial problems.

The politics of the assimilating political community also differs significantly from those of other black political communities in that the primary political focus of the group is on social acceptance. They are not concerned with advancing the social cause of the larger black community; instead, their interests lie in achieving the American economic dream and being recognized for their personal achieve-ments. They do not care about addressing past racial grievances. Members of the assimilating political community are more concerned with matters pertaining to their individual material (economic) well-being, and less about the social welfare of the larger black community. Their interest in their economic class status takes precedent over their racial interests. As a result, their identity with the racial group is low and likewise their level of racial consciousness is low.

Politically, these individuals are more likely to identify with the Republican Party or register as Independents, and their level of political participation (voting, attentiveness to politics, etc.) is higher than that of the general black population. Politically they are more conservative than the larger black population. They are more likely to support the conservative agenda on social welfare programs. They are anti-welfare and feel that blacks are responsible for solving the problems facing their community, and often do not feel that the government should take special action to help the black community. They are more likely to be economically conservative adopting an anti-tax, pro-business, and protection of property stance. They are far less liberal than the larger black community on civil rights matters. Although they support civil rights, they differ with mainstream black leaders over how best to achieve civil rights for blacks. They prefer to use quiet diplomacy. They are also likely to be moderate in their political orientation on social issues. This group's political decision making is driven less by race and concern for the larger black community and more by individual and economic desires.

The Accommodating Political Community

The accommodating political community is the second largest black political community. Because of improved socioeconomic opportunities for blacks since the civil rights era, this is the fastest growing group representing 25 to 30 percent of the whole. Attitudes toward total assimilation among this group would range from moderate to moderately high. Members of the accommodating political community are less likely than members of the assimilating community to totally abandon their racial group's cultural identity. As a matter of fact, many are strong defenders of maintaining and preserving their racial culture. Nevertheless, they have embraced the process of economic assimilation into society. Like the assimilating political community, the accommodating political community is proportionately made up of members of the new black middle class. Their level of education, income, and occupation gives them a higher socioeconomic standing in the community. They are overwhelmingly Baby-Boomers or younger. Members of the accommodating political community are more likely to reside in suburbia, in urban communities with other blacks of similar socioeconomic standing, or racially-diverse urban communities. Their social and cultural connections to the larger black community are moderately high. Many members of the accommodating political community are first generation middle-class. The vast majority of them grew up in predominantly black communities and they still have familial and social connections (via church, civic and social organizations, schools, etc.) to the larger black community. However, for many, their place of residence and socioeconomic status impede their social connection to the larger black community. That is, their social connection with the larger black community is often minimized by their place of employment and residence.

This sub-community tends to be motivated equally by their social and economic interests. Social justice and social acceptance constitute the essence of the accommodating political community's political focus. Focus on social justice assures protection and opportunities in areas such as education and employment that are important to the maintenance of a moderate-to-high socioeconomic living standard. But it is equally important to the accommodating political community that discrimination and racism do not prevent them from enjoying the fruits of their socioeconomic prosperity. Their status as a racial minority continues to make them sensitive to social injustices and the need for reform. The mindset of the accommodating political community is also driven by economic concerns. Economically they aspire to live the American dream; therefore, the accumulation of wealth and material goods is important to them. In many ways they are torn between a commitment to their racial group interests on one hand, and their class group interests on the other. Despite the fact that the environment in which this group functions is racially mixed, their levels of racial consciousness and racial identity are moderate because of their ties to the larger racial group. For this group there could be psychological conflict between their racial and socio-economic statuses.

Members of the accommodating political community are more likely to iden-tify themselves as Democrats; however, their support for the Democratic Party ranges from moderate to moderately strong. Larger portions of this group, when compared to blacks in the other political communities, identify themselves as Independents, and a significant proportion of this group identify themselves as Republicans. Their level of political participation is fairly high because of their level of education and interest in political and social affairs. Blacks in this group continue to be liberal on civil rights issues and moderately liberal on social issues. They tend to be moderately liberal on social welfare issues because of their concerns and connectivity to the larger black community. At the same time, they are more moderate on economic issues because of their socioeconomic standing.

The Mainstream Political Community

The mainstream political community is the largest of the four communities repre-senting around 50 percent. There is much interest in upward socioeconomic mobility among this group. They tend to have moderate levels of education and are employed in lower white-collar, upper blue-collar, and some in lower blue-collar positions. Their incomes are at or above the national median income. Attitudes towards assimilation within this group are more diverse because of the size of the group. This political community will have members whose attitudes toward assimilation will range from upward mobility, to upward mobility with lagged acculturation and downward mobility. The younger and more economi-cally prosperous will favor either upward mobility or upward mobility with lagged acculturation. The older and less economically prosperous tend toward upward mobility with lagged acculturation or downward mobility.

Many in this political community tend to be either from the older generations (including old Baby-Boomers) and they tend to reside in urban communities or the fringe of older suburban communities. They have high social and cultural connections to the black community because they live and function socially in predominantly black neighborhoods. These individuals support the established social and cultural institutions of the black community. Economic justice is very important to them and is often sought through political empowerment. The mainstream political community seeks upward social and economic mobility, but institutional discrimination and racism prevent this from happening. The main-stream political community sees the political system as the primary means through which their quality of life will be improved. This community differs from the accommodating political community in that its members often feel they have not been afforded access to or that they have not received their fair share of the resources that the government and society in general allocate for the public good. Racial justice is also part of their political focus, largely due to their strong (and continuing) ties to the civil rights agenda.

The politics of the mainstream community tend to be driven by social and economic concerns; however, concerns for social matters take precedence over economic matters. Because of their personal experiences, they are more concerned about the social and economic interests of the larger black community than their individual interests. The mainstream political community's economic concerns are driven by a sense of social consciousness. Thus, their positions on economic issues are driven by their concerns for helping those who are less well-off socially and economically and geared more toward improving the life chances of the racial group. They function in a predominantly black environment because they tend to live in racially segregated communities. They often work in environments where other black and low- and semi-skilled workers constitute a significant majority. Individuals in this group have a high level of identification with the racial group and an equally high level of racial consciousness.

Members of the mainstream community overwhelmingly support Democratic Party politics. However, their level of political participation can be described as moderate because they are frustrated with the political process despite seeing it as the means to social and economic salvation. This group is more likely to feel politically inefficacious. They are moderately liberal on social issues and especially liberal on those issues that affect blacks as a racial group. They are more liberal on civil rights issues than any of the other political communities. They are also liberal on social welfare issues because of their closeness to the black apolitical community and because of their own socioeconomic circumstances. Finally, they are liberal on economic bread and butter issues.

The Apolitical Political Community

The apolitical political community is the remaining 20 to 25 percent of the population, not as large as the accommodating political community, and is experiencing a decline in size as time moves on. This community tends to be characterized by its lower socioeconomic status. Poverty, crime, high unemployment, and poor educational opportunities are all concerns of this group. They tend to be older (from the Silent and/or Greatest generations) or younger (from younger Baby-Boomers or Generation X). Most in the older population were trapped in these communities because very low educational attainment and income opportunities prevented them from moving on. On the other hand, some of the older population were very established and chose not to leave. The vast majority of the younger blacks in this community have low human capital skills, and many have problems related to making poor decisions in their lives (e.g., teenage pregnancy, criminal records, dropping out of high school, drug abuse). Most reside in predominantly black inner cities or rural areas. Their social and cultural connections to the black community are high. However much of their culture is often defined by their lower socioeconomic status. As a result, social and economic justice is the primary political focus of this group. This community is primarily interested in public policy that will address their socioeconomic plight.

Because of their socioeconomic standing, perceived prospects for improvement, and social isolation, the path toward assimilation for this group can be described as downward. The political worldview of this community is driven by social, social welfare, and community concerns. That is, for many their primary concern is public safety and improving their social well-being. This community often seeks compassion and the understanding of others as the solutions to their problems. They often see their socioeconomic status as a direct result of their race. However, they are well aware that class is also a factor. Those in the apolitical political community function in a racially segregated environment, thus the level of identity with blacks as a racial group is high. Likewise, their level of racial consciousness is also high. They often see improvements of their condition as being tied to that of other black sub-communities.

The apolitical political community is highly committed to Democratic Party politics. However, their level of political participation is very low. They tend not to register to vote, and if they register they do not turn out to vote with great regularity. They tend to have strong feelings of powerlessness, and they lack confidence in the social, political, and economic institutions of society. They are most liberal on social welfare issues because they see these types of policy as most likely to address their socioeconomic plight. Likewise, they are liberal on economic issues because these issues are as well perceived as the key to improving the quality of their lives. They are perhaps more moderate to conservative on social issues than are the other black political communities. They are often liberal on civil rights issues because they usually associate the struggle for civil rights as the means to improving their socioeconomic status.

Conclusion

The black community has changed considerably since the end of the civil rights movement. As discussed in this chapter and previously, a new black middle class has emerged. The emergence of this new black middle class coincided with the black Baby-Boomer generation's coming of age. Black Baby-Boomers represent the black community's connection between its social, political, and economic past and the future. That is, black Baby-Boomers are old enough to have experienced life under America's system of apartheid, and at the same time they came of age at the height of the dismantling of the system. The black Baby-Boomer generation is a product of two worlds and thus we can think of this generation as the "bridge generation." They are better educated and they have greater economic resources than their predecessors do, and their world is not confined to the "black world" or black experience. As a result, demographic and geographic changes will be among the defining characteristics of black politics in the future. Therefore, it is inevitable that in the Socioeconomic Transition Era of black politics we will see the emergence of sub-political communities among blacks. Although we are still rather early into the Socioeconomic Transition Era, the implications are that this is the time for the emergence of truly "new black politics". A new black politics, not just centering around political activity, but a new black politics with an enlarged focus on gender issues and human rights, diversity in black worldviews, and attention given to blacks as a global community, functioning as global political actors (i.e. Pan-Africanism and global black politics).

4

ATTITUDES AND PERCEPTIONS IN BLACK AND WHITE

What They Suggest About Race and Politics

Throughout this nation's history, there has been an expectation that minorities and immigrants would eventually adapt to the character, structure, and culture of "white America" (as the dominant racial and social group). For blacks and other ethnic and racial minorities this meant that adapting the behavioral patterns of white America was a necessity and relinquishing familiar ethnic customs or at least watching one's children assimilate was inevitable.[1] As more blacks take advantage of the new social and economic opportunities afforded them, what impact will it have on their political attitudes and behavior? Furthermore, what impact would greater interaction with blacks have on the political attitudes and behavior of whites? Finally, what do political attitudes and behavior suggest about race relations and black politics in the Socioeconomic Transition Era?

Using these general questions as a starting point, the aim of this chapter is to examine patterns of public opinion among blacks and whites to evaluate the extent to which race still matters in American politics today. The objectives of this chapter are threefold: first, to assess the extent to which the political values of blacks and whites are consistent on select groups of issues in the Politics and Socioeconomic Transition Eras of black politics; second, to ponder the extent to which the political views of blacks and whites today are an indication of the continuing or declining significance of race; finally, to reflect on what the differences or similarities in the political attitudes and perceptions of blacks and whites to this point in the Socioeconomic Transition Era suggest about the future of black politics.

Political Orientation

Over the years, the political attitudes of blacks have differed considerably from those of whites (especially on race-relevant issues). Blacks' distinctive political attitudes and behaviors have been partially attributed to the group having had to overcome an oppressive political system.[2] Consequently, blacks have been considered one of the more liberal groups in America, mainly because of their strong support for continued civil rights progress.[3] When asked to place themselves on a political orientation scale (with the choices being liberal, moderate, or conservative), blacks' political orientation differed significantly from that of whites in the latter part of the Politics Era (mid-1980s) and it continued into the Socioeconomic Transition Era. Overall, a greater percentage of blacks thought of themselves as liberal when compared to whites, as shown in Figure 4.1. In the Politics Era,[4] 37.4 percent of the blacks identified themselves as liberal. Since the end of the Politics Era, the percentage of blacks identifying themselves as liberal has declined. Into the Socioeconomic Transition Era (mid-2000), the percentage of blacks identifying themselves as liberal had decreased to 32.2 percent. On the other hand the percentage of whites identifying themselves as liberal hardly changed between the end of the Politics Era and the current phase of the Socioeconomic Transition Era. Roughly 25 percent of whites identified themselves as liberal.

Since fewer blacks are self-identifying as liberal, does this mean more are self-identifying as conservative? The data in Figure 4.1 suggest this is not the case, but today blacks are increasingly identifying themselves as moderate. Toward the end of the Politics Era, only 36.0 percent of the black population identified themselves as moderate. Today the percentage of blacks identifying themselves as moderate has increased to 43.7 percent. Much of the increase in the percentage of blacks identifying themselve as moderate between the Politics and the current phase of the Socioeconomic Transition Era has come at the expense of the percentage of blacks identifying themselves as liberal. Among whites, there was only a very slight change in the percentage identifying themselves as moderate. The percentage of

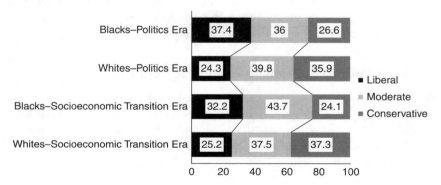

FIGURE 4.1 Blacks' and Whites' Self-Placement on the Liberal/Conservative Scale in the Politics and Socioeconomic Transition Eras

Source: Combined 1985, 1986, 1987 General Social Survey for the Politics Era, and the Combined 2004 and 2006 General Social Surveys for the Socioeconomic Transition Era

whites identifying themselves as moderate has actually declined by 2.3 percent since the end of the Politics Era of black politics.

Between the end of the Politics Era and today, there has been a slight change in the percentage of blacks and whites identifying themselves as conservative. Among blacks, the percentage self-identifying declined from 26.6 percent in the latter part of the Politics Era to 24.1 percent today. For whites, the percent self-identifying as conservative increased from 35.9 percent in the latter part of the Politics Era to 37.3 percent in the current phase of the Socioeconomic Transition Era. Overall, blacks as a group became less liberal in terms of self-identification and more moderate. The change among whites was less pronounced and as a group they have become less moderate and slightly more conservative. These data suggest that blacks' shift away from liberalism was greater than whites' shift toward conservatism.

As discussed in previous chapters, the future of black politics depends largely on the activities and behavior of blacks in the upper socioeconomic stratum. While the patterns of political orientation among upper socioeconomic status blacks did not deviate much from that of blacks as a group in the Socioeconomic Transition Era, such was not the case for upper socioeconomic status whites. Roughly 45 percent of the blacks in the upper socioeconomic group[5] identified themselves as moderate compared to only 27 percent of their white counterparts.[6] Around 40.8 percent of upper socioeconomic status whites self-identified as conservative compared to 23.1 percent of the blacks in the upper socio-economic status group. Approximately 32 percent of the blacks and whites in the upper socioeconomic status identified themselves as liberal. It is very apparent that significant differences exist in the political orientation of the upper socio-economic status blacks and whites. The data suggest two things about blacks' and whites' political orientation since the end of the Politics era. First, although there may have been a shift in political orientation, there has not been a convergence. Second, there is no indication of a convergence in the political orientation of upper socioeconomic status blacks and whites.

The Most Important Problem Facing the Country

When asked to identify the most important problem facing this country, blacks and whites differed significantly across all three eras of black politics. As shown in Table 4.1a, in the late Protest Era (1966 to 1977) almost half (48.5 percent) of the white population felt the most important problem facing this nation was related to foreign affairs/national defense. The second largest percentage of whites (15.2 percent) in the late Protest Era identified public order. The Vietnam War and public disturbances surrounding civil rights and the war protest movement may have contributed to nearly two-thirds of the white population identifying either foreign affairs/national defense or public order as the most important problem facing the nation. Around 11.5 percent of the white population felt that issues

TABLE 4.1A Snapshot of Blacks' and Whites' Perceptions of the Most Important Problem Facing America in the Late Protest Era

	Blacks	Whites	Difference
Agricultural	.0	.9	.9
Economic/business	8.2	11.5	3.3
Foreign affairs/National defense	33.4	48.5	15.1
Government functioning	1.7	2.6	.9
Natural resources	.2	2.1	1.9
Public order	10.4	15.2	4.8
Racial problems	11.6	6.7	4.9
Social welfare	31.2	11.4	19.8
Other	3.2	1.2	2.0
Sum of differences			53.6

Source: American National Election Studies Combined 1966, 1968 and 1970 study years
$p < .000$

related to economics/business were the most important facing the nation. Then 11.4 percent of the white population felt that social welfare was the most important problem and 6.7 percent identified a racial problem. Less than 8 percent identified agriculture, government functioning, labor issues, or other concerns as the most important problem facing the nation in the late Protest Era.

Blacks differed significantly from whites in their selection of the most important problem facing the nation in the late Protest Era. Two-thirds of blacks identified either a social welfare or public order issue as the most important problem facing the nation. Similar to whites, in the waning years of the late Protest Era, the largest percentage of blacks (33.4 percent) identified a foreign affairs/national defense matter as the most important problem facing the nation. However, an equally large percentage of blacks (31.2 percent) identified a social welfare issue as the most important problem. Surprisingly, only 11.6 percent of blacks in the late Protest Era identified a racial concern among the most important problem. Public order was the most important problem facing the nation according to 10.4 percent of blacks, and 8.2 percent identified an economic/business concern as the most important problem. During the late Protest Era, the sum of response differences between blacks and whites was 53.8 percent. The largest difference (or gap) between blacks and whites was in the percentage that identified a social welfare issue as the most important problem facing the nation (19.8 percent). The second largest response difference (15.1 percent) was on foreign affairs/national defense. The difference between the groups in the Protest Era on the other issues did not exceed 5 percent.

During the second phase of the Politics Era (1980 to 1984), foreign affairs became less important for both blacks and whites. Economic/business and social welfare concerns became more important in different ways. The percentage identifying a racial problem diminished sharply for both racial groups in the second phase of the Politics Era. As shown in Table 4.1b, the largest percentage of whites identified an economic/business issue as the most important concern facing the nation. Between the latter part of the Protest Era and second phase of the Politics Era of black politics, the percentage of whites identifying a foreign affairs/national defense issue as the most important problem declined from 48.5 percent to 30 percent. This represented an 18.5 percent decrease in the percentage of whites who identified foreign affairs/national defense matters as the most important problem facing the nation. Among whites in the second phase of Politics Era, the percentage that identified a social welfare matter as the most important problem increased by nearly 14 percent, from 11.4 percent to 24.9 percent. The percentage of whites that identified either a public order or a racial issue as the most important problem had declined to less than 5 percent by the second phase of the Politics Era.

Among blacks, there was a major drop in the percentage identifying a racial problem as the most important problem. Between the latter part of Protest Era and the second phase of the Politics Era, the percentage of blacks identifying racial problems as the most important problem dropped by just over 10 percent. In the second phase of the Politics Era less than 1 percent of blacks identified a race-related issue as the most important problem facing the nation. There was also a decline between the two eras in the percentage of blacks that identified a foreign affairs issue as the most important problem, dropping by just around 10 percent. There was a shift in the perceptions of the most important problem for blacks between the latter part of the Protest Era and the second phase of the Politics Era toward economic/business and social welfare issues. The percentage of blacks identifying economic/business issues as the most important problem increased from 8.2 percent in the late Protest Era to 20.2 percent by the

TABLE 4.1B Snapshot of Blacks' and Whites' Perceptions of the Most Important Problem Facing America in the Latter Half of the Politics Era

	Blacks	*Whites*	*Difference*
Agricultural	.6	1.0	.4
Economic/business	20.2	37.2	17.0
Foreign affairs	24.9	30.0	5.1
Government functioning	.8	2.4	1.6
Natural resources	.6	1.3	.7
Public order	4.2	2.6	1.6
Racial problems	.8	.1	.7
Social welfare	47.0	24.9	22.1
Other	.8	.5	.3
Sum of difference			49.5

Source: American National Election Studies Combined 1980, 1982 and 1984 study years
$p < .000$

mid Politics Era. While the largest percentage of blacks in the late Protest Era identified a social welfare issue as the most important problem, the percentage identifying a social welfare issue grew even larger by the second phase of the Politics Era. Almost half (47 percent) of blacks in the second phase of the Politics Era identified a social welfare issue as the most important problem facing the nation. The largest differences between blacks and whites were on the issues of social welfare (22.0 percentage points) and economic/business (17 percentage points). Between the late Protest Era and latter part of the Politics Era, the sum of differences declined from 53.9 percent to 49.5 percent. Thus, there was some closing of the gap in what blacks and whites identified as the most important problem facing the nation between the waning years of the Protest Era and the latter part of the Politics Era.

In the Socioeconomic Transition Era (between 1996 and 2000), the combined difference in the percentage of blacks or whites identifying agricultural, government functioning, labor issues, natural resources, or "other" matters as the most important problem did not rise above 10 percent. Among blacks or whites the proportion identifying a foreign affair/national defense issue had declined to less than 10 percent. Although the percentage of blacks identifying racial problems as the most important problem remained below 10 percent, the percentage rose between the second phase of the Politics Era from 0.8 percent to 9.4 percent in the Socioeconomic Transition Era as shown in Tables 4.1b and c.[7] The difference in the percentage of blacks and whites identifying a racial matter actually increased from 0.7 percent in the second phase of the Politics Era to 7.7 percent in the Socioeconomic Transition Era. In the Socioeconomic Transition Era, only 1.7 percent of the white respondents identified a race relations issue as the most important problem facing the nation. Between the latter half of

TABLE 4.1C Snapshot of Blacks' and Whites' Perceptions of the Most Important Problem Facing America in the Socioeconomic Transition Era

	Blacks	Whites	Difference
Agricultural	.0	.3	.3
Economic/business	9.7	17.1	7.4
Foreign affairs/National defense	6.9	9.5	2.6
Government functioning	4.4	7.8	3.4
Natural resources	.0	2.1	2.1
Public order	26.1	22.6	3.5
Racial problems	9.4	1.7	7.7
Social welfare	43.4	38.8	4.6
Other	.0	.1	.1
Sum of differences			31.7

Source: American National Election Studies Combined 1996, 1998 and 2000 study years
p < .000

the Politics Era and the Socioeconomic Transition Era, the percentage of blacks identifying an economic/business issue dropped to less than 10 percent and the percentage of whites declined to less than 20 percent.

During the Socioeconomic Transition Era, social welfare concerns were identified by 43.4 percent of the blacks as the most important problem facing the nation, which was a slight decline from the 47.0 percent in the latter part of the Politics Era of black politics. There was a large increase in the percentage of whites who identified a social welfare issue as the most important problem facing the nation between the second part of the Politics Era and the Socioeconomic Transition Era. The percentage of whites identifying a social welfare issue increased (by 13.9 percent) to 38.8 percent between the two periods. The biggest increase was in the percentage that identified a public order issue as the most important. Among blacks the percentage identifying a public order issue as the most important problem rose from 4.2 percent in the latter Politics Era to 26.1 percent in the Socioeconomic Transition Era. The increase in the percentage of whites identifying a public order matter was comparable to that of blacks. Among whites, the percentage identifying a public order matter increased by 20 percent between the second phase of the Politics Era and the Socioeconomic Transition Era.

Although whites identified the same three issues that blacks identified as the most important problems facing the nation (social welfare, public order, and economic/business) in the Socioeconomic Transition Era, the magnitude of the percentages differed. The data show that the sum of difference between what blacks and whites felt was the most important problem declined over the three eras. The sum of difference declined 21.9 percent between the waning years of the Protest Era and the point under examination in the Socioeconomic Transition Era. The importance of this is twofold. First, although significant differences still exist between blacks and whites over what they perceive as the most important problem, the magnitude of difference has declined significantly. Second, blacks and whites to this point in the Socioeconomic Transition Era identify the same three issue groups as the most important problems facing the nation.

What was identified as the most important problems differed significantly between upper socioeconomic (or higher-educated) blacks and whites and other social classes in the Socioeconomic Transition Era. Among both groups, the largest percentage felt that social welfare concerns were the most important problems facing the nation.[8] Forty-four percent of the blacks in the upper socioeconomic status group and 39 percent of the similar status whites identified a social welfare issue as the most important problem facing the nation. Actually, the percentage of both groups identifying a social welfare problem was comparable to the respective percentage in the general population. Similarly, comparable percentages of upper socioeconomic status blacks and whites identified public order as the most important problem facing the nation. Slightly more than 20 percent (around 23 percent) of both groups identified a public order issue as the most important problem facing the nation. This is where the similarities between higher-educated blacks' and whites' identification of the most important problem ended. Among higher-educated blacks 11.2 percent identified an economic/business problem compared to 18.9 percent of higher-educated whites. Likewise, 11.2 percent of higher-educated blacks identified a race relation problem compared to only 1.6 percent of their white higher-educated counterparts. Overall, the patterns of identification of the most important problems facing the nation between higher-educated blacks and whites were very similar to those found among the general population.

Trust in Institutions

Throughout the history of America, the government has subjugated or allowed the subjugation of blacks' social, political, and economic rights. Prior to the Politics Era, blacks were alienated from the political process and left with few opportunities to influence governmental decisions. As a result, blacks have for a long time had reasons not to trust government and to feel that government and the political process had ignored them. Some 40 plus years beyond the Protest Era of black politics, to what degree are blacks still less trusting of some of society's key political institutions? Furthermore, to what degree do differences remain between blacks' and whites' trust in these institutions? To answer this question, blacks and whites were asked about specific institutions, "How much of the time do you think you can trust them?"[9] The possible responses were "always," "most of the time," "sometimes," and "never." The data in Figure 4.2 show the percentage of blacks and whites responding either "sometimes" or "never."

When asked if they trusted the government in Washington, overall 60.6 percent of all respondents (regardless of race) in the Socioeconomic Transition Era responded either "sometimes" or "never." Nevertheless, blacks and whites differed significantly in their response. As shown in Figure 4.2, 78.1 percent (more than

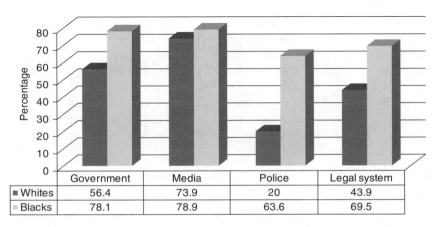

	Government	Media	Police	Legal system
■ Whites	56.4	73.9	20	43.9
▨ Blacks	78.1	78.9	63.6	69.5

FIGURE 4.2 Blacks' and Whites' Trust in Institutions: Responding Sometimes or Never

three-fourths) of the blacks responded that they trusted government in Washington sometimes or never. The percentage of blacks that indicated a lack of trust in the government in Washington was 21.7 percentage points higher than the percentage of whites. Similarly, a significantly larger percentage of blacks either trusted the media "sometimes" or "never." Blacks' distrust of the media was comparable to their distrust of the government in Washington. Some 78.1 percent of the blacks said they only "sometimes" or "never" trusted the media. Of all the institutions examined, whites' lack of trust in the media was almost comparable to that of blacks. Some 73.9 percent of the white respondents said they either "sometimes" or "never" trusted the media.

Perhaps surprisingly, blacks as a group appeared to be a little more trusting of the police and the legal system than they were of government or the media. Despite this observation, nearly two-thirds of the blacks said they either "sometimes" or "never" trusted the police or legal system. As shown in Figure 4.2, 63.6 percent of blacks said they only "sometimes" or "never" trusted the police and 69.5 percent said they only "sometimes" or "never" trusted the legal system. On the other hand, whites are far more trusting of the police and legal system than blacks. Whites actually have a significantly greater trust in the police and legal system than they have in the government in Washington and the media. Only 20 percent of the white respondents said they only "sometimes" or "never" trusted the police and only 43.9 percent had a lack of trust in the legal system. The difference in blacks' and whites' lack of trust in the legal system was slightly greater (at 25.6 percent) than their lack of trust in the government in Washington. However, the lack of trust gap between blacks and whites in the police was huge. The gap between the percentage of blacks and whites with a lack of trust in the police was 43.9 percent.

When examining the level of trust in key institutions by race and socio-economic status (as measured by level of education), the data showed higher-educated blacks differing significantly from higher-educated whites. Overall, higher-educated blacks were less trusting in the government in Washington, the media, the police and the legal system than their white upper educated counterparts. The difference between higher-educated blacks and whites was larger than the difference between blacks and whites in general. The difference in the percentage of higher-educated blacks and whites responding they only "sometimes" or "never" trusted government in Washington was 24.6 percent, 9.3 percent on the media question, 47.4 percent on the police question, and 28.2 percent on trust in the legal system question. On matters of trust in key institutions, race appears to trump socioeconomic status in determining attitudes.

General Spending Priorities of Government

To further ascertain the level of convergence in blacks' and whites' public opinions, attitudes on the general spending priorities of government were examined. Since 1972, Americans have been asked to respond to a series of questions designed to assess opinions on the general spending priorities of the government.[10] For the purposes of this study, blacks' and whites' attitudes were examined on eight questions that were grouped into two categories. The first group, the social concerns group, included questions about protecting the environment, halting the rising crime rate, dealing with drug addiction, and solving the problems of big cities. In the second group, referred to as the social-welfare concerns group, respondents were asked about government spending on programs to provide services for the benefit of its citizens. Among the items in this group were spending to improve the nation's educational system, improving the conditions of blacks, welfare, social security, and protecting the nation's health. For each question, respondents were asked if they felt the government spent "too little," "about right," or "too much" to solve these problems.

As shown in Table 4.2, the response of blacks and whites differed significantly in relation to government spending to address social concerns. Blacks were more likely to feel that the government spent too little protecting the environment, halting crime, dealing with drug addiction, and solving the problems of big cities. The difference between the proportion of blacks and whites who felt the government spent

TABLE 4.2 Blacks' and Whites' Attitudes Toward General Spending Priorities of the Government in the Socioeconomic Transition Era

	Whites	Blacks	[a]Coefficient	[b]Higher-educated whites	[b]Higher-educated blacks	[a]Coefficient
Spend too little protecting the environment	63.0	69.3	−.030*** (.011)	65.4	75.6	−.036* (.105)
Spend too little halting crime	57.0	72.8	−.078*** (.011)	48.0	71.9	−.088*** (.017)
Spend too little dealing with drug addiction	57.7	70.6	−.064*** (.012)	52.7	70.9	−.066*** (.017)
Spend too little dealing with big city problems	42.7	63.8	−.108*** (.013)	39.5	73.5	−.132*** (.019)
Spend too little improving the educational system	71.8	82.6	−.058*** (.009)	73.2	85.4	−.047*** (.013)
Spend too little on welfare	20.3	42.0	−.130*** (.013)	20.2	35.8	−.061** (.020)
Spend too little improving health care	75.2	81.6	−.058*** (.009)	73.9	91.2	−.064*** (.011)
Spend too little on social security	60.7	79.0	−.096*** (.007)	52.1	78.1	−.096*** (.012)
Spend too little improving conditions of blacks	26.9	75.6	−.0192*** (.011)	29.4	77.9	−.198*** (.020)

Source: Combined 2002, 2004 and 2006 General Social Survey
[a] Kendall's Tau-c Coefficient
[b] Higher-educated defined as having a junior college degree or higher
*p < .05 **p < .01 ***p < .001

too little on protecting the environment was 6.3 percent. Spending to protect the environment was the issue on which blacks and whites were most in agreement even though the percentage who responded that government spent too little was significantly different. Among blacks, 63.0 percent felt the government spent too little protecting the environment compared to 69.3 percent of whites. Likewise, there was a significant difference in the opinions of blacks and whites about government spending on dealing with drug addiction. While 70.6 percent of blacks felt the government spent too little, only 57.7 percent of whites felt the same. The difference in blacks' and whites' attitudes regarding spending to halt crime was slightly larger than the gap between the two groups on the drug addiction question. The difference in the percentage of blacks and whites saying that the government spent too little was 15.8 percent. The largest difference in attitudes between the two groups on the social issues was on the question of spending to solve the problems of big cities. There was a 21 percentage-point difference between blacks and whites feeling the government spent too little to solve the problem of big cities.

In the Socioeconomic Transition Era, significant differences exist between blacks' and whites' opinions on issues to improve the social welfare of society and the average difference in opinion was slightly larger than differences on the social issues. As shown in Table 4.2, the largest difference between the races in Socioeconomic Transition Era was on the question of spending to improve the conditions of blacks. The percentage of blacks feeling the government spent too little to improve the conditions of blacks was 75.6 percent. On the other hand, the percentage of whites feeling the government spent too little to improve the conditions of blacks was 26.9 percent. The difference between the proportion of blacks and whites saying that the government spent too little to improve the conditions of blacks was 48.7 percent. The second largest difference between the two was on the question of government spending on welfare. While more than half of the whites felt the government spending on welfare was either too much or about right, a little less than half of the blacks felt government spent too little. Well over half of both blacks and whites felt the government spent too little on social security, but the difference in the proportion of the two groups with this attitude was 18.3 percent. Although significant differences existed in the proportions of blacks and whites feeling that the government spent too little to improve education and to protect the nation's health, the difference was only around 10 percentage points. Seventy percent or more of both racial groups felt the government spent too little improving the nation's education system and protecting health.

Overall, the data presented in Table 4.2 show that blacks and whites differed significantly over governmental spending priorities to this point in the Socioeconomic Transition Era of black politics. Blacks were significantly more inclined to believe that the government spent too little to address both social and social welfare problems. Nowhere was this more apparent than in the differences in the opinions of higher-educated blacks and whites. On average, the gap between blacks and whites on the social concerns questions was 14 percent. Between higher-educated blacks and whites the gap was 21.7 percent. When compared to the responses of the total population, the proportion of higher-educated blacks responding that the government spent too little was much higher. However, among higher-educated whites, the proportion responding that the government spent too little was lower than the percentage of the larger white population. This pattern held true when examining the social welfare government spending issues (excluding spending to improve blacks' conditions). A slightly larger proportion of higher-educated blacks and whites were more inclined than the general population to say the government spent too little to improve conditions for blacks; the gap between higher-educated blacks and whites was comparable to that of the total population.

Social Issues

Table 4.3 shows differences in the attitudes of blacks and whites on matters of social interest. The issues presented in Table 4.3 are representative of two categories of social interests. The first group of issues pertains to the punishment

TABLE 4.3 Snapshot of Differences in Blacks' and Whites' Opinions on Select Social Issues in the Socioeconomic Transition Era

	Whites	Blacks	[a]Coefficient	[b]Higher-educated whites	[b]Higher-educated blacks	[a]Coefficient
Oppose death penalty for murder	27.2	57.5	.230★★★ (.015)	33.3	55.8	.135★★★ (.025)
Favor gun permits	78.1	85.9	−.069★★★ (.015)	80.0	92.2	−.093★★★ (.021)
Legalize marijuana	39.3	28.5	.079★★★ (.017)	41.3	27.8	.082★★ (.028)
Pornography legal for anyone over 18	60.4	65.8	.039★★ (.017)	66.6	67.5	.011 (.029)
Disapprove law opposing bible prayer in school	57.7	78.3	.151★★★ (.015)	43.9	71.2	.162★★★ (.028)
Support abortion married— if want no more children	44.0	37.6	.046★★ (.017)	53.9	49.5	.024 (.029)
Support abortion if woman's health endangered	88.8	86.9	.021 (.018)	90.4	94.5	−.041 (.024)
Allow incurable patients to die	71.7	50.7	.164★★★ (.019)	73.5	62.1	.077★ (.032)

Source: Combined 2002, 2004 and 2006 General Social Survey
[a] Kendall's Tau-c Coefficient
[b] Higher-educated defined as having a junior college degree or higher
★*p* < .05 ★★*p* <.01 ★★★*p* <.001

and/or regulation of social activity or behavior. The social issues included in this group are attitudes regarding the death penalty for murder, gun control, legalization of marijuana, and the legalization of pornography. Blacks and whites differed significantly in their attitudes regarding the punishment and regulation of certain types of social behavior. The social issue on which blacks and whites differed most strongly was capital punishment. The percentage of blacks in opposition to the death penalty for murder was twice that of whites. As a matter of fact, of all the issues examined in Table 4.3, the difference in the percentage of blacks and whites opposing the death penalty for murder was the largest. Well over half of the black respondents opposed the death penalty for murder while just over one-fourth of the white respondents concurred. This difference in opinion could largely be attributed to the direct implications this issue has for blacks as a community. A disproportionate number of blacks have received the death penalty over the years.

The issue of gun permits and the legalization of marijuana also have implications for large segments of the black community. With the high rate of crime in many black communities attributed to drug-related activities and deplorable economic conditions, it should be no surprise to find a large proportion of the black population favoring some sort of gun control and opposing the legalization of marijuana. Although more than three-fourths of the black and white respondents favored legislation requiring a person to obtain a permit before buying a gun, blacks were more likely to favor a law requiring such action. The percentage of blacks favoring a permit to purchase a gun was 7.8 percentage points higher than whites. The gap between the percentage of blacks and whites supporting the legalization of marijuana was larger than the percentage gap between the two groups on the gun permit question. Only 28.5 percent of the black respondents favored the legalization of marijuana compared to 39.3 percent of the white respondents. The percentage of the two groups favoring the legalization of pornography for any one over the age of 18 was much smaller than it was for the other three issues. Although significant, the difference between the percentage of blacks and whites in favor of making pornography legal for anyone over 18 was less than 6 percentage points. It is worth noting here, of the three issues regarding social behavior, this issue had no direct implications for blacks or whites as a group.

Blacks' and whites' opinions on the second group of issues, the social moral issues, were also significantly different. Whereas blacks tended to be significantly more liberal than whites on the social issues, on the social moral issues blacks were more conservative. A larger percentage of blacks (more than three-fourths) dis-approved of a law banning bible prayer in school when compared to whites (just over half). While 71.7 percent of the white respondents would favor allowing an incurable patient to die, only 50.7 percent of the black respondents concurred. Blacks and whites did not differ significantly in their approval of abortion where a woman's health is endangered. Well over 80 percent of both groups supported abortions if the mother's health were endangered. On the "soft" abortion question, blacks were significantly less inclined than whites to support abortion. That is, only 37.6 percent of the black respondents said they would support an abortion if the woman was married and did not want any more children.

On the three social issues that had either direct or indirect implications for blacks as a group (the death penalty, gun permits, and legalizing marijuana), the difference in response between higher-educated blacks and whites was significant. The gap between the two groups on these issues ranged from 12.2 percent to 22.5 percent as shown in Table 4.3. However on the social issues that had no direct implications for blacks as a racial group, the difference in blacks and whites' responses was not significant. On the social moral questions, for the most part, the difference in higher-educated blacks' and whites' responses was not as great. On the abortion questions, there were no significant differences between the responses of higher-educated blacks and whites. The percentage of both groups responding that they would allow an incurable patient to die was significant, but smaller than the gap between blacks and whites in general. The largest difference in the proportions of blacks' and whites' responses was on the bible prayer in school question, and perhaps religiosity was the key factor here. Overall, the data indicate that blacks tend to be more liberal than whites on social issues that have a direct impact on blacks' quality of life, but more conservative on social issues that intertwine with morality and religiosity.

National Defense and Security

Informed public opinion on matters of foreign affairs and national defense is unusual. Americans are often uninformed about foreign affairs and national defense largely because they are inattentive to events happening abroad.[11] Despite this, blacks and whites still differed significantly in their opinions on these matters, but differences tend to depend on the nature of the issue. For example, Table 4.4 shows several questions from the 2004 National Politics Study that were divided into two categories. The first group had a national security focus and access concerns about protection in the homeland from foreign agents/invaders. The questions group asked: 1) should English be the official language of the United States?; 2) is it alright to imprison a non-citizen terrorist suspect indefinitely?; 3) should non-citizens be allowed to serve in the military?; and 4) should the government increase spending for border patrols? The second group of questions pertains to matters of national defense. Among the questions asked in this group were: 1) whether war should be used to "put other nations in their place"; 2) attitudes about the U.S. decision to put the military in Iraq; and 3) attitudes about government spending for defense.

The difference in blacks' and whites' opinions regarding the national security questions ranged from not significant, to significant with a weak relationship, to

TABLE 4.4 Differences in Blacks' and Whites' Opinions on National Security and National Defense-Related Issues in the Socioeconomic Transition Era

	Whites	Blacks	[a]Coefficient	[b]Higher-educated whites	[b]Higher-educated blacks	[a]Coefficient
Agree English should be official language	92.2	87.4	.078** (.025)	90.9	91.4	−.009 (.030)
Agree with imprisoning non-citizen terrorist suspects indefinitely	63.3	65.1	−.019 (.025)	58.3	61.8	−.035 (.030)
Non-citizens should not be allowed to serve in military	40.4	43.4	−.030 (.025)	38.0	43.6	−.057 (.031)
Increase spending for border patrol	64.6	86.5	−.247*** (.022)	61.2	86.4	−.272*** (.026)
Agree war puts other nations in their place	42.8	32.9	.101*** (.025)	36.8	27.8	.094** (.030)
US military in Iraq—did the right thing	49.7	15.9	.354*** (.022)	44.9	13.3	.332*** (.026)
Increase govt spending for defense	38.1	31.8	.095*** (.023)	33.3	27.8	.076** (.029)

Source: The National Politics Study, 2004
[a] Kendall's Tau-c Coefficient
[b] Higher-educated defined as having a junior college degree or higher
*$p < .05$ **$p < .01$ ***$p < .001$

significant with a very strong relationship. There were no significant differences between blacks' and whites' responses to imprisoning non-citizens indefinitely if suspected of being a terrorist. Slightly less than two-thirds of both groups supported this action by government. Similarly, blacks and whites did not differ significantly in their attitudes about allowing non-citizens to serve in the military. Around 40 percent of both groups agreed that non-citizens should not be allowed to serve in the military. Although the question of declaring English as the official language could be considered a domestic issue, it also has implications for national security. Treating it as such, the data show that the overwhelming majority of blacks and whites felt that English should be the official language of the nation. There were differences between the two groups, however. Blacks were less inclined than whites to agree with declaring English as the official language. The largest difference in blacks' and whites' responses to a matter of national security was on the question of spending for border patrol. The difference in the percentage of blacks and whites responding that the government should increase spending for the border patrol was more than 20 percentage points. Eighty-six percent of the black respondents felt that government should increase spending for border patrols compared to 64 percent of the white respondents.

While the differences in blacks' and whites' opinions on matters of national security varied from being significant to not significant, this was not the case on the national defense questions. As a group, blacks seem to be less likely to support military action or increased defense spending than whites. Forty-two percent of the white respondents compared to 32 percent of the black respondents agreed that it is alright to use war to "put other nations in their place." Similarly, a larger percentage of whites were significantly more inclined to favor increasing government spending for defense. Nearly 85 percent of the black respondents said the U.S. military should have stayed out of Iraq compared to just under half (49.7 percent) of the white respondents who felt the U.S. did the right thing sending in our military.

The group of issues on which one would expect the attitudes of higher-educated blacks and whites to be more consistent was foreign policy/relations, national security, and national defense issues. As a group, higher-educated blacks and whites tended to lean toward the liberal perspective on national security and defense issues. Nevertheless, the pattern of differences between higher-educated blacks and whites was not dissimilar from the opinion patterns of the larger group. On the national security questions, the two groups' responses did not differ significantly. The exception was on the increased spending for border patrol question. Three-fourths of the higher-educated black respondents compared to less than two-thirds of the higher-educated white respondents felt the government should increase spending for border patrols. Where the two groups differed significantly in their responses was on the national defense questions. A significantly larger proportion of higher-educated whites than higher-educated blacks was inclined to agree that war "puts other nations in their place," to feel that the U.S. did the right thing by sending our military into Iraq, and to favor the increase of government spending for the military.

Matters of Equality

V.O. Key wrote that the politics of the South revolved around the issue of race.[12] However, issues of race and racial inequality are not limited to the politics of the South. They also play a role in national politics as well. Table 4.5 shows the attitudes of blacks and whites toward issues of equality in the Socioeconomic Transition Era. The first four issues probe blacks' and whites' attitudes toward societal pursuit of equality (or equal life chances). The latter four ascertain blacks' and whites' attitudes regarding efforts to extend equal opportunity.

Blacks and whites differed significantly in their attitudes regarding societal pursuit of achieving equal life chances for everyone. A significantly larger percentage of blacks were more likely to support increasing opportunities for equality in society. For example, as shown in Table 4.5, only 44.6 percent of the white respondents disagreed with the notion that we have gone too far pushing for equal rights compared to 66.8 percent of the black respondents. The difference in the

TABLE 4.5 Differences in Blacks' and Whites' Attitudes on Matters of Equality in the Socioeconomic Transition Era

	Whites	Blacks	[a]Coefficient	[b]Higher-educated whites	[b]Higher-educated blacks	[a]Coefficient
[c]Disagree we have gone too far pushing for equal rights	44.6	66.8	.112★★★ (.015)	49.7	80.7	.135★★★ (.016)
[c]Disagree it is a big problem if chances are not equal	44.1	12.4	−.197★★★ (.015)	45.7	12.7	−.176★★★ (.018)
[c]Disagree it is okay if some people have more of a chance	51.1	66.6	.072★★★ (.015)	53.7	77.7	.100★★★ (.016)
[c]Disagree we should worry less about inequality	40.6	58.1	.088★★★ (.020)	46.3	72.9	.113★★★ (.016)
[c]Disagree blacks should not have special favors	16.5	41.3	.143★★★ (.016)	20.5	54.0	.140★★★ (.020)
[c]Disagree that blacks have gotten less than they deserve	56.1	17.8	−.234★★★ (.012)	53.5	17.3	−.180★★★ (.020)
[d]Favor preference in hiring and promotion	23.9	51.1	−.367★★★ (.025)	25.6	56.6	−.380★★★ (.025)
[d]Same-sex couples should be able to legally marry	33.6	22.2	.234★★★ (.027)	38.5	20.4	.294★★★ (.027)

[a] Kendall's Tau-c Coefficient
[b] Higher-educated defined as having a junior college
[c] Combined 2000, 2002 and 2004 American National Election Studies
[d] The National Politics Study, 2004
★$p < .05$ ★★$p < .01$ ★★★$p < .001$

percentage of higher-educated blacks and whites disagreeing that we have gone too far pushing for equal rights was greater than 30 percentage points. Slightly less than half (49.7 percent) of the higher-educated white respondents compared to slightly more than 80 percent of the higher-educated black respondents disagreed that we have gone too far pushing for equal rights. The difference in the attitudes of the two groups was even greater on the question "Is it a big problem if chances are not equal?" Among the white respondents, 44.1 percent disagreed that it was a big problem if chances were not equal. However, only 12.4 percent of the black respondents shared that position. As a matter of fact, 81.1 percent of the black respondents agreed that it was a big problem if chances were not equal compared to 41.8 percent of the white respondents. The difference in the percentage of higher-educated blacks and whites sharing this position was comparable to the difference between the general populations.

Blacks and whites also differed in their attitudes towards whether it was okay "if some people had more or less of a chance in life." A significantly larger number of blacks disagreed with the general idea that it was okay if some people had more of a chance in life. Around two-thirds of the black respondents disagreed that it was okay if some people had more of a chance. Slightly more than half of the white respondents felt the same. Whereas the gap between the response of blacks and whites in general was around 15 percent, the gap between higher-educated blacks and whites responding it was okay if some people had more of a chance than others was 24 percentage points. Blacks were also more inclined to disagree that we "should worry less about inequality." While only 40.6 percent of the white respondents disagreed that we should worry less about inequality, 58.1 percent of the black respondents disagreed with the statement. Once again the gap in the percentage of the larger group of blacks and whites disagreeing with the statement was about 17.6 percent; the difference between higher-educated blacks and whites was 26.6 percent.

The issue of equal opportunity and equal treatment has always been important to blacks, given the history of racism and segregation. Many blacks feel that part of the reason for their lack of good jobs, income, and housing opportunities is due to having fewer opportunities than whites. When blacks' and whites' attitudes regarding efforts to extend equal opportunity were examined, the difference between the two groups was even more pronounced, as shown in Table 4.5. The percentage of blacks disagreeing that "blacks should not have special favors to overcome prejudice" was twice that of the percent of whites. Only 16.5 percent of the white respondents disagreed with this statement compared to 41.3 percent of the black respondents. Although a larger percentage of both higher-educated blacks and whites disagreed that "blacks should not have special favors to overcome prejudice," the percentage of higher-educated blacks taking this position was 12.7 percent higher than the percentage of black respondents in general taking this position. The difference between higher-educated whites and the general white population was only 4 percent on this question. Blacks were also less likely to disagree "that blacks had gotten less than they deserved." Only 17.8 percent of blacks compared to 56.1 percent of whites took this position. The difference in the percentage of blacks and whites accepting this position was slightly less than 40 percent. The difference in the percentage of higher-educated blacks and whites accepting this position was slightly smaller at 36.2 percent.

As shown in Table 4.5, when asked about attitudes toward preferences in hiring and promotions, the percentage of blacks favoring preferences in hiring and promotion was 27.2 percentage points higher than the percentage of whites. When the percentage of higher-educated blacks was compared to higher-educated whites, the difference in those favoring the measure was 31 percent. Blacks are not always more supportive of efforts to extend equality than whites. When the extension of equality pertains to blacks, blacks were significantly more likely to support the measure than whites; however this pattern did not always hold true when the question of extending equality did not pertain to blacks. For example, when the question of extending equal rights to same-sex couples was asked, blacks were less supportive than whites. Only 22.2 percent of the black respondents said that same-sex couples should be able to legally marry, and only 27.5 percent felt same-sex couples should be allowed to form a civil union but not marry. Overall, 50.3 percent of the black respondents said same-sex couples should not be able to marry or form a civil union. Whites were far more open to same-sex marriage and/or the forming of a civil union. Some 33.6 percent of the white respondents felt it was okay for same-sex couples to marry and another 39.4 percent of whites would allow same-sex couples to form a civil union but not marry. Only 27 percent of the white respondents said same-sex couples should not be allowed to marry or form a civil union. The gap between higher-educated blacks and whites in their approval of same-sex marriage was even larger than the gap between the larger populations. The gap between the percentage of blacks and whites, in general, on the question of allowing same-sex couples to marry was 11.4 percent compared to 18.1 percent between higher-educated blacks and whites.

There are several things worthy of note about the differences in the attitudes of blacks and whites on matters of equality. First, the sharpest and the most consistent divisions between blacks' and whites' opinions are on those issues that have implications for blacks as a racial group. Second, differences between blacks and whites remained evident in the Socioeconomic Transition Era. Third, for the most part, differences in higher-educated blacks' and whites' attitudes on matters of equality were greater than those between blacks and whites in general. Finally, these response patterns suggest that there are significant differences in blacks' and whites' perceptions of equality and how matters of inequality should be addressed.

Conclusion

The findings show that since the Politics Era, blacks have become less likely to identify themselves as liberal and more likely to identify themselves as moderate. Change in whites' self-placement on the liberal/conservative scale changed only slightly. There was a slight increase in the percentage of whites identifying themselves as conservative. Despite the moderate changes in blacks' and whites' self-placement on the liberal/conservative scale (or in their political orientation), the two groups differed significantly in the Politics Era and they continued to differ significantly in the Socioeconomic Transition Era.

Blacks' and whites' perceptions of the most important problem facing the country have been similar yet very different. Matters pertaining to social welfare, public order, economic/business and foreign affairs/national defense have been chosen by the largest percentage of whites across the three eras of black politics. However, the order of the distribution has changed across the three eras. Among blacks, social welfare and public order have been consistently identified by the largest proportion of the group as the most important problem facing the nation. During the Politics and Protest Eras, for blacks, the issue of foreign affairs/national defense was among the top four categories and it was replaced during the Protest and Socioeconomic Transition Eras by economic/business issues. Racial problems were among the top four issues for blacks during the Protest and Socioeconomic Transition Eras. Despite the similarities in the most important problems identified by blacks and whites, the distribution of the percentages identifying an issue category as the most important was often dissimilar.

The data presented in this chapter also show that blacks are less trusting than whites in some of the key institutions in society (the government in Washington, the media, the police, and the legal system). Blacks are significantly more supportive of increased government spending to address many of the social problems facing the nation. Likewise, blacks are significantly more liberal than whites on social issues that have direct or indirect implications for blacks as a racial group. Blacks are significantly more conservative on moral issues than whites. Blacks and whites are closest in their attitudes on national security matters (protecting the homeland), but they differ significantly from one another on matters of national defense (taking military action). Finally, blacks are significantly more likely to feel that society should do more to promote equality and to take action to extend opportunity (especially to blacks as a group).

Blacks and whites continue to differ significantly in their opinions in the Socioeconomic Transition Era of black politics. Despite this fact, there are several things worthy of note about the differences between the two races. First, although there was a significant gap in the two groups' opinions, the differences do not constitute a chasm. In most instances, the relationship between race and political opinion was either weak or moderately strong. Second, the response patterns of the two groups suggest the continuing significance of race; however this continuing significance of race in the Socioeconomic Transition Era is probably a carryover from the Protest and Politics Eras. In other words, race still matters but in different ways than it mattered in the earlier eras of black politics. Finally, over the years, there has been some concern that the growing socioeconomic divisions occurring within the black community would lead to increased diversity of opinion among blacks. Although the findings of this chapter do not specifically address this issue, they do suggest that the increased number of blacks in the upper socioeconomic status is not changing the nature of the politics of race. If anything, the data indicate that the differences between upper socioeconomic status blacks and whites are greater than the differences between that of the general black and white populations. The implication of this chapter is that race remains a factor in the black community's external politics (that is, how they interact politically with groups outside of the community). The next chapter examines patterns of public opinion within the black community with an eye toward understanding the implications of socioeconomic divisions on the internal dimensions of black politics.

5

BLACKS' PUBLIC OPINION TODAY

A Question of Consensus

The future of black politics hinges largely on the attitude and behavior of the emerging black middle class. It has been suggested that a class-related schism in blacks' attitudes would develop only if the classes differentiated from each other in their dependence on government services and support.[1] However, it has also been suggested that blacks' economic self-interest would operate to prevent such class-based cleavages from emerging within the community,[2] and increasing life chances for blacks and the escalation of class divisions would not factor into their political behavior.[3] However, one must consider as we move further away from the Protest Era of black politics how changes in the socioeconomic and socio-demographic characteristics of the black community will impact the group's collective political attitudes and behavior. Thus, it is posited that the changing role of race and class in society and the intersection of the two in the Socioeconomic Transition Era will make black politics more complex and less likely to conform to the traditional models of political behavior.

In the Politics Era, there was little evidence to support the contention that major cleavages in blacks' public opinion existed or were developing along class lines.[4] There were no significant differences in middle-class and working-class blacks' attitudes in support of government spending on social and social welfare issues such as improving health care, solving big city problems, halting rising crime, dealing with drug addiction, and improving education.[5] Overall, both groups voted for the same candidates and had the same liberal preferences.[6] Blacks, regardless of socioeconomic standing, were solidly liberal and solidly Democrat.[7] However, there were issues on which lower and upper socioeconomic status blacks' public opinion differed significantly. For example, in the Politics Era, upper socioeconomic status blacks' views differed from those of lower socioeconomic status blacks on certain social welfare issues and those concerning affirmative action.[8]

Dawson suggested that class (or "economic group") interests will ultimately influence, directly or indirectly, such basic political phenomena as blacks' party identification, candidate evaluations, and voting behavior.[9] So as class increasingly becomes a factor in black politics, there is no reason to doubt that it will also become a factor influencing blacks' public opinion at the individual level. Despite this assertion, we still should not expect to find major cleavages in blacks' public opinion along class lines, due to the continuing significance of race in society. The magnitude of difference in blacks' opinion along class lines will largely depend on the nature of the issue in question.

There are several reasons to believe that changes in the social and socioeconomic structure of the black community would eventually lead to significant changes in black public opinion in the Socioeconomic Transition Era. First, the new black middle class has become a significant part of the nation's social and economic fabric, and changes in the social and economic characteristics of the black population have resulted in changes in the cultural, demographic, and geographic structure of the black community. With such changes come new life experiences and the evolution of differing world views. There have always been some philosophical divisions in black politics and often along class lines. For example, in the Politics Era, on the issue of black political autonomy, blacks with higher socioeconomic standing were found to be more distant from the black masses and black elites than blacks of lower socioeconomic status.[10] Improved life chances have the potential to put even more political distance between the emerging sub-communities of blacks, and affect the political cohesion of the larger community. Second, new opportunities and improved life chances will eventually have some impact on the significance of race in society[11] and this is bound to affect the influence of race on political behavior. It has been suggested that as blacks become largely free of legal segregation (once an integral part of the meaning of "blackness"), race will wane as a principal basis for blacks' political consciousness.[12] For example, Allen, Dawson and Brown found that as individual blacks experience upward social mobility they are less likely to take a stance of separating from whites.[13] Even if race does not wane as the principal basis of political consciousness, the impact of race will vary from individual to individual and socioeconomic group to socioeconomic group, due to differing life circumstances. Finally, changing life experience will ultimately lead to increased diversity of opinion and differences in political behaviors among blacks (especially on non-race based issues). With variation of socioeconomic status comes variations in interests at the individual and subgroup level. In this context it is suggested that improvements in blacks' life chances will lead to a maximization of individual and/or subgroup interests and the minimization of larger group interests.

This chapter examines patterns of public opinion among blacks based on socioeconomic stratification in the Socioeconomic Transition Era. It will contemplate how changes in the socioeconomic characteristics of the black community will affect the groups' public opinion. The ultimate aim of the chapter is to give consideration to what the patterns of public opinion among blacks today tell us about the future of black politics. It is believed that differences in blacks' public opinion based on socioeconomic status are more likely to be found on those issues that have no implications for blacks as a racial group. It is also believed that blacks may or may not differ significantly on issues that have indirect implications for the group, although this depends on the nature of the issue: the more individualized or personal the issue is, the greater the chances that differences in opinion will exist along the lines of socioeconomic status. However, it is suggested that we will find no significant differences in blacks' public opinion on most issues that have direct implications for blacks as a racial group. The reasons for this expectation are simple: race still matters in this society and blacks continue to feel that it has some impact on life chances and opportunity at the group level. In this chapter, education will be used as the measure of socioeconomic status. The three educational groupings comprised individuals in: 1) the lower-educated (lower socioeconomic status) group, who had less than 12 years of school; 2) the moderately educated (or moderate socioeconomic status) group, who had 12 to 15 years of school; and 3) the higher-educated (or upper socioeconomic status) group, who had 16 or more years of school.

Perceptions of the Most Important Problem Facing the Nation

Over the years, the American people have been asked what they consider to be the most important problem facing the nation.[14] For purposes of analysis there were six categories into which responses fell: economic/business, foreign affairs, public order, race relations, social welfare, and other problems.[15] These six categories were further divided into two groups based on their direct and indirect implications for blacks. The group that was deemed to have direct implications for blacks included public order, race problems, and social welfare. It was felt that identifying a problem that fell into one of these groups was usually tied to one's connectedness (direct or indirect association) to the group or the plight of the larger group. The groups of problems that had indirect implications for blacks as a group included: economic/business, foreign affairs/national defense, and other problems. The implications of these problems extended beyond racial or class-based concerns, being relevant to the well-being, safety or general functioning of the larger society.

Between 1960 and 2000, there has been a drastic shift in what blacks perceive as the most important problem facing the nation. As shown in Figure 5.1, there was a dramatic change in blacks' opinions on the issues that had direct implications for blacks as a group. During the early 1960s, upward to 43 percent of blacks felt that race-related problems were the most important problems facing the nation. By the late 1960s, the percentage of blacks identifying a race-related

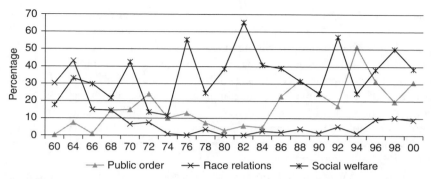

FIGURE 5.1 Attitudes About "The Most Important Problem Facing the Nation" on Issues That Have Direct Implications for Blacks as a Group: 1960 to 2000

problem as the most important problem facing the nation had declined to around 14 percent. In the early 1970s, the percentage of blacks identifying such a problem as the most important facing the nation had declined to around 6 percent. Between the mid-1970s and the mid-1990s, the percentage of blacks identifying a race-related problem had declined to well under 5 percent. There were several occasions in the late 1970s and early 1980s when less than one percent of blacks identified a problem related to race as the most important facing the nation. Surprisingly, since the mid-1990s the percentage of blacks identifying a race relations problem has increased. Between 1996 and 2000, on average 9 percent of blacks identified such a problem as the most important facing the nation.

The percentage of blacks identifying a public order matter as the most important problem facing the nation has gradually increased over the years. In the early 1960s, on several occasions less than one percent of blacks identified a public order matter as the most important problem facing the nation. Between 1968 and 1976, there was a gradual spike in the percentage of blacks identifying a public order issue as the most important problem. In 1968, 14.5 percent of the blacks identified a matter related to public order as the most important problem facing the nation. By 1972, the percentage had reached a high of 24 but slowly declined to 12.9 in 1976. Between 1978 and 1984, those identifying a public order problem averaged around 5 percent, much lower than the percentage of blacks identifying either an economic/business or foreign affairs issue as the most important problem facing the nation. Between the mid-1980s and through the 1990s, the second largest percentage of blacks identified a public order problem as the most important facing the nation. Between 1986 and 2000, on average, 28.7 percent of blacks identified a public order problem as the most important facing the nation.

Social welfare-related concerns have consistently been identified by blacks as one of the most important problems facing the nation. In the 1960s, on average, one-fourth of blacks identified a social welfare problem as the most important facing the nation. While the percentage of blacks identifying a race-related problem has been steadily declining since the 1960s, the percentage of blacks identifying a social welfare issue has been consistently increasing. Except for a very brief period in the early 1970s, the largest percentage of blacks has identified a social welfare problem as the most important facing the nation. In 1976, 1984, and 1992 more than 55 percent identified a social welfare problem as the most important problem. Blacks' concerns about social welfare matters tend to spike or correspond with problems in the economy (i.e., the recessions of 1973–1975, 1981–1982 and 1990–1991).[16]

On those issues that had no direct implications for blacks as a group, a much smaller percentage of blacks identified such a problem as the most important facing the nation. For example, on issues such as agriculture, government functioning, labor, natural resources and others, the combined percentage of blacks identifying a concern in one of these areas was very small. Since the mid-1970s, the percentage of blacks identifying an issue in the "other" category has failed to rise above 5 percent as shown in Figure 5.2. Between 1970 and 1980, those blacks identifying an economic/business or consumer-related problem as the most important averaged around 35 percent. However, in 1974 and 1978 the percentage of blacks identifying a business/economic matter was close to 60. Otherwise, since the early 1980s the percentage of blacks identifying an economic/business issue has averaged 14.7. Overall, the percentage of blacks identifying an economic/business problem has been fairly consistent. The percentage of blacks identifying a business/economic problem as the most important tended to spike when the percentage of blacks identifying a social welfare concern declined.

The percentage of blacks identifying a foreign affairs/national defense problem as the most important problem facing the nation tended to be event driven. That is, nearly one-third of blacks identified a foreign affairs/national defense problem

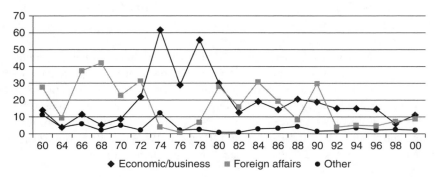

FIGURE 5.2 Attitudes About "The Most Important Problem Facing the Nation" on Issues That Have Indirect Implications for Blacks as a Group: 1960 to 2000

between 1966 and 1972 (the height of the Vietnam War) and around one-fifth identified a foreign affairs/national defense issue during the 1980s (the height of the Cold War). During the 1980s, the percentage of blacks identifying a foreign affairs/national defense problem as the most important fluctuated from as high as 30.7 percent to as low as 8.2 percent. In 1990, the percentage of blacks identifying a foreign affairs/national defense problem as the most important got as high as 29.7 percent, but during the remainder of the decade it failed to get above 10 percent.

In sum, the data suggest that blacks tended to identify most with issues that have direct implications for the group. Since the mid-1980s, a clear majority of blacks have identified an issue that has implications for blacks as a group as the most important problem facing the nation (i.e., public order, race relations, and social welfare). Furthermore, blacks were most likely to identify a problem pertaining to public order and social welfare as the most important problem facing the nation. However, there are occasions when problems that have indirect implications for blacks as a group (i.e., economic/business, foreign affairs/defense, and other) were identified as the most important problems facing the nation. During the late 1960s and early 1970s (the height of the Vietnam War) and again in the 1980s (during heightened Cold War tension), a significant proportion of blacks (averaging 33 and 21 percent respectively) felt that foreign affairs or national defense matters were the most important facing the nation. Likewise, during the troubled economic times of the mid-to-late 1970s and again in the mid-1980s to early 1990s, a significant proportion of blacks (40 and 18 percent respectively) identified an economic/business problem as the most important facing the nation. This is significant because it suggests that although issues with direct implications for blacks as a group tend to be the primary concern of the vast majority of the group, blacks are also attentive to issues that do not have direct implications for the group and they are willing to identify these issues among the most important facing the nation. The data suggest that in times of national crisis, for example, blacks will put their group concerns aside in the interests of the larger society. Further evidence of this was blacks' reaction during the crisis periods of World War I, World War II, and the Great Depression.

The focus now turns to examining perceptions of the most important problems facing the nation when blacks were divided into three groups based on their level of education.[17] As shown in Table 5.1, the congruency in blacks' attitudes regarding the most important problem has changed considerably from one era to another based on level of education. In the Protest Era of black politics, there was no significant difference in blacks' attitudes regarding the most important problem based on level of education. Despite the response patterns being not statistically significant, it is worth noting that in the Protest Era a large percentage of higher-educated blacks identified a race problem as the most important facing the nation, while the largest percentage of lower-educated blacks selected a social welfare problem.

TABLE 5.1 The Most Important Problem Facing Our Nation: Based on Level of Education (in percent)

Protest Era	Lower-educated	Moderately educated	Higher-educated
Economic/business	7.9	8.6	6.9
Foreign affairs	29.6	28.3	24.1
Public order	9.3	8.6	3.4
Race relations	16.2	20.6	34.5
Social welfare	32.4	28.6	24.1
Other (includes agricultural, governmental functioning, natural resources, etc.)	4.6	5.3	6.9

Source: American National Election Combined 1948–1970 Studies. Chi-square prob = .685 n = 584 missing = 818

Politics Era	Lower-educated	Moderately educated	Higher-educated
Economic/business	30.5	28.1	38.7
Foreign affairs	13.4	17.7	16.8
Public order	17.6	10.7	6.7
Race relations	2.3	1.6	1.7
Social welfare	35.5	38.2	32.8
Other (includes agricultural, governmental functioning, natural resources, etc.)	.8	3.7	3.4

Source: American National Election Combined 1972–1986 Studies. Chi-square prob = .006 Phi = .136 n = 1,353 missing = 438

Socioeconomic Transition Era	Lower-educated	Moderately educated	Higher-educated
Economic/business	13.0	13.9	24.4
Foreign affairs	19.0	10.3	6.4
Public order	26.0	30.7	19.4
Race relations	2.0	4.6	7.5
Social welfare	39.0	37.6	37.5
Other (includes agricultural, governmental functioning, natural resources, etc.)	1.0	3.0	4.4

Source: American National Election Combined 1988–2004 Studies. Chi-square prob = .000 Phi = .167 n = 1137 missing = 833 (lower-educated less high school diploma, moderately educated high school diploma or some college, and higher-educated includes those with a bachelors degree or higher)

In the Politics Era, blacks' perceptions of the most important problem differed significantly based on level of education. Nearly one-third of blacks in all three groups identified a social welfare problem as the most important problem facing the nation. However, while the largest proportion of lower- and moderately educated blacks identified a social welfare problem, the largest proportion of higher-educated blacks identified economic/business concerns as the most important problem. Economic/business concerns were identified as the most important problem by the second largest percentage of lower- and moderately educated blacks. Foreign affairs/national defense matters were chosen by the third largest contingency of all three groups as the most important problem facing the nation. During the Politics Era, the percentage of lower-educated blacks identifying a public order issue as the most important problem facing the nation was 10 percentage points higher than that of higher-educated blacks.

In the Socioeconomic Transition Era, not only was there a significant relationship between blacks' level of education and what they perceived as the most important problem, but the strength of the relationship was stronger than it was in the Politics Era. Furthermore, in the Socioeconomic Transition Era, the difference in what higher- and lower-educated blacks perceived as the most important problem became more evident. Since the Protest Era, the percentage of blacks identifying foreign affairs/national defense as the most important problem facing the nation continued to decline. In the Socioeconomic Transition Era, the difference in the opinions of lower- and higher-educated blacks regarding the importance of foreign affairs/national defense was 12.6 percent. That's three times larger than it was in the Politics Era. Surprisingly, concerns among blacks about race-related problems rose between the Politics and Socioeconomic Transition Eras. A significantly higher percentage of higher-educated blacks, when compared to lower- and moderately educated blacks, identified a race-related problem as the most important facing the nation.

In the Socioeconomic Transition Era, the largest percentage of lower-, moderately, and higher-educated blacks identified a social welfare concern as the most important problem nation. More than one-third of the blacks in all three groups identified a social welfare issue. The second largest contingency of higher-educated blacks identified economic/business and the third largest percentage identified a public order problem. The second largest percentage of lower- and moderately educated blacks identified public order as the most important problem facing the nation. More than one-fourth of lower- and moderately educated blacks identified a public order concern as the most important problem facing the nation. Among moderately educated blacks, the third largest group selected economic/business concerns.

If one looks at blacks' public opinion patterns of the most important problem facing the nation over time, one can see several patterns emerging. First, race-related problems have not been chosen as the most important problem facing the nation by a significant portion of blacks since the Protest Era. Second, overall and especially today, race-related problems appear to be more important to higher-educated blacks than to lower- and moderately educated blacks. Third, social welfare concerns were important to a large percentage of blacks regardless of their level of education. Fourth, public order problems have increasingly become among the most important facing the nation identified by blacks, especially for those in the lower- and moderately educated groups. Finally, a significantly larger percentage of higher-educated blacks felt that economic/business matters were the most important problems facing the nation than lower- and moderately educated blacks.

Moral Issues (No Direct Implications)

There are some issues that are important to blacks at the individual level, but these issues have no implications for blacks as a racial group. These issues offer blacks no special protection or due process of law. They do not offer to redress for past grievances to the racial group, nor do they seek to improve the life chances of blacks trapped in poor socioeconomic conditions. Often these issues are important at the individual level and driven by personal interests or conditions. They may be driven by common cultural or social bonds associated with race. They could also be driven by geographic interests, historical factors, or personal experiences. For example, as a group blacks are fervent supporters of the Democratic Party but their policy stance is consistent with Republicans on some moral issues.[18] On these issues that have no direct implications for blacks as a racial group, they (as a group) can be rather liberal but they can also be rather conservative. To test the notion that the lack of congruency in blacks' public opinion is most likely to occur on issues that have no direct implications for the racial group, blacks' public opinion on a number of moral issues was examined. It is suggested that this is one of those areas where divisions in public opinion are most likely associated with the individuals' socioeconomic status. The moral issues examined basically fell into one of two categories. One group of issues was tied to religious matters and the other issues address morals in a behavioral context (although one could argue that there is some overlap here).

There were two questions among this group that were clearly grounded in religion. This is important because religiosity is important in the lives of many blacks and influential in defining black culture. When asked if they would approve of a law against prayer in school, only 21.7 percent of blacks (regardless of their level of education) said they would approve of this measure. Although a larger percentage of the higher-educated blacks would approve of such a law, the differences in opinion on this question were not significant based on the level of education as shown in Table 5.2. On the question about allowing an atheist to make an anti-religion speech, level of education was significantly associated with approval of this measure. Overall, 67 percent of blacks would allow an atheist to make an anti-religion speech. More than 83 percent of the higher-educated blacks would allow an atheist to make such a speech compared to slightly more than half (51.2 percent) of lower-educated blacks and a little more than two-thirds (68.2 percent) of the moderately educated blacks.

There were several (morally based) questions that looked at attitudes toward controlling or mediating behavior. One group of questions looked at protecting the sanctity of life. This group included two questions regarding abortion and one

TABLE 5.2 Attitudes on Issues That Have Moral Importance but *No Direct Implications* for Blacks as a Group

	Lower-educated blacks	Moderately educated blacks	Higher-educated blacks	Kendall Tau Coefficient
Pornography should be legal to all over the age of 18	57.4	68.5	69.5	.084★ (.043)
Approve of abortion any reason	22.9	41.6	47.3	−.166★★★ (.042)
Approve of abortion if woman's health in danger	79.3	87.5	96.0	−.104★★★ (.030)
Approve of allowing incurable patients to die	41.4	51.6	60.2	−.118★★ (.044)
Approve of law against prayer in school	22.7	19.0	30.5	−.038 (.046)
Allow atheist to make anti-religion speech	51.2	68.2	83.8	−.207★★★ (.041)
Allow homosexual to make a speech supporting homosexuality	56.7	80.7	92.3	−.235★★★ (.038)

Source: Combined 2002–2006 General Social Surveys
Prob. ★< .05 ★★< .01 ★★★< .001 (Standard error in parentheses)

about euthanasia. In general, 86 percent of the black respondents would approve of an abortion if a woman's health was in danger. As a group, higher-educated blacks were significantly more likely to approve of an abortion if the mother's health was in danger. More than 96 percent of higher-educated blacks would allow an abortion given these circumstances. Moderately educated blacks were more likely to approve of the measure than lower-educated blacks as shown in Table 5.2. On the question of approving of an abortion for any reason, blacks were overall less approving. Only 38 percent of all blacks would approve of an abortion for any reason. Approval of abortion for any reason among higher- and moderately educated blacks was measurably greater than it was among lower-educated blacks. While more than 40 percent of the higher- and moderately educated blacks would approve of an abortion for any reason, less than 25 percent of the lower-educated blacks would approve an abortion for any reason.

When asked, "If a person has a disease that cannot be cured, do you think doctors should be allowed by law to end the patient's life by some painless means if the patient and his/her family request it?" blacks were divided in their opinions. Overall, blacks were split down the middle in their response on this question about euthanizing an incurable patient. Around 50.7 percent of blacks would approve of the measure, while 49.3 percent would disapprove. On the euthanasia question, blacks differed significantly in their opinions along educational lines. Higher-educated blacks were more likely than lower-educated blacks to approve of allowing incurable patients to be euthanized. The difference between higher-educated and lower-educated blacks was roughly 20 percent, and the difference in the percentage of moderately educated blacks approving of the measure was 10 points lower than that of higher-educated blacks and 10 points higher than that of lower-educated blacks on this measure.

On the two moral questions that measured the appropriateness of a behavior, blacks differed significantly in their opinion based on level of education. On the question of whether pornography should be legal to all over the age of 18, 65.8 percent of blacks thought this should be the case. Higher- and moderately educated blacks were significantly more likely than lower-educated blacks to approve of making pornography legal to everyone over the age of 18. While around 69 percent of the higher- and moderately educated blacks felt pornography should be made legal to those over 18 years of age, only 57.4 percent of lower-educated blacks approved of this measure. Seventy-six percent of blacks would allow a homosexual to make speech supporting homosexuality. Blacks' responses differed significantly based on level of education. By more than 30 percent, higher-educated blacks were more likely than lower-educated blacks to allow such a speech to be made. Taken as a whole, the data in Table 5.2 support the notion that blacks' opinions often differ significantly on those issues that have little or no implications for blacks as a racial or as a social or economic group.

Governmental Spending Priorities

The previous chapter illustrated how blacks and whites differed significantly on the governmental spending priorities to solve social and social welfare problems. Blacks were significantly more likely than whites to feel the government spent "too little" money addressing most social and social welfare concerns. The question addressed here is how the attitudes of blacks differ on governmental spending priorities based on educational attainment. This question is especially significant since many of these government spending initiatives have no direct policy implications for blacks as a group; however they do have implications for blacks at the individual or subgroup levels. Thus, these governmental spending priorities (or the implied policy initiatives) have greater implications because of a common bond or shared position in life.

Overall, the data in Table 5.3 show that blacks were especially supportive of increasing governmental spending to address social and social welfare problems. In fact, the only spending question where the majority of blacks felt government spending was either "about right" or "too much" was on the welfare issue. In the mid-2000s, 31.1 percent of blacks felt the amount that government spent on welfare was about right and 26.9 percent felt the government spent too much. However, the attitudes of blacks to government spending on welfare differed significantly along educational lines. Lower-educated blacks were more inclined to feel that the

TABLE 5.3 Attitudes on Issues That Have Policy or *Indirect* Implications for Blacks as a Group

Socioeconomic Transition Era	Lower-educated blacks	Moderately educated blacks	Higher-educated blacks	Kendall Tau Coefficient
Too little improving the educational system	72.4	85.6	84.4	−.099★ (.043)
Too little dealing with drug addiction	62.9	74.1	67.4	−.049 (.042)
Too little halting rising crime rate	65.0	76.6	68.4	−.048 (.042)
Too little solving the problems of big cities	54.4	64.6	72.3	−.113★★ (.038)
Too little protecting the nation's health	79.2	87.8	91.5	−.105★★ (.040)
Too little on welfare	46.3	43.2	31.9	.071★★ (.037)
Government spends too little protecting the environment	52.1	73.1	76.6	−.156★★★ (.040)

Source: Combined 2002–2006 General Social Surveys
Prob. ★< .05 ★★< .01 ★★★< .001 (Standard error in parentheses)

government spent too little on welfare. Approximately 46 percent of lower-educated blacks felt the government spent too little compared to 31.9 percent of higher-educated blacks. At 43.2 percent, the response pattern of moderately educated blacks was closer to that of lower-educated blacks than that of higher-educated blacks.

The data in Table 5.3 showed no significant difference in blacks' response to the drug addiction and halting crime spending questions based on level of education. Around 70.6 percent of all blacks felt that the government spent too little dealing with drug addiction and 72.8 percent felt the government spent too little to halt crime. This finding is relevant because of the seven government spending questions examined the questions on dealing with drug addiction and halting crime had the most direct implications for blacks as a group. Drug addiction and rising crime are concerns of blacks regardless of educational level. Most blacks are not the direct victims of drug abuse or crime; however most blacks have a strong awareness of the problems as they exist in the larger black community.

On the questions of government spending to improve education, protect the environment, solve big city problems, and protect the nation's health, on average 75.5 percent of blacks felt the government spent too little. Again on the two issues that had direct implications for blacks at the individual level but no direct implications for the group, the percentage of blacks indicating the government spent too little was in excess of 80 percent. Eighty-two percent of blacks felt the government spent too little to improve education and 86.6 percent felt the government spent too little protecting the nation's health. On the other hand, on the two questions that had the least implications for blacks as a group, the percentage of blacks feeling that the government spent too little was less than 70. That is, only 63.8 percent of blacks felt the government spent too little to solve the problems of big cities and 69.3 percent felt the government spent too little protecting the environment.

A significantly larger percentage of higher-educated blacks felt the government spent too little on big cities, improving the nation's health, and protecting the environment than lower-educated blacks. The percentage of moderately educated blacks feeling that the government spent too little protecting the nation's health and the environment was much closer to the percentage of higher-educated blacks than it was to that of lower-educated blacks. The percentage of moderately educated blacks saying that the government spent too little on solving the problems of big cities was approximately 10 points greater than the percentage of lower-educated blacks and about 8 points less than that of higher-educated blacks. On the whole, the data in Table 5.3 show significant differences along educational lines among blacks toward governmental spending priorities on social and social welfare matters. Higher-educated blacks were significantly more likely to feel that the government spends too little improving education, protecting the environment, dealing with drug addiction, solving the problems of big cities, and protecting the nation's health.

Race-Related Issues

It is understandable why blacks (as a group) are likely to support issues protecting and securing rights for the racial group, those providing governmental assistance to the racial group or creating special policies to help blacks. Similarly, it is understandable why blacks are also likely to be very supportive of initiatives addressing the social problems affecting the larger black community. However, the level of support varies from issue to issue. For example, when asked would they favor an open housing law prohibiting discrimination versus letting the owner decide to whom to sell their house, 80.1 percent of blacks favored an open housing law. On another measure designed to ensure rights for blacks, a larger percentage of the group took a surprisingly less supportive position. When asked if they supported or opposed blacks being given preference in hiring, 56.6 percent of the black respondents opposed the measure.

The majority of blacks did not always take the most supportive position on questions concerning government assisting or assistance to blacks. For example, when asked if government should help blacks or whether blacks should receive no special treatment, the results were mixed. Only 14.5 percent of the black respondents felt blacks should receive no special treatment. Forty-five percent of the black respondents felt the government should aid blacks; however 40 percent of the black respondents felt the government should help and blacks should also help themselves. On another question concerning government assistance to blacks, respondents were asked if government spends too little improving conditions of blacks. Around 75.6 percent of the black respondents felt the government spent too little, and only 2.8 percent said the government spent too much.

On those issues addressing problems confronting blacks as a community, the degree to which blacks' responses were most supportive depended on the nature of the problem and the proposed solutions. For instance, 71.5 percent of the black respondents felt that marijuana should not be made legal. It would not be unreasonable to assume that this high disapproval rate is due to drug problems and the crimes associated with it in black inner-city communities. When asked if they would favor or oppose a law requiring gun permits, 85.9 percent would favor such a law. On the death penalty for murder issue, black respondents were more equally divided; 57.5 percent opposed capital punishment while 42.5 percent were in favor.

How supportive (or non-supportive) blacks were depended on the degree to which the issue has direct or explicit implications for the group. Furthermore, the data in Table 5.4 show no significant difference based on level of education in blacks' response to issues that had direct or explicit implications for blacks. Overall, the data reveal several things about blacks' public opinion on race-related issues. First, blacks are most supportive of measures that protect or enhance the racial

TABLE 5.4 Attitudes on Issues That Have *Explicit* Implications for Blacks as a Group

	Lower-educated blacks	*Moderately educated blacks*	*Higher-educated blacks*	*Kendall Tau Coefficient*
Government should help blacks	50.5	42.1	50.0	.008 (.044)
Favor open housing law	68.8	84.3	79.0	.091 (.055)
Government spends too little improving conditions of blacks	69.9	72.2	76.8	−.054 (.041)
Support preferences in hiring blacks	42.1	40.6	55.4	−.070 (.043)
Oppose death penalty for murder	57.3	59.0	51.9	−.024 (.036)
Favor gun permits	86.6	83.6	93.8	−.046 (.037)
Marijuana should be legal	30.2	28.7	25.7	.028 (.044)

Source: General Social Survey 2002–2006
Prob. *< .05 **< .01 ***< .001
(Standard error in parentheses)

group's rights and quality of life. This is especially true of questions that asked if whites have a right to deny blacks something because of their race. This is less the case where blacks were asked how they should proceed in addressing quality of life issues. Second, higher-educated blacks are no more or less supportive than lower- or moderately educated blacks on issues that have explicit or direct implications for the racial group.

Conclusion

The data presented in this chapter show blacks to be most liberal in their public opinion on certain types of issues. In particular, blacks were most liberal on those issues that have direct or explicit implications for their own racial group. The data presented in this chapter suggest political congruency is not always the case because there are variations in political attitudes and behavior within the group. Higher-educated blacks were more likely to differ from lower-educated blacks in their attitudes toward most policy and political issues that have no direct or explicit implications for the racial group. Nevertheless, there was no evidence of an ideological cleavage within the black community based on level of education. The findings suggest that the types of issues where cleavages are most likely to develop among blacks are on those issues that are least important to blacks as a racial group.

The findings of this chapter show the complexity of the politics of the black population. Although the nature of the study was simplistic from a methodological perspective, the findings are important because they suggest that the surface political behavior of blacks may not be evidence of what is happening below the surface. This does not mean that the black political community is on the verge of major political fragmentation. However, it does suggest that the black political community may be ready for some type of political transformation as the result of socioeconomic, demographic, and geographic changes. Significant changes in patterns of social and economic development within the community are beginning to become noticeable among blacks, and the factors that produce a sense of commonality in the population are beginning to change. As a result, it is reasonable to expect some transformation in the political behavior and patterns of public opinion among blacks.

6

BLACK POLITICS AND THE CONTINUING STRUGGLE FOR POLITICAL INFLUENCE IN THE SOCIOECONOMIC TRANSITION ERA

Immediately after the Protest Era of black politics, blacks got politically dressed up only to discover they had no place to go. In the late 1960s and early 1970s, blacks had opportunities to gain political power like they never had before. Taking advantage of the recently passed Civil Rights Act of 1964 and the Voting Rights Act of 1965, they began registering and turning out to vote in large numbers. During this period, there were enormous increases in the number of black elected officials. The augmentation of blacks' influence in the political system (especially at the local level) was eventually met by partisan adjustments and ideological shifts among whites. By the late 1980s and early 1990s, blacks' political activism had begun to subside and the political influence as a group had began to level off. In the Socioeconomic Transition Era of black politics, blacks' political influence rested more with subgroups than with the collectivity. There are three questions regarding blacks' continuing struggle for political influence that this chapter ponders. First, what are the implications of blacks' stabilized political activity and the changing dynamics of the black community on the group's continuing struggle for political influence today? Second, what is the future for blacks as a political bloc in the Socioeconomic Transition Era? Finally, based on the political activity and behavior of blacks in the Socioeconomic Transition Era, what are the chances of blacks serving as a balance of power in the political system?

In the late 1960s, Chuck Stone scrutinized blacks' quest for political power and raised questions about the future of black politics.[1] He argued that the black vote and its potential to serve as a balance of power would never pose a serious threat to whites' political dominance. Moreover, he felt that blacks posed no threat to the white power base because blacks would eventually lose their sense of racial identity and solidarity as they moved out into mainstream society. Stone felt that blacks as a voting bloc could expect to be nothing more than a minor influence in elections; in addition, for blacks to become a true political power, three conditions must be met: 1) there would have to be political cohesion among group members—blacks must constitute a bloc, 2) there would have to be a two-way split of the white vote, and 3) there would have to be some political oscillation of fragile loyalties (that is, the black vote would have to swing back and forth between the two major parties).

Stone noted the absence of all three factors in the Protest Era because the black vote had been more of a loyal ally than a neutral balance of power. He even questioned whether blacks were loyal allies because they had not been able to translate their votes at the polls into jobs. In other words, he implied that although blacks had been loyal, they had not received much in return. Stone asked what have blacks gained in political rewards for holding the balance of power. His answer was "virtually nothing, considering their proportionate size in the population and the crucial proportion their votes made between victory and defeat."[2]

In the late 1970s, Edwin Dorn followed with a similar assessment. He wrote that the rules of voting and the substantive results were open.[3] Dorn felt that having the right to vote could be the key to political equality and protection or it could lead to "creeping mediocrity . . . and a host of other evils." To that end he identified the "rules of suffrage" (or conditions necessary) to produce the desired policy outcomes that were important to blacks. He identified five general conditions: 1) having the right to vote; 2) exercising the right to vote; 3) making the vote count as members of the winning coalition; 4) having members in the dominant coalition in the representative assembly; and 5) ensuring that the group's policy desires appeared on the agenda. Dorn concluded nothing in "rules of suffrage" would lead him to believe the black vote would have a meaningful effect on policy. He wrote, "If black voting is to have predictable effects on policy, certain conditions must be satisfied and they have not been." Dorn (like Stone) suggested that if blacks were to achieve success they had to take advantage of political divisions and form the pivotal point of a winning coalition.[4]

In the initial phase of the Politics Era, blacks showed much promise in converting their potential political power to real political power, but since the early 1980s the black community has not measured up politically in ways that have significantly improved their overall social and economic well being. They have not become a significant political force despite their efforts during the late Protest and early Politics Eras. As a result, the black community as a political entity has not achieved its maximum political potential. This chapter contemplates how the changing demographics and improved life chances for blacks in the Politics Era has influenced blacks' struggle for political power in the Socioeconomic Transition Era. The aim of this chapter is to take a closer look at the state of blacks' continuing struggle for political power (influence) today. Stone and Dorn's measures of political strength will be the criteria used to determine the state of black politics in the Socioeconomic Transition Era. More specifically this chapter examines blacks' struggle for political influence and power by: 1) looking at how blacks have exercised their right to vote since the end of the Protest Era; 2) discussing blacks' behavior as a political bloc; 3) considering the future of blacks as part of the winning political coalition in the electorate; and 4) discussing the potential for the black community to engage in the politics of oscillation in the Socioeconomic Transition Era.

Exercising the Right to Vote

Blacks' political and social demands during the Protest Era, as they culminated in the 1964 Civil Rights Act,[5] included outlawing racial segregation in education, public accommodations, employment, and increased voting rights. Because the political arena was also going to be the primary means for blacks to gain economic and social equality, the push for voting rights took center stage. Black leadership in the Protest (1950s through 1960s) and early Politics Eras (1970s and 1980s) perhaps overstressed the importance of political development to the extent of understressing the importance of social and economic development. At the federal level, the vote would give blacks greater opportunity to influence the social and economic values of the nation by choosing elected officials. At the local level, the vote would provide blacks with an opportunity to determine directly how local resources were allocated through black elected and non-elected officials. Given the importance of blacks' political development (i.e., the vote and elected repre-sentation) to the group's overall social and economic quality of life, a simple indi-cator of the struggle for political influence would be to examine the political activity and behavior of blacks in a comparative context to that of whites. It is reasonable to expect that the road to blacks' achieving their maximum political potential begins with increasing their collective political activity and participation in the political system. As a result, their voter registration and turnout, at minimum, would have to be comparable to that of whites.

Voter Registration

In 1968 (roughly the end of the Protest Era and immediately after the passage of the Voting Rights Act) the voter registration rate among blacks was 70.2 percent.[6] In the 40-year period between 1968 and 2008, the only other times the voter registration rate among blacks has exceeded 70 percent were in 1984 and 1992. In the initial phase of the Politics Era (1972 to 1980), voter registration among blacks averaged 65.3 percent. Between 1972 and 1976, the voter registration rate declined from 69.5 percent to 62.2 percent. This decline could reasonably be attributed to the passage of the Twenty-Sixth Amendment which lowered the voting age to 18.[7] The 1980 voter registration rate among blacks increased slightly to 64.1 percent, which was still 6.1 percent below the 1968 voter registration rate. There was a resurgence in voter registration among blacks in the second phase of the Politics Era (the early to mid-1980s), and this resurgence was largely brought on by Jesse Jackson's bid for the Democratic Party presidential nomination in 1984. As shown in Figure 6.1, between 1980 and 1984 the voter registration rate among blacks rose by 7.9 percent to 72 percent. Although Jackson sought the party's nomination again in 1988, the voter registration among blacks actually declined by 3.2 percent to 68.8 percent.

Since the start of the Socioeconomic Transition Era (the late 1980s), blacks' voter registration has averaged about 67.5 percent. Since the 1992 presidential election, voter registration among blacks has failed to exceed 70 percent despite the candidate for the Democratic Party being a black man in the 2008 presidential election. In the Socioeconomic Transition Era, voter registration among the black citizen population was lowest in 1996 at 66.4 percent and this was down 3.6 percent from 1992. As shown in Figure 6.1, since 1996 black voter registration has increased by roughly 1 percent every presidential election year. The voter registration pattern for off-year elections since 1992 has shown a different pattern. Since 1998, the black voter registration rate for off-year elections has been in decline. Between 1992 and 2006, the off-year voter registration rate among blacks has an average of 62 percent. During this period, the off-year voter registration has ranged from a high of 63.6 percent in 1998 to a low of 60.9 percent in 2006.[8] Despite improvements in blacks' level of education and increased opportunities to register to vote (i.e., "motor voter" legislation and less burdensome voter registration laws), we have not seen significant changes in blacks' voter registration activity.

Among whites, average voter registration during the latter phase of Politics Era (1980 to 1988) was 74.3 percent as shown in Figure 6.1. In the latter phase of the Politics Era, the average voter registration rate among whites was 6 percentage points higher than the voter registration rate of blacks. Interestingly enough, in

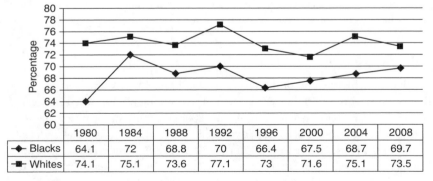

FIGURE 6.1 Black and White (non-Hispanic) Citizen Population Reported Registered to Vote: 1980 to 2008

Source: Table A1. Reported Voting and Registration, by Race, Hispanic Origin, Sex and Age for Groups: November 1964 to 2008, U.S. Census Bureau, Current Population November 2008 and earlier reports: Internet release date: July 2009

the latter phase of the Politics Era, blacks' voter registration pattern has tended to mirror that of whites in terms of rising and falling. The highest voter registration rate among whites in the latter phase of the Politics Era was 75.1 percent in 1984 and that rate declined to 73.6 percent in 1988. During the Socioeconomic Transition Era, the rate of voter registration of whites continued to exceed that of blacks. The average voter registration among whites in presidential election years since the 1992 election was 74.1 percent. The voter registration rate for whites in the Socioeconomic Transition Era of black politics was on average 5.6 percentage points higher than it was for blacks. Even in 2008, with a black candidate heading the ticket for a major political party, the voter registration rate for whites exceeded that of blacks. At no time since the passage of the civil rights legislation and the passage of the Voting Rights Act has the black voter registration rate exceeded that of whites. Nevertheless, the black/white voter registration gap has closed since 1980 when it was 10 percent. Since the 1992 presidential election year, the gap between blacks and whites voter registration has averaged 5.6 percent. The largest black/white voter registration gap in the Socioeconomic Transition Era was in 1992 (7.1 percent) and the smallest gap was in 2008 (3.8 percent). Since the latter phase of the Politics Era of black politics, the smallest black/white voter registration gap was 3.1 percent in 1984.

As shown in Table 6.1, differences in the reported voter registration rate between blacks and whites produced some surprising results based on select demographic and geographic characteristics. It is reasonable to expect some subpopulations in the black community to register and turn out to vote at a rate that far exceeds their white contemporaries. For example, one could reasonably expect middle-aged (45-to-64), Southern, and higher-educated blacks to have voter registration and turnout rates that were at least comparable, if not exceeding, those of their white counterparts. This assertion is based on the assumption that middle-aged and older blacks' experiences (directly or indirectly) with racial inequality and awareness of blacks' struggle for civil rights would augment their interests, sense of obligation, and participation in politics. Likewise, one could argue that blacks in the South would have higher (or comparable) voter registration and turnout rates than their white counterparts because that region was the battleground for the civil and voting rights movements. In the same way one would also expect higher-educated blacks to have voter registration and turnout rates that were comparable to those of their white counterparts because of their increased awareness as a group of the importance of political activism to improving blacks' social and economic position in society. That is, the nature of blacks' struggle for civil and voting rights should be a stronger motivator to register and turn out to vote among some subpopulations as opposed to others. On the other hand, one must acknowledge that there are a number of factors that may preclude blacks from registering and turning out in levels comparable to those of whites despite population characteristics.

With a black candidate heading the ticket of a major political party in 2008 not only would one expect the level of voter registration to rise among blacks (similar

TABLE 6.1 Percentage of Black and White (non-Hispanic) Citizen Population Reporting They Registered to Vote: Based on Selected Characteristics

	2004			2008		
	Blacks	*Whites*	*Difference*	*Blacks*	*Whites*	*Difference*
Age 18 to 24 years	53.1	52.5	0.6	61.3	58.3	3.0
Age 25 to 44 years	62.2	62.0	0.2	69.5	68.7	.8
Age 45 to 64 years	69.2	74.6	−5.4	72.3	76.0	−3.7
Age 65 to 74 years	73.2	78.4	−5.2	75.0	79.7	−4.7
Age 75 years plus	74.5	78.4	−3.9	72.7	77.8	−5.1
Sex—males	60.0	66.2	−6.2	66.2	70.2	−4.0
Sex—females	67.9	69.5	−1.6	72.4	73.7	−1.3
Region—Northeast	54.9	68.6	−13.7	62.1	72.0	−9.9
Region—Midwest	71.6	74.0	−2.4	71.5	74.5	−3.0
Region—South	65.3	66.7	−1.4	71.9	71.3	.6
Region—West	64.3	62.7	−1.6	66.2	70.3	−4.1
Education—less than 9th grade	51.7	31.5	20.2	55.1	49.3	5.8
Education—9th to 12th (no diploma)	55.1	44.6	10.5	57.6	49.6	8.0
Education—high school graduate	61.1	62.7	−1.6	67.4	64.3	3.1
Education—Some college/ associate degree	70.9	73.6	−4.7	75.1	76.1	−1.0
Bachelor degree	72.2	80.9	−8.7	77.7	82.8	−5.1
Advanced degree	73.9	85.5	−11.6	76.7	87.7	−11.0

Source: Tables 2, 3 and 6. "Reported Voting and Registered by Race, Hispanic Origin, and Sex for United States November 2004. U.S. Census Bureau, Current Population Survey, November 2004, Internet release date: May 25, 2005; and Tables 2, 3 and 6. "Reported Voting and Registered by Race, Hispanic Origin, and Sex for United States November 2008. U.S. Census Bureau, Current Population Survey, November 2008, Internet release date: July, 2009

to that of 1984 when Jesse Jackson ran for the party nomination), but one could reasonably expect black voter registration and turnout to exceed that of whites. Furthermore, one would expect black voter registration to exceed that of whites across the board if for no other reason than the nation's racial history and blacks' struggle for political influence. However, this was not the case. Despite the voter registration rate for blacks increasing and the percentage for whites declining between 2004 and 2008, the percentage of blacks registering to vote did not exceed that of whites. The registration gap between the two groups did decline from 6.4 percent in 2004 to 3.8 percent in 2008, and the percentage of blacks and whites reporting they were registered to vote changed in nearly every category between the 2004 and 2008 presidential election as shown in Table 6.1.

When blacks' and whites' voting age populations were divided into five age groups,[9] the difference in voter registration rates across these age groups in 2008 ranged from 0.8 to 5.1 percent.[10] The smallest voter registration gap in 2008 was between the 25-to-44 age group, and this pattern was consistent with the 2004 voter registration pattern. In 2004 and 2008, the difference in the voter registration rate between blacks and whites in this age group was less than 1 percent. The percentage of both groups registering to vote actually increased by 7 percent between 2004 and 2008. Overall, the smallest voter registration rate was among 18 to 24-year-olds, and surprisingly blacks in this age group had a higher voter registration rate than their white counterparts. The voter registration difference between blacks and whites in the 18-to-24 group was 0.6 percent in 2004 and rose to 3.0 percent in 2008. In 2004 the difference in the voter registration between blacks and whites in the 45-to-64 age group was 5.4 percent (the largest difference of the five groups), but it closed considerably in 2008 to 3.7 percent. Perhaps most surprising here was that the percentage of whites registered to vote was higher than that of blacks. This was surprising because this group included the first wave of the new black middle class. The difference in voter registration between blacks and whites in the 65-to-74 age group also declined between 2004 and 2008. This closure was due to the percentage of blacks in this age group registering to vote increasing by more than 2 percent in 2008, while the percent of whites in the age group increased by less than one percent. It was in the 75-plus category that the voter registration rates actually declined between 2004 and 2008 for both blacks and whites. These were the stable mature adults (over 24 years of age) at the start of the Politics Era. They were old enough to have been part of the initial voter registration surge among blacks in the late 1960s and early 1970s. One would expect this group of blacks to have a heightened awareness because of their experiences and effort put forth to get this group acclimated to and participating in the political process. There are several patterns worthy of note here. First, younger blacks' (under the age of 45) levels of voter registration are comparable to those of their white counterparts. Second, although there is a difference in the voter registration rates of older blacks and whites the difference does not constitute a gap.

Between 2004 and 2008 the largest growth in registration rates between the sexes was among black males. Nevertheless, the percentage of black males and females reporting they registered to vote was lower than the percentage of white males and females. The difference in voter registration between black and white males was larger than the difference between black and white females. The voter registration gap between black and white males was 4.0 percent in 2008 down from 6.2 percent in 2004. The gap between black and white females was only 1.6 percent in 2004 and 1.3 percent in 2008. While the difference in the voter registration rates between black males and females was 6.2 percent in 2008, it was only 2.5 percent between white males and females. Across regions, voter registration rates for blacks were also smaller than those for whites. In 2008, the largest voter registration gap between blacks and whites was in the Northeast (9.9 percent). The smallest voter registration gap between blacks and whites was in the South (0.6) percent. Voter registration among blacks ranged from a high of 71.9 percent in the South to a low of 62.1 percent in the Northeast.

It should be noted that in the South the percentage of blacks reporting they registered to vote in 2008 exceeded that of whites. In the Midwest and the West, the reported voter registration gap between blacks and whites actually increased (in favor of whites).

A rather surprising pattern emerged when the voter registration gap was measured based on educational attainment. Lower-educated blacks (those with a high school education or less) had a voter registration rate that was higher than their white counterparts. The difference in voter registration between blacks and whites with 8 or less years of school in 2008 was 5.8 percent and this was down from 20.2 percent in 2004. In 2008, while the voter registration rate among blacks in the less than 9 years of school group increased by 3.4 percent, the voter registration rate among their white counterparts increased by close to 18 percent. At the other extreme, the voter registration gap was greatest between higher-educated blacks and whites (those with advanced degrees); this did not change much between 2004 and 2008 and was the largest among the six educational groups. The registration gap between blacks and whites with advanced degrees was 11.0 percent in 2008. The gap between blacks and whites with bachelor degrees in 2008 was 5.1 percent down from 8.7 percent in 2004. The difference in voter registration between blacks and whites with associate degrees almost disappeared in 2008 (1 percent). Surprisingly, the data suggest that as the level of education among blacks and whites increased the voter registration gap also increased. In 2008, lower-educated blacks continued to report registering at a higher rate than lower-educated whites; however lower-educated whites; closed the gap between 2004 and 2008. Higher-educated whites (those with at least some college education) continued to report registering to vote at a higher rate than higher-educated blacks; however, the gap between the two racial groups closed noticeably between 2004 and 2008. Finally, blacks responded with increased voter registration across the board in 2008 when a black candidate headed the ticket of one of the major political parties.

Voter Turnout

In the twelve presidential elections between 1964 and 2008, the average voter turnout among blacks (the citizen population) was 57.9 percent compared to 66.3 percent for whites (the citizen population).[11] Furthermore, the voter turnout rate for blacks has never exceeded that of whites. As shown in Figure 6.2, since the latter phase of the Politics Era, the largest voter turnout among blacks was in the 2008 election when 64.7 percent of black citizens reported voting. In addition to the 2008 presidential election, the black citizens' voter turnout rate has equalled or exceeded 60 percent in only four other presidential elections: 1964 (62.3 percent), 1968 (61.4 percent), 1984 (60.6 percent), and 2004 (60 percent). The average voter turnout rate among black citizens in the Politics Era (1972 to 1988) was 55.6 percent compared to 58.7 percent in the Socioeconomic Transition Era. As shown in Figure 6.2, during the latter phase

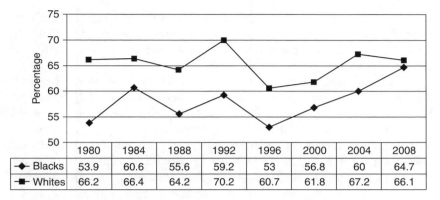

	1980	1984	1988	1992	1996	2000	2004	2008
◆ Blacks	53.9	60.6	55.6	59.2	53	56.8	60	64.7
■ Whites	66.2	66.4	64.2	70.2	60.7	61.8	67.2	66.1

FIGURE 6.2 Black and White (non-Hispanic) Citizen Population Reported Voting: 1980–2008

Source: Table A1. Reported Voting and Registration, by Race, Hispanic Origin, Sex and Age for Groups: November 1964 to 2008, U.S. Census Bureau, Current Population November 2008 and earlier reports: Internet release date: July 2009

of the Politics Era, voter turnout among blacks was an up and down affair. The average voter turnout among the black citizen population in the three presidential elections in the 1980s (the latter phase of the Politics Era) was 56.7 percent.

Since the 1996 presidential election black voter turnout has been on a slight upward path. Starting with the 1992 presidential election (the first presidential election in the Socioeconomic Transition Era), voter turnout among the black citizen population has averaged 58.7 percent. During the same period, the average voter turnout in presidential elections for the white (non-Hispanic) citizen population was 65.2 percent. The average voter turnout among the white (non-Hispanic) citizen population during the 1980s (the second phase of the Politics Era) was 65.6 percent. While there was a slight increase in the average voter turnout among the black citizen population between the Politics Era and the Socioeconomic Transition Era, the average voter turnout among whites remained fairly constant at around 65 percent. Overall, the average difference in blacks' and whites' voter turnout in the two Protest Era elections examined (1964 and 1968) was 10 percent (the average voter turnout for the black citizen population during this era was 61.8 percent and 71.8 percent of the white citizens population). The average turnout for the black citizen population actually declined between the Protest and Politics Eras to 55.6 percent, and similarly it declined for the white citizen population to 65.3 percent. In the Socioeconomic Transition Era, there was an increase in the average turnout for black citizens while the voter turnout rate for the white citizen population remained constant. In the Socioeconomic Transition Era, the average voter turnout for the black citizen population was 58.7 percent compared to 65.2 percent for the white population. As shown in Figure 6.2, if you disregard the 2008 presidential election, since the 1980 presidential election there has been no clear indication that the voter turnout gap between blacks and whites has either closed or widened significantly. The differences in the turnout between the two groups have largely been election driven.

When examining sub-population characteristics, the data show a significant change in blacks' and whites' voter turnout rates between 2004 and 2008. Younger blacks' (those between the ages of 18 and 44) voting behavior has been either comparable to or exceeded that of their white counterparts. In 2004, as shown in Table 6.2, there was a slight difference in the voter turnout between blacks and whites (in favor of blacks) in the 18-to-24 age group and no difference between the two racial groups in the 25-to-44 age group. However, in the 2008 presidential election the voter turnout for blacks between the ages of 18 and 24 was 7.7 percentage points higher than that of their white counterparts and 3.9 percent higher for blacks in the 25-to-44 age bracket. Although middle-aged blacks (in the 45-to-64 age group) turned out to vote in larger proportions for the 2008

TABLE 6.2 Percentage of Black and White (non-Hispanic) Citizen Population Reporting Voting: Based on Selected Characteristics

	2004			2008		
	Blacks	Whites	Difference	Blacks	Whites	Difference
Age 18 to 24 years	44.1	42.6	1.5	55.4	47.7	7.7
Age 25 to 44 years	54.0	54.0	0.0	64.0	60.1	3.9
Age 45 to 64 years	62.9	68.9	−5.7	68.7	70.2	−1.5
Age 65 to 74 years	66.2	72.4	−6.2	70.9	73.8	−2.9
Age 75 years plus	60.9	68.4	−7.4	63.8	69.0	−5.2
Sex—males	51.8	58.6	−6.8	60.5	62.4	−1.9
Sex—females	59.8	62.0	−2.2	68.1	66.3	1.8
Region—Northeast	48.4	61.8	−13.4	58.6	64.6	−6.0
Region—Midwest	64.7	66.2	−1.5	67.3	66.6	0.7
Region—South	55.9	57.6	−1.7	66.0	62.3	3.7
Region—West	57.9	57.1	−0.8	63.0	65.0	−2.0
Education—less than 9th grade	38.5	22.7	15.8	46.4	37.6	8.8
Education—9th to 12th (no diploma)	43.1	33.1	10.0	49.8	37.6	12.2
Education—high school graduate	52.4	53.4	−1.0	61.3	54.6	6.7
Education—some college/associate degree	63.6	68.0	−4.4	71.2	68.5	2.7
Bachelor degree	68.7	76.7	−8.0	76.2	78.5	−2.3
Advanced degree	72.6	82.7	−10.1	75.1	84.9	−9.8

Source: Tables 2, 3 and 6. Reported Voting and Registered by Race, Hispanic Origin, and Sex for United States November 2004. U.S. Census Bureau, Current Population Survey, November 2004, Internet release date: May 25, 2005

presidential election than they did in the 2004 presidential election, they still lagged behind their white counterparts. The differences in turnout between black and white males and black and white females were drastically different in 2008 when compared to 2004. In 2008, the black females' turnout to vote was almost 2 percentage points higher than that of white females. The percentage of black males turning out to vote still lagged behind white males in the 2008 presidential election; however the difference was down to 1.9 percent in 2008 compared to 6.8 percent in 2004.

Regionally blacks in the South and Midwest erased their deficit in voter turnout between the 2004 and 2008 presidential elections. The difference in voter turnouts between blacks and whites in the Northeast in the 2004 presidential election (13.4 percent) was cut almost in half in the 2008 presidential election. The West was the only region of the country where the difference in voter turnout actually grew in favor of whites. Overall higher-educated blacks registered and voted in greater proportions than lower-educated blacks; however, higher-educated blacks failed to vote in greater proportions than their higher-educated white counterparts. On the other hand, lower-educated blacks registered and voted in greater proportions than did their lower-educated white counterparts. Two things are worthy of noting here: first, even with a black candidate heading a major party's ticket, black voter turnout did not exceed that of whites. Nevertheless, it should not go without saying, the black candidate running for president significantly increased the percentage of blacks registering and voting. Secondly, much of the change in the average voter registration and turnout gap was not due to major increases in blacks' voting behavior; rather it was due to downward changes in the voter registration and turnout behavior of whites.

The Future of the Political Bloc

The success of black politics depends heavily on the level of political cohesion within the group. As a political minority, it is essential that blacks remain congruent in their political behavior. In the Protest and Politics Eras, it was easy to achieve political congruency because black politics was driven primarily by racial concerns. In the Socioeconomic Transition Era, race continues to be a driving force in black politics, but it is also driven equally by economic concerns. Because of the changes in the societal factors influencing black politics and the emergence of subgroup politics (based on differing social and economic interests), the potential for a weakening of blacks as a political bloc is greater. Furthermore, as blacks become more mainstream in society they will be less interested in collectivism and more individualized.[12] An examination of political orientation and party identification across the Politics and Socioeconomic Transition Eras is a good gauge of sustained political cohesion. Furthermore, it is an indicator of the degree to which the political bloc is strengthening or weakening over time. One of the major complexities of black politics in the Socioeconomic Transition Era is that blacks' outward (external) political behavior does not always reflect the internal politics of the community.

Changes in Political Orientation

Blacks have been identified as one of the more liberal groups; however, they are not as liberal today as they were in the Politics Era.[13] Between 1974 and 2004, the percentage of blacks identifying themselves as liberal declined from 51.5 percent to 25.2 percent as shown in Figure 6.3. The greatest decline occurred between 1974 and 1984 when the percentage identifying as liberal went from 51.5 percent to 31.1 percent. Increasingly, more blacks are identifying themselves as moderate or conservative. Since 1974, the percentage of blacks identifying themselves as conservative has gradually risen. In 2004, there was a two percentage-point difference in the proportion of blacks identifying themselves as liberal versus conservative. In 1974, the difference in the percentage of blacks self-identifying as liberal versus conservative was 32.3. Between 1974 and 2004, the percentage of blacks identifying themselves as moderate rose from 29.4 percent to 47.6 percent. The fact that more blacks are identifying themselves as moderate and the percentage identifying themselves as liberal or conservative is almost equal suggests a potential for greater division among blacks in terms of their political orientation. If nothing else, it could suggest a weakening in the group's political solidarity in terms of their political orientation.

To what degree does the political orientation of higher-educated blacks differ from lower-educated blacks? As shown in Figure 6.4, in the mid-2000s, blacks did not differ significantly in political orientation based on level of education. Around 40 percent of higher- and lower-educated blacks described their political orientation as liberal. In summary, since 1980, the percentage of blacks identifying themselves as liberal has been in constant decline, while the percentage of blacks

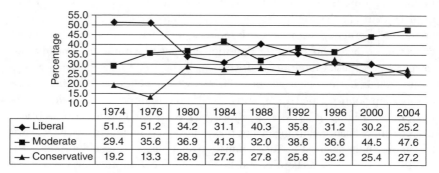

	1974	1976	1980	1984	1988	1992	1996	2000	2004
◆ Liberal	51.5	51.2	34.2	31.1	40.3	35.8	31.2	30.2	25.2
■ Moderate	29.4	35.6	36.9	41.9	32.0	38.6	36.6	44.5	47.6
▲ Conservative	19.2	13.3	28.9	27.2	27.8	25.8	32.2	25.4	27.2

FIGURE 6.3 Change in Blacks' Political Orientation: 1974–2004

The figures are averages of the political orientation questions in the General Social Survey 1972–2006 and American National Election Study 1948-2004 for the selected years

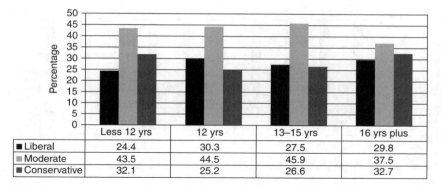

	Less 12 yrs	12 yrs	13–15 yrs	16 yrs plus
■ Liberal	24.4	30.3	27.5	29.8
■ Moderate	43.5	44.5	45.9	37.5
■ Conservative	32.1	25.2	26.6	32.7

FIGURE 6.4 Blacks' Political Orientation by Years of School Completed

Source: Combined 2002, 2004 and 2004 General Social Surveys *n* = 732

identifying themselves as moderate has increased. The percentage of blacks self-identifying as conservative has also risen, but not at the same rate as those identifying themselves as moderate. Finally, in the Socioeconomic Transition Era, there has been no significant change in the self-identified political orientation patterns of higher-educated blacks when compared to lower-educated blacks.

Party Identification

There is little doubt about blacks' commitment to the Democratic Party since the end of the Protest Era of black politics. Since the early 1970s around 80 percent of blacks have consistently identified themselves as Democratic partisans, as shown in Figure 6.5. The vast majority of blacks identified with the Democratic Party during the Politics Era, and party identification patterns among blacks have not changed today. In 1972, 79.5 percent of blacks identified themselves as Democratic (or Independent leaning Democratic), 12.0 percent as Independent, and 8.6 percent as Republican. In 2008, 80.9 percent of blacks identified their party affiliation as Democratic or leaning Democratic. In the same presidential election year, 13.3 percent of blacks identified themselves as Independent, and only 5.8 percent identified themselves as Republican. Since 1972, blacks' party identification has remained fairly constant. Since 1972, the percentage of blacks identifying themselves as Republican has exceeded 10 percent only once in 1988 when 10.6 percent of blacks identified with the party. During the 1980s, it appears that a slight downward trend in the percentage of blacks identifying with both the Democratic and Republican Parties was starting and a modest upward trend in the percentage of blacks identifying themselves as Independent.

In addition to blacks' identification with the Democratic Party remaining stable over the years, the nature of their party identification has also remained stable.

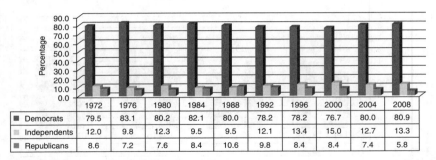

	1972	1976	1980	1984	1988	1992	1996	2000	2004	2008
■ Democrats	79.5	83.1	80.2	82.1	80.0	78.2	78.2	76.7	80.0	80.9
▨ Independents	12.0	9.8	12.3	9.5	9.5	12.1	13.4	15.0	12.7	13.3
▩ Republicans	8.6	7.2	7.6	8.4	10.6	9.8	8.4	8.4	7.4	5.8

FIGURE 6.5 Blacks' Party Identification in Presidential Election Years: 1974–2008

When asked about the strength of this identification with the Democratic Party, on average 49.3 percent of those asked in presidential election years said they were strong Democrats.[14] The percentage that described the strength of their Democratic Party identification as strong has not changed much across the Politics and Socioeconomic Transition Eras. During the Politics Era, in presidential election years, 48.8 percent of blacks identified themselves as strong Democrats. The percentage identifying themselves as strong Democrats never exceeded 53 percent (in 1972) nor went below 40.4 percent (1976). There was however a noticeable trend among those identifying themselves as weak Democrats in the Politics Era: there was a steady decline from a high of 42.8 percent in this category in 1976 to 31.2 percent by the 1988 presidential election. Similarly, during this period those identifying themselves as leaning or weak Democrats went from an average low of 8.5 percent in 1972 to 18.9 percent in 1988. During the Socioeconomic Transition Era (the presidential election since 1988), slightly more than half of the blacks who identified themselves as Democrats said they identified strongly with the party. In 2008, the percentage saying they were strong Democrats declined to the lowest during this era (44.2 percent) and this was down 10 percentage points from the 2000 figure. In the average presidential election during the Politics Era, roughly 14.9 percent of those blacks identifying themselves as Democrats said they were leaning or Independent Democrats. In the presidential election years between 1992 and 2004, the average percentage of blacks identifying themselves as leaning or Independent Democrats rose to 17.4 percent. Between the 1992 and the 2004 presidential elections, those blacks identifying themselves as leaning or Independent Democrats has risen from 14.8 percent to 20.8 percent. The data suggest that blacks' strong feelings toward the Democratic Party are beginning to weaken.

It is reasonable to expect some variation in party identification among blacks based on the level of education. One would attribute this expectation to differences in experiences and exposure via education, occupation, residence, etc., and the tendency for persons in the upper socioeconomic echelon to affiliate with the Republican Party. On the other hand, other factors might predict less variation in blacks' party identification based on level of education. With higher education comes an increased awareness (and perhaps a greater sense of consciousness) about the black experience in the larger context. Therefore, if the Democratic Party was perceived as the party most likely to introduce policy that would improve blacks' quality of life, then it is reasonable to expect a larger percentage of higher-educated blacks to support the Democratic Party. Such was the case as shown in Figure 6.6. In the 2000/2004 election period, there was a significant difference in party identification among blacks based on level of education. Identification with the Democratic Party was significantly lower among blacks with 12 or less years of school. Although this group was not significantly more inclined to identify with the Republican Party, a higher percentage (25 percent) did identify themselves as Independent. Of the four education groups examined, blacks with 13 to 15 years of school were less inclined to identify themselves as Republican. While between 9 and 11 percent of the blacks in the other educational categories identified themselves as Republican, less than 6 percent of the blacks in the 13 to 15 years of school category identified with the Republican Party. Blacks in the 13 to 15 years of school group had the highest identification with the Democratic Party (79.5 percent). Even though the differences in the distribution of blacks' party identification based on level of education were significant, the relationship was weak. Thus, there was no definitive pattern of party identification based on level of education.

To sum up, the data lead us to several conclusions about blacks' party identification since the end of the Protest Era of black politics. First, blacks' party identification did not change significantly during the Politics Era or to this point in the Socioeconomic Transition Era of black politics. Second, a larger proportion of higher-educated blacks identified with the Democratic Party, while lower-educated blacks were more likely to identify themselves as Independent. This pattern has remained consistent across the Politics and Socioeconomic Transition

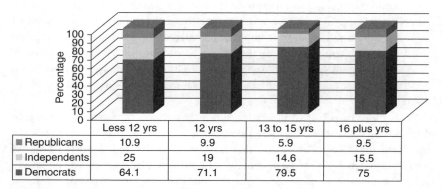

	Less 12 yrs	12 yrs	13 to 15 yrs	16 plus yrs
■ Republicans	10.9	9.9	5.9	9.5
Independents	25	19	14.6	15.5
■ Democrats	64.1	71.1	79.5	75

FIGURE 6.6 Blacks' Party Identification Based on Level of Education in the Socioeconomic Transition Era

Eras of black politics. Finally, the real story here may not be blacks' continuing identification with the Democratic Party, rather the fact that since 1992 the percentage of blacks "strongly" identifying with the Democratic Party has started to decline. Patterns of self-identified political orientation and party identification among blacks suggest that the future of the political bloc should be watched carefully, especially if the significance of race in society overshadows the significance of class.

Blacks' Electoral Support and the Winning Political Coalition

It is increasingly difficult for blacks to be part of a winning political coalition for two reasons. First, race matters in politics, and it is particularly important in the black/white racial context, especially in the South and municipalities with large black populations outside of the South. Second, blacks' unparalleled loyalty to Democratic candidates and to Democratic Party politics has made it difficult to forge long-term meaningful relationships with other groups. The contextual function of race in contemporary politics is extremely subtle. Reeves noted that political candidates and their staffs are very adept and inventive in the deployment of race-related campaign tactics and strategies to get white electoral support. In campaigns between two white candidates, appeals to race may be subtle or blatant, but in a race between a black candidate and a white candidate race often becomes a key factor in the campaign.[15] Lee Atwater (former Chairman of the Republican National Committee and George H. Bush's campaign), in an interview with Alexander Lamis in 1981, said what others are reluctant to say:

> You start out in 1954 by saying "Nigger, nigger, nigger." By 1968 you can't say "nigger"—that hurts you. Backfires. So you say stuff like forced busing, states' rights, and all that stuff. You're getting so abstract now [that] you're talking about cutting taxes, and all these things you're talking about are totally economic things and a by-product of them is [that] Blacks get hurt worse than whites. And subconsciously maybe that is part of it. I'm not saying that if it is getting that abstract, and that coded, that we are doing away with the racial problem one way or the other. You follow me—because obviously sitting around saying, "we want to cut this," is much more abstract than even the busing thing and a hell of a lot more abstract than "Nigger, nigger."[16]

With more than half of blacks residing in Southern states, race continues to play a pivotal role there.[17] V. O. Key in his classic work stated that Southern politics was about the "Negro." Key said that Southern politics and Southern political institutions were deliberately designed to subordinate blacks in the region and to block threatening interferences from the outside.[18] Southern politics is about protecting whites' control and dominance of the social, political, and economic institutions and resources in the region. What has happened in Southern politics since the end of the Protest Era continues to bear this out. Blacks and whites are sharply divided politically along party lines in the South, and race and improving the quality of life for the economically disadvantaged is the basis for this division.

The rise of Republicanism in the South was accelerated after the passage of the Civil Rights and Voting Rights Acts of the 1960s. As the Democratic Party pursued policies and positions that undermined or challenged the continuing dominance of conservative white males, the traditional Democratic Party identifiers in the South began to leave the party to the extent that today the political party of conservative whites is the Republican Party.[19] The rise of Republicanism in the South has been attributed to electoral realignment, but the salience of racial issues in the evolution of American politics also cannot be ignored.[20] Although some have argued that racial issues are more important to blacks,[21] there is ample support for the view that race in contemporary Southern politics is just as important to whites. As Lamis notes, whites continue to have "resentment from the days of the integration of the schools, the competition for scarce economic development dollars, increasing cost of entitlement programs . . . and for Blacks . . . their listing of resentments would be different, flowing as they would from being on the receiving end of discrimination in the era of segregation and earlier."[22]

To say that race is not a factor in the politics of the South is a major understatement. Richard Nixon's Southern strategy and the subsequent politics of the Republican Party in the region were about realigning white conservative voters. Murphy and Gulliver wrote that this strategy catered in subtle ways to the segregationist leaning of white Southern voters, including finding candidates for the Supreme Court, and moving to slow down the process of school desegregation or any kind of desegregation. Nixon's instincts were to remold the entire South into the new national support base for the Republican Party.[23] Ronald Reagan capped out this strategy by attracting substantial majorities from the conservative and moderate white electorate and conceding blacks and liberal whites to the Democrats.[24] According to Lamis, the Republican Party's growth in the South was propelled in the early years of the two-party South first by white Southerners' resentment against the Kennedy, Johnson and Humphrey Democratic integrationists and second by support for conservative economic issues tied to a restrictive view of the role of government.[25]

Outside of the South, race has a more subtle influence in politics, especially in communities with large black populations (primarily in Midwestern and Northern metropolitan areas). Kenneth Clark best summarized the situation in a 1984 interview with the *New York Times* when he said:

> Northern forms of racism are deep, pernicious, subtle and supported by intellectual, academic rationalizations which are much more difficult to cope with than the more flagrant forms of Southern Racism.[26]

In a discussion of voting discrimination against black candidates in general, Reeves wrote, "In the absence of direct information about the motivations and sentiments underlying individual voting behavior, the claim that whites disregard race on entering the voting booth remains more of an assertion than a rigorously established empirical fact."[27] Walton and Smith noted that coalitions with whites are necessary for blacks to achieve their policy goals, but when coalitions with whites are formed, they tend, because of racism and white supremacist thinking, to be tenuous, unstable, and short lived. As a result, blacks find themselves constantly rebuilding coalitions.[28]

It is also difficult for blacks to unite with others to forge a meaningful political coalition because of their overwhelming dedication to Democratic Party candidates. The average support among blacks for Democratic presidential candidates between 2000 and 2008 was 89 percent. In the mid-to-latter phase of the Politics Era (1976 to 1988) on average the Democratic Presidential candidate received 86 percent of the black vote and this was also true during the Socioeconomic Transition Era (1992 to 2008). Over the eight elections between 1976 and 2008, the lowest percentage of the black vote received by Democratic presidential candidates was 83 percent in both 1976 and 1992. Since 1976, the highest percentage of black votes received by Republican presidential candidates was 16 percent (in 1976), and the highest by an Independent candidate was 7 percent in 1992.[29]

Blacks are most likely to forge a political coalition with a group on the basis of religious/moral or ethnic/racial grounds. Figure 6.7 shows the difference in the percentage of votes received by Democratic presidential candidates between blacks and selected religious and ethnic/racial groups between 1972 and 2004. Of the three religious groups examined (Jews, Catholics, and White Protestants), the smallest gap in support of Democratic candidates was between blacks and Jewish voters. The average difference in the percentage of black and Jewish votes received

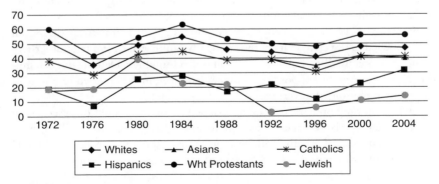

FIGURE 6.7 Difference Between Blacks' and Select Groups' Support for the Democratic Presidential Candidate: 1972–2004

Source: Combined 2000 through 2004 General Social Survey. $p < .001$ n = 1198

by Democratic presidential candidates between 1972 and 2004 was 17.3 percent. The percentage difference between blacks and Jewish voters has been as low as 3 percent in 1992 and as high as 40 percent in 1980. During the Politics Era, the difference between the percentage of black and Jewish votes received by the Democratic presidential candidate averaged 24.4 percent. The percentage difference during the Politics Era increased from 18 in the 1972 presidential election to 22 in the 1984 election. The average difference between the two groups between 1992 and 2004 had declined to 8.5. However, since 1992 the difference in the percentage of black and Jewish votes received by Democratic presidential candidates has risen from 3 percent to 14 percent in 2004. Although Jewish voters, like black voters, are inclined to vote for the Democratic presidential candidate, a larger percentage of Jewish voters were more inclined to break this pattern and support the Republican presidential candidate (especially in those elections won by the Republican candidate).

When compared to other religious groups with whom blacks could forge a coalition, the greatest difference in the percentage of votes received by Democratic presidential candidates was between blacks and white Protestants. The average difference in the percentage of votes received by the Democratic candidate between the 1972 and 2004 presidential election cycle was 53.5 percent. Differences in the percentage of votes cast for Democratic candidates between blacks and white Protestants have ranged from as high as 63 percent in 1984 to as low as 42 percent in 1976. The average difference in the percentage of votes cast for Democratic presidential candidates between blacks and white Protestants declined slightly between the Politics and Protest Eras of black politics. In the Politics Era the average difference between these two groups was 54.4 percent and it was 52.5 percent in the Socioeconomic Transition Era. The average difference in the percentage of votes cast for Democratic presidential candidates between blacks and Catholics between 1972 and 2004 was 38.4 percent. The smallest gap in the percentage of votes cast for the Democratic presidential candidate between blacks and Catholics was 29 percent in 1976. Since 1976, the difference in the vote of blacks and Catholics cast for the Democratic presidential candidate has ranged from 39 to 45 percent (this is excluding the 1996 election where the difference was 31 percent). Overall, between the Politics and the Socioeconomic Transition Eras, the gap between the percentage of votes cast for the Democratic presidential candidate between blacks and white Protestants and blacks and Catholics has remained fairly large and stable. Thus, Jews are the only religious group that blacks could reasonably expect to join with in a stable political coalition.

Figure 6.7 also shows differences in support for Democratic presidential candidates between blacks and selected ethnic/racial groups in the nine presidential elections between 1972 and 2004. The percentage difference in support of the Democratic Party candidates was smallest between blacks and Hispanics, averaging 20.7 percent. The smallest difference in votes for a Democratic presidential candidate between black and Hispanics was in 1976 when it was 7 percent; since that time, the difference has been in excess of 20 percent in five of the seven elections. In the Politics Era, the average difference in the percentage of votes cast for Democratic presidential candidates between blacks and Hispanics was 19.4 percent. The average difference between the percentage of blacks and Hispanics casting votes for Democratic presidential candidates actually grew between the 1992 and 2004 elections to 22.2 percent. The 1996 presidential election was the only one during this period where the gap was less than 20 percent. The greatest difference in support for Democratic candidates was between black and white voters; the average difference was 46.3 percent in the elections between 1972 and 2004. Over the years, there has been no significant closure of the difference in the percentage of votes cast for Democratic candidates between blacks and whites. The lowest vote difference between blacks and whites was 36 percent in 1976. The average vote difference between blacks and whites in the Politics Era was 47.4 percent and it slightly declined between the elections of 1992 and 2004 to 45 percent. The average difference between blacks and Asians in the Socioeconomic Transition Era (the 1992 to 2004 elections) was 39.3 percent.[30] The difference in the percentage of votes cast for Democratic presidential candidates by blacks and Asians has ranged from a low of 35 percent in 1996 to a high of 42 in 2000.

For blacks to reach their fullest political potential as a political unit, they must form coalitions with other racial and ethnic minorities. Even this strategy, however, requires a substantial percentage of the white electorate or other racial minorities voting with blacks, as was the case in the 2008 election. With a black heading the Democratic Party's ticket, the 2008 election shed light on the groups with which blacks are most likely to forge a coalition. In the 2008 election, the difference in the percentage of blacks and whites supporting the Democratic Party's candidate actually grew over the 2004 figure. In the 2004 presidential election, the difference in the percentage of blacks and whites voting for the Democratic Party's candidate was 47 percent compared to 52 percent in 2008. In the 2008 presidential election 95 percent of the votes cast by black voters were for the Democratic candidate compared to only 43 percent of the white votes. However, it is worth noting that young white voters (under 30 years of age) were far more inclined to support the black Democratic presidential candidate (at 54 percent) than whites over the age of 30 (averaging around 41 percent voting for the Democratic candidate). The difference between the percentage of blacks and Hispanics voting for the Democratic candidate in 2008 was smaller than the difference in 2004. In 2004, the difference between the percentage of blacks and Hispanics supporting the Democratic candidate was 32 percent. In the 2008 presidential election the gap declined to 28 percent. This was also the case between blacks and Asians. In the 2004 presidential election, the difference in the percentage of blacks and Asians supporting the Democratic presidential candidate was 40 percent and this difference declined by 7 percent to 33 percent in the 2008 presidential election.[31] In 2008, it was the votes of whites under the age of 30, Hispanics and Asians along with blacks that determined the election outcome.

To see the extent and relevance of the differences in the percentage of electoral support for Democratic candidates between blacks and whites, one could also examine differences in the level of support for Democratic presidential candidates by region. Blacks' ability to form meaningful coalitions with whites has varied across regions. Blacks' greatest chances of forming a coalition with whites are in the Northeast and West. Even in these regions, the gap between the percentage of votes cast for Democratic presidential candidates between blacks and whites votes was very large. In the eight presidential elections between 1976 and 2004, the average difference in the percentage of votes cast between blacks and whites for Democratic presidential candidates was 38.9 percent in the Northeast and 40.3 percent in the West. In the Midwest the different averaged 46.1 percent.

In no region has the disparity between black and white voters been as large as in the South, where the difference averaged 52.4 percent since the 1980s. The 1980 presidential election marked the beginning of clearly defined and accelerated differences in blacks' and whites' level of support for Democratic presidential candidates. This was especially true of voting differences between the two groups in the South. In the 1976 election, the difference between blacks and whites in the South was 34 percent. By 1980, the difference had risen to 54 percent despite a native Southerner heading the Democratic ticket. Since the 1980 election, the smallest difference in Southern blacks' and whites' support for a Democratic presidential candidate was 49 percent (in 1992 in which there was a native Southerner heading the ticket). Between 1980 and 2004, the vote disparity has been in excess of 50 percent in six of the seven presidential elections.

The Politics of Oscillation

Both Stone and Dorn maintained that blacks' ability to move their collective votes between parties was essential for political success. The politics of oscillation is especially important for black politics because it offsets blacks' inability to establish a meaningful political coalition with other minority or subgroups within the majority. The politics of oscillation is also not easy to achieve among blacks as a political unit, because of their unwavering support for Democratic Party politics and candidates. The failure to move their votes between political parties and candidates has not worked to their advantage. Between 1980 and 2004, the Republican Party was the majority party in the U.S. Senate for seven of the twelve sessions. In the 16 states constituting the South,[32] nearly 60 percent of the members of the U.S. House of Representatives and 53 percent of the U.S. Senate were Republicans in 2000. Although Democrats held 58 percent of the state legislative and 59 percent of the state senatorial seats, the conservative nature of party politics at the state level does not necessarily give advantage to blacks in the political process. In the elections between 1980 and 2000, the Republican candidates won four of the six presidential elections, and the Republican candidates received an average of 53 percent of the vote. The Democratic candidates won in only two of the 16 Southern states.

Failure to move the black vote from one party to the other is consistent with blacks' attitudes and perceptions about the political parties. For political oscillation to be effective, group members must recognize that moving their votes between political parties is a viable option. This is not the case for blacks. In the 1996 National Black Election Study,[33] when asked what they thought was the best strategy to increase blacks' political power, 61 percent of blacks felt that the best strategy for increasing the group's political power was to support the Democratic Party. Thirty-two percent felt the best strategy should be to support an independent black political party, and only 7 percent felt that supporting the Republican Party was the best strategy to increase the group's political power. Among blacks, the second best strategy, with 51 percent, was to support an independent black political party. Only 17 percent of blacks' surveyed felt that supporting the Republican Party was the second best strategy.

When blacks were asked in the 1996 National Black Election Study whether blacks should form their own party, only 34 percent agreed. This was significant because the majority of blacks do not favor the formation of a black political party; but a majority would favor forming an independent black political party over joining the Republican Party to increase blacks' political power. Despite significant differences in blacks' perception of how the group should go about increasing its political power, this pattern held true even when level of education was taken into consideration. A clear majority of blacks, regardless of their level of education, felt that the primary political strategy was to support the Democratic Party. However, as level of education increased, support for this Democratic Party strategy decreased. Only 27.3 percent of blacks in the lower-educated group supported the formation of an independent black political party; 33.4 percent of blacks in the moderately educated group and 32.2 in the higher-education group favored the formation of an independent black political party as the first strategy.

Support for the Republican Party as the primary strategy to achieve political power ranged from a low of 5.1 percent among moderately educated blacks to 11.7 percent among the lower-educated blacks. The three educational groups did not differ significantly in what they felt was the second best way for blacks to increase their political power. Overall, the data from the 1996 National Election Study suggest several things. First, blacks felt the best way to increase their political power was by working within the Democratic Party. Second, blacks felt the second-best strategy was to form an independent black political party. Third, blacks are not very comfortable with the idea of forming an independent black political party. Finally, blacks have little confidence in using the Republican Party to increase their political power.

Party oscillation is also difficult to achieve because the majority of blacks perceive the Democratic Party as best suited to deal with many of the problems facing the nation, especially those important to blacks as a political unit. As shown in Table 6.3, more than 70.0 percent of blacks felt that the Democratic Party would be better at handling health care, improving race relations, and handling poverty. On average, only 6.1 percent of blacks felt that Republicans would do a better job in these areas. On the other hand, slightly more than 20 percent felt that neither party would do a better job. Sixty-three percent felt that Democrats would do a better job of reforming the welfare system, and 58.9 percent said that Democrats were better at handling the economy. Only 12.9 percent felt the Republican Party would do a better job handling the economy, and 15.9 percent felt that Republicans would do a better job reforming welfare. However, 28.2 percent felt that neither party would do a better job handling the economy. Twenty-one percent felt the same about both parties reforming the welfare system. The greatest support for the Republican Party came on the issue of handling of foreign affairs, where 19.4 percent felt that it would do a better job. However, this was still well short of the 45.8 percent favoring the Democratic Party in this area. Approximately one-third (34.7 percent) displayed little confidence in either party on the issue of handling foreign affairs.

Despite a majority of blacks feeling that the Democratic Party would be better at handling a number of issues important to the nation, there were variations in blacks' perceptions of which political party would do a better job based on level of education. Although there were significant differences in the responses, there was no discernible pattern of differences. For example, higher-educated blacks were more likely to feel that Democrats would do a better job at making health care more affordable and improving race relations. On the other hand, the lower-educated blacks were more likely to feel that Democrats would do a better job at handling the economy, foreign affairs, and improving the welfare system. Attitudes about which party would do a better job at handling poverty did not differ along educational lines. The higher-educated blacks were more likely than the lower-educated blacks to feel that neither the Democratic nor Republican Party would do a better job dealing with the economy, foreign affairs, or reforming the welfare system. On the issue of making health care more affordable and improving race

TABLE 6.3 Blacks' Perceptions of Party Positions on Issues (in percentages)

	Democrats	Republicans	See no difference
Better at handling economy	58.9	12.9	28.2
Better at handling foreign affairs	45.8	19.4	34.7
Better at making health care more affordable	77.1	6.3	16.5
Better at improving race relations	70.3	4.7	25.0
Better at reforming welfare system	63.1	15.9	21.0
Better at handling poverty	70.5	7.3	22.2
Better at handling budget deficit	52.8	14.6	32.6
More likely to cut Social Security	7.6	68.9	23.5
More likely to raise taxes	10.7	47.7	41.6

Source: National Black Election Study, 1996

relations, less than 2 percentage points separated the two groups in feeling that neither party would do a better job. A greater proportion of higher-educated blacks when compared to lower-educated blacks thought that the Republican Party would do better handling the economy, handling foreign affairs, and reforming the welfare system.

The data show several interesting patterns. First, it suggests that even though blacks feel most comfortable with the Democratic Party, there is evidence that a significant percentage of the group are not totally satisfied. Second, few blacks see the Republican Party as an alternative to the Democratic Party. Third, on average, almost 30 percent of blacks did not think that either party would do a better job at handling key problems facing the nation, suggesting that a substantial proportion of the black population feels that neither party is a realistic option. Blacks' level of education was associated with their feelings about which party would do a better job of handling certain key issues facing the nation.

Conclusion

This chapter began by making the assertion that the potential for political fragmentation is greater today than at any point since the end of the civil rights movement. Not only could demographic, geographic, and socioeconomic changes in the population create conditions that could make it difficult for blacks to function effectively as a political bloc, but blacks' political behavior could do the same. Racial concerns, as the basis of black politics, are no longer the dominant factor influencing black politics. As a result, blacks' struggle for political power is taking on different meanings and desired outcomes for various subgroups within the population. Although blacks appear to be homogeneous in their political behavior today, the reality is that the population is becoming more heterogeneous. Furthermore, changes in the nature of politics have presented a situation where blacks' options in their struggle to gain political power are changing. For example, blacks are no longer "the minority" group that the majority must contend with. In examining the extent to which blacks have made significant progress in their struggle for political influence and power, the findings in the chapter suggest several trends emerging.

Stone felt the key to blacks' struggle for political power was the group's ability to function as a political bloc. There is little doubt that blacks' political behavior suggests that a high level of racial consensus still drives their political behavior. However, the degree of consistency may be more about the nature of the political system and less about political harmony. The nature of the two-party system offers blacks few alternatives. As a result, one party takes them for granted and the other gives token consideration. In the end, the civil rights movement may have provided blacks with the power to vote, but political and social circumstances may be preventing them from using their vote as a meaningful way of advancing their agenda.

The civil rights legislation was supposed to strengthen the social, political, and economic development of the black community; instead, it indirectly created conditions that weakened the community at the group level and strengthened it at the individual level. As a result, the potential for blacks to continue functioning as a political bloc in the future is becoming weaker. Led by geographic and socio-economic changes in the community, blacks are less galvanized today as a political bloc than during the Protest or Political Eras. Matters pertaining to race no longer drive black politics; instead, matters of class are increasingly driving black politics. Personal circumstances for some blacks make issues pertaining to improving socioeconomic quality of life more important while for others dealing with social justice continues to be of most importance.

Blacks have gained the right to vote, but they have not exercised that right in a way that augments their struggle for political power. They still register and vote at a rate lower than do whites. Blacks are making only modest progress in getting blacks elected to office outside of large communities with a very large black population, but most importantly blacks are making little progress in preventing candidates that could be described as less supportive of their political agenda from getting elected to political office. The face and tactics of the black counter-move-ment has changed and is much more subtle as we move further into the Socioeconomic Transition Era. In addition, blacks' loyalty to the Democratic Party may be hindering their struggle for political power. The white vote is not splitting to the extent of empowering the black vote, so blacks are increasingly finding themselves in the electoral minority. As a result, blacks are not finding themselves as members of winning representative or electoral coalitions.

Thus, the implications of this chapter are less about the future of blacks as a political bloc and more about what they will be able to accomplish in the political system as a bloc. Today, one could reasonably argue that increased socioeconomic status among some segments of the black population has not significantly altered the political activity or behavior of blacks as a group and for the most part at the individual level. That is, it has not altered the political behavior and activity of blacks with higher socioeconomic status enough to cause them to participate at rates that exceed their white counterparts or in ways that are significantly different from blacks with lower socioeconomic status. Furthermore, despite blacks' struggle for civil and political rights in the Protest Era they have yet to position themselves as a group to influence the balance of power in the political system.

7

BLACK POLITICAL LEADERSHIP TODAY

Since the mid-1980s, political cohesiveness among blacks has been increasingly threatened by changes in the community's social and economic structure. Blacks are no longer a segregated self-contained community driven to work toward the same political goals. The black population is increasingly becoming a collection of sub-communities that are often divided by factors tied to socioeconomic status, with differing social, political, and economic agendas that are connected by the continuing significance of race in society. These factors alone make effective black political leadership necessary, yet it also makes it difficult for such leadership to emerge in an environment where interests and values are changing. Effective leadership is extremely important in black politics because it is essential for blacks (as the political minority) to be able to influence the conduct of the majority. In post-civil rights black America, black political leaders are the community's face and voice, and it is they who are expected to vigorously champion the causes of the black community and effectively present the demands and desires of the community to the outside world.

Ascension to a political leadership position in the black community is similar to that of leaders of other groups. According to Bass, some people have personality traits that naturally project them into leadership roles (Traits Theory). Others become leaders because they rise to the occasion during a crisis or important event (Great Events Theory), while others choose or learn to become leaders (Transformational Leadership Theory).[1] Yet there is a uniqueness about the styles and types of black leader that often makes them difficult to classify.

Robert Smith noted that, while there is no universal agreement on the meaning of black leadership, there is agreement that black leadership involves influencing the attitudes and behavior of blacks regarding the community's social and political goals; moreover, black leadership is not limited to blacks but also includes whites.[2] In the post-Civil Rights Era, the path to leadership has been twofold. There are those whom the "community" deems "leaders." These individuals have the authority or power (whether formally or informally) to serve as a point person for the group. They usually have very close contact with the "people" (or the "community"). On the other hand, there are those in leadership positions because they are "public figures." These individuals tend to be de facto representatives of the black community. They usually occupy positions in society that give them high visibility and because of these positions and visibility they are automatically seen as leaders or representatives of the group (especially by the outside community). This chapter discusses how styles and types of black political leadership have changed and evolved since the Protest Era, and how these changes are crucial to understanding the current state of black politics today.

Leadership Styles

Styles of leadership involve modes of thinking about the problems facing the community. Leadership style also involves how a leader chooses to convey their thoughts, and how they present themselves when conveying their message. Within the black community, style can affect an individual's leadership potential. Leadership styles are particularly important in the black community because of the community's expressive culture. That is, oral and verbal patterns and individual aesthetics can make or break one's ascension to the role of community leader. In most instances, an effective leader within the black community must be able to verbally connect with the "soul" of the community. The ability to speak with a poetic flow augments one's charisma, something often utilized by the black clergy, for example, whose verbal patterns frequently incorporate a kind of rhythm and rhyme that makes them particularly adept at connecting with the individual. Similarly, street hustlers, politicians, leaders of civic and social organizations, business and professional leaders working within the community usually employ similar verbal communication skills, with the difference coming through the message.

Effective leadership in the black community is also determined by personal aesthetics. That is, physical modes of presentation (i.e., body movements, facial expressions, style of clothing, etc.) are also important. This is not to say the substance of the message is unimportant, rather it is to say that the substance of the message is enhanced by verbal abilities and personal aesthetics. In addition, leadership styles in the black community are often influenced by interpersonal qualities that tie the individual emotionally and spiritually to the community. Because of blacks' emotional and spiritual connectedness to their leaders, they tend to be loyal to them and stick by them through good and bad times. People outside of the black community often do not understand how or why the black community stands by its leaders through improper behavior or even when that leader is no longer effective in their position. Once black leaders have ascended to the position of leadership they have done more than demonstrate an under-standing and ability to articulate the larger community's problems; they have "connected" with their followers on a different level.

Styles have gradually changed among black leaders since the Protest Era. This change can be attributed to at least three factors. The first factor is change in the nature of interactions between blacks and whites. As segregation declined and increased interracial interaction occurred, styles of communication among black leaders have also changed accordingly. Today black leaders' styles of communica-tion vary according to the audience they are appealing to (within the black community and outside of the black community). The second factor that has contributed to the gradual change in black leadership styles is the rise of the new black middle class. The new middle class is better educated, more affluent, and more likely to live and/or work in an environment that is far removed from the traditional segregated environment. This new black middle class is more likely to be drawn to a black leader because of their message and not because of verbal skills and personal aesthetics. As a result, this group is more likely to be critical and turned off by leaders without a pertinent message. The final factor is the emer-gence of sub-political communities within the black community. Black leadership styles have changed since the 1970s because the black community itself has changed. As discussed in previous chapters, the black community is no longer a community unified by racial issues alone; rather it has become a number of sub-communities unified by race but driven by other interests. As a result, leadership styles in the black community have begun to change to appeal to multiple communities within the black community.

In the 1940s, Gunnar Myrdal developed a typology of black leadership styles based on blacks' subordinate position and the fact that this position limited them to either accommodating (accepting and not rejecting their position) or protesting (dissatisfied and rejecting their position).[3] James Q. Wilson, in a study of black civic leadership in the late 1950s, identified two political styles that "more or less" emerged as the dominant political styles: the *militant* and the *moderate*.[4] Wilson's description was based on several factors: 1) the nature of the issues confronting them and their values; 2) the goals they deemed appropriate to seek via civic action; 3) the means employed to achieve these goals, and 4) the motives, goals, and attributes of other political actors. According to Wilson, the militant black leader style perceived issues confronting blacks in rather simplified terms; they presented the government with many demands; they shared values with white liberals and radicals; and they sought to integrate blacks into society first and to improve the welfare of the black community second. According to Wilson, the moderate leader style, on the other hand, understood there were no easy solutions to the problems facing blacks. They spoke most often of specific and concrete problems, rather than long-range, multi-faceted problems. The moderate style, according to Wilson, tended to see the world as it was, and it sought to improve the general welfare of blacks first and change blacks' status (i.e., seeking integration) second. Wilson noted that the moderate style was most evident among blacks in positions of prominence, and such leaders exhibited aspects of a "bargainer." In the Protest Era of black politics, the moderate style of black leadership placed little confidence in legislation to solve problems; instead, it sought to persuade, educate, and bargain with industry.

Subsequent literature categorized black leadership styles in the Protest and early Politics Eras into four general categories. The first style was the least likely to outwardly voice opposition to blacks' subordinate status and tended to accept blacks' subordinate position in society. The leader was referred to as the *conservative*[5] or *Uncle Tom*[6] and their style was about appeasing the outside (white) community. Often the label of leader was most likely bestowed upon them by the white community. The second leadership style relied on education and persuasion to bring about change. It favored gradual change in the system resulting from activities like voting, lobbying, and limited protest and such leaders were often referred to as *moderates*[7] or *race diplomats*.[8] The third style of leader during the Protest and Politics Eras had a very strong identification with the community. They aggressively rejected the subordinate status of blacks and called for immediate action and mass protests. These leaders were referred to as *radicals*,[9] *race-men*,[10] or *militants*.[11] The final style of leader advocated changing blacks' status via conventional political means. These individuals relied on moral suasion and appealed to the national government to correct local problems of discrimination and segregation. They engaged in actions to improve blacks' conditions within the existing context of blacks' subordinate status. This leadership style fell somewhere between the moderates and the militants in their behavior, and they were referred to as *liberals*[12] and *traditionalist*.[13] Using the Million Man March in 1995 as the backdrop, Joseph McCormick created a typology of black leadership styles today based on the relationship between black leadership and "followership."[14] McCormick used the notions of political leadership tendencies (patterns of belief and political behavior) and multi-faceted black predicament (those aspects of conditions that shape one's life experiences) to create categories of black leadership styles. He categorized black leaders as the *racially conscious*, the *moderate*, the *conservative*, and the *ambiguous nationalist*.

Likewise, I identify four dominant styles of black leadership that appear to have emerged in the Socioeconomic Transition Era. My typology of the emerging black leadership style today is based on several factors: 1) perceptions of race and racism as the cause of blacks' conditions and status in society; 2) style or methods used to bring attention to blacks' concerns; and 3) the black subgroup that the leader appeals to. Some black leaders perceive blacks' social, political, and economic problems as exclusively tied to race and racism. Those with this view place nearly all of the responsibility for the community's problems on forces external to the black community. Leadership styles employing this view usually do not encourage blacks to take responsibility for their plight, and they usually do not offer any solutions. Those employing this style have a tendency to use the "race card" when necessary. Other leadership styles advance the idea that race and racism play only a minor role in determining blacks' status in society; other factors also contribute. For those who adopt this position, among the other factors explaining blacks' social, political, and economic status are class, education, culture, poverty, segregation, alienation, and isolation, with self-esteem playing some role.

The style used by black leaders today to bring attention to the issues of the black community can range from cooperation to provocation. On the one hand, some leadership styles can be described as conciliatory. These styles of leadership do not challenge the current racial status quo. The message of those employing a conciliatory style is often geared toward assimilating blacks into the larger community. There are those black leaders whose style is more accommodating. That is, those utilizing this leadership style are more apt to engage in bargaining, compromising, and negotiating methods to bring about change in blacks' status in society. Other leadership styles used today to bring attention to the problems of the black community are similar to those used in the Protest and Politics Eras, and can be described as "caustic voices." Although this leadership style does not hesitate to use the "bully pulpit" to get attention, those employing this style are not against bargaining, compromising, and negotiating behind the scenes on behalf of their constituency. There are those leadership styles today that are very confrontational in their approach and challenge for immediate results. This style can range from "in your face" to "talking at you."

The final factor used to categorize black leadership styles in the Socioeconomic Transition Era of black politics is the black sub-community they are appealing to. Gone are the days when one leadership style, for the most, would enable one to represent the larger black community. The black community has always been very diverse, but the diversity in the black community during the Protest and early Politics Eras of black politics was contained by segregation and lack of opportunity. In the Socioeconomic Transition Era, diversity in ideology, life chances, etc. has created an environment for diversity in leadership styles. As a result, some styles are conducive to the evolving *assimilationist* black community, while others appeal to the *accommodationist, mainstream,* and/or *apolitical* sub-communities.

Consequently, I identify four styles of black political leaders today: the *conservative,* the *moderate,* the *advocate,* and the *race-man/activist.* The *conservative* has the least appeal within the black community. This leadership style is more appealing to the outside community. Nevertheless, there is a small group of blacks that this style of leader appeals to. More specifically, this leadership style has its greatest appeal among blacks in the assimilationist political sub-community. Leaders employing the conservative style perceive race and racism as minor factors in determining the status of blacks in society. This style of black leader often ignores the legacy of race and racism. The conservative style of leader often adopts the position that blacks must use economic systems to improve their position in society. Of all black leadership styles, the conservative is the most conformist to the status quo. Their political orientation is to the right on economic issues and more central on civil rights and social welfare issues. This style of leader will more likely support Republican Party candidates or very conservative Democratic candidates. The conservative is most effective in predominately white and/or racially conservative environments. They are often perceived by other blacks as more interested in improving their personal position than advancing the good of the larger black community.

It should be noted that the conservative leadership style is not always consistent with the traditional definition of conservatism. What defines this style of leadership is their approach to solving the problems facing the black community. This could range from the extent that they choose to explicitly downplay (or ignore) race to the extent they choose to be very low-key in the efforts to deal with issues of race. For example, in recent years, many black candidates and other black community leaders have employed a political strategy referred to as "deracialization." McCormick and Jones described deracialization as a style of campaigning that defuses the polarizing effect of race by avoiding explicit references to race-specific issues.[15] Kilson referred to this approach as "transethnic politics" because of its appeal to a broader category of ethnic and racial groups in an effort to garner support to address the issues facing the black community.[16] For those employing the conservative style, this may be more than a strategy: this is their reality. They deliberately choose to deracialize their message to reduce racially polarizing terminology in campaigns and other activities which have had a clear negative effect on public opinion and the range of acceptable discussions on political issues.[17] They feel that racializing the message could be detrimental to efforts to develop coalitions with other minorities or segments of the majority.[18] Those that employ this style do so because they believe matters of race are best ignored and/ or focusing on race is counterproductive to achieving racial equality and harmony.

The moderate style of leadership has its greatest appeal among the young and the growing black middle class. This is often true for those in these groups whose socioeconomic circumstances (residence, work, etc.) remove them from the larger black community but who nevertheless have a strong emotional attachment to it (i.e., through cultural affinity, family, etc.). Leaders employing the moderate style often see race and racism as factors continuing to influence blacks' status as a community. The moderate does not downplay race as an issue, nor do they downplay the ultimate goal of improving the social, political, and economic conditions of the black community. However, those employing the *moderate style* acknowledge that other factors (attitudes, beliefs, values, the nature of the social, political, and economic systems, etc.) are equally important in determining the status of blacks. The moderate style is middle-of-the-road in its political orientation and practice. Moderates are likely to advocate the use of legitimate political means (i.e. protests, voting, boycotts, running for office, community organizing, etc.) to achieve their goal. They rely on diplomacy, the ability to bargain, compromise, and negotiate to get support from inside and outside the community. Those using the moderate style tend to possess what Matthew Holden referred to as the technical bureaucratic skills enabling them to have a certain measure of power as well as moral authority.[19] Furthermore, those using this style would exemplify the type of leader Holden referred to as part of the "protobureaucracy," which Holden describes as "a network of people who possess the management competencies necessary to anticipate, counteract, and outmaneuver others." Although they would most likely work within the context of Democratic Party politics, they would consider working to improve blacks' status via the Republican Party. The moderate is most likely to operate in an environment that is racially mixed, but blacks remain in the minority. The moderate style would appeal mostly to the *accommodationist* black political sub-community. The moderate style seeks personal rewards from both the black community and the external communities.

The advocate leadership style (which McCormick would refer to as "racially conscious") is most visible within the black community and is most effective in representing the general character of the black community. This leadership style has a large following within the community. The greatest appeal within the black community is to the *mainstream* black sub-community. The appeal of the advocate is that their rhetoric and perceptions of the problems reflect those of the dominant black community. Those making use of this style acknowledge that other factors contribute to blacks' status in society, but they place the majority of the blame on race and racism. The advocate views and understands the problems of blacks from a "community" perspective; whereas the conservative and some moderates are more likely to view the problems of blacks from an individualistic perspective. This type of leader is more likely to see blacks' status in society as an outcome of cultural or institutional racism. Furthermore, they are more likely to attribute the black community's problems to past behaviors and policy practices of the social, political, and economic system. They are more caustic in their approach to getting attention for their cause and they prefer to work exclusively within Democratic Party politics. This style of leader is most effective in predominately black environments; that is, where either the larger community is predominately black or blacks live in large community clusters. This style is effective in environments that range from racially conservative to racially liberal. The advocate style looks to gain more personally from within the black community, but personal gains could also come from the external community.

The final leadership style today is the race-man/activist style (this is very similar to McCormick's ambiguous nationalist) and this style appeals to a smaller portion of the black community. Its greatest appeal would be among the *apolitical* black sub-community who are often not educationally credentialed and whose contact with the larger society is limited. The environment that is most suitable for the race-man/activist style is predominately black, with very little interaction with the external communities, and sometimes isolated within the larger black community. When this type of leader is communicating to their followers, it could be described as "preaching to the choir." Followers of this kind of leader are very loyal. They tend to be "street smart," and sometimes they are better informed but their under-standing is ideologically biased. The race-man/activist style of leadership tends to suggest that race and racism are largely responsible for black social, political, and economic status in society. Thus, race and racism are at the forefront of the political activity and rhetoric of this approach. For those employing this style, racism, racial discrimination, hatred and prejudice are the causes of the problems facing the black community. As a result, the rhetoric of the race-man/activist advocates racial independence and sometimes racial separation and blames black people's problems on the "white man" and "his corrupt social, political and economic systems." Those employing this approach are not interested in working within the "system" to bring about change to their community. This style of leader rarely advocates using such traditional means as working through the system to improve the quality of life for blacks. They demand, nevertheless, that the system address the problems of the black community. Because they do not expect the "racist system" to reply, they will call upon the black community to solve the problem by itself. These leaders rarely have the organizational skills to produce tangible results for the community; nevertheless, their rhetoric and presence are useful in getting issues on the public agenda. This leadership style often has a "militant-in-your-face" approach when addressing the problems of the black community.

Styles among black leaders today are more fluid than in previous eras of black politics. Furthermore, black leaders' leadership styles can fluctuate between and/ or straddle categories. For example, it is not uncommon for a leader to engage his constituents using one style, yet appeal to his sponsors or benefactors using another. In the Politics Era, the most successful black leaders have the ability to adopt multiple leadership styles to appeal to multiple sub-communities within the black population and sometimes to appeal to certain segments of the white community. In the Socioeconomic Transition Era, black leaders often employed a combination of the advocate style (when interacting with the black community) and the moderate style (when interacting with the white community).

Leadership Types

Leadership type is another dimension of style that focuses on the qualities or distinctive characteristics of the individual. The focal point of leadership type is the source for authority and preferred method for advancing the black agenda. James Q. Wilson described a type of black civic leader in the Protest Era called the "volunteer leader."[20] This category of leader excluded politicians, bureaucrats, and paid voluntary association staff members whose civic life was tied to their formal positions. Wilson's typology of volunteer civic leaders included the *prestige*, the *token*, and the *organizer*. The prestige leader had high personal achievement in busi-ness or professional life and tended to avoid controversy. Their associations in the black community were in non-controversial civic enterprises. They contributed money to race organizations, but their greatest assets were their contacts with the white community. Prestige leaders were often solicited by white leaders for their advice and backing on civic projects. The token leaders were selected by whites to represent blacks in civic activities. Unlike prestige leaders, token leaders' contacts with the white community were narrow and focused, and they were chosen by whites for their utility. The token leaders did not represent the outspoken element of the black community, nor were they considered leaders by the black community. They were typically drawn from the ranks of professional and business people, and rarely were active in race organizations. The organizer raised issues and created, directed, and sustained organizations to achieve civic goals of the black community. They lacked the status, income, or power of the prestige leaders, but their civic activity was a way of acquiring status and power, and they had a high degree of commitment to what they wanted to achieve. Wilson described the organizer as often restless, ambitious, eager to improve or gain more, and very imaginative.

Wilson wrote of the gradual emergence of a "new" black leadership.[21] Wilson wrote of a new leader emerging in the black community who would respond to intangible incentives for civic action and contribute time and money, without hope of personal gain. The new black leaders, according to Wilson, would work with whites as equal partners. In the Socioeconomic Transition Era, the changing social dynamics of society have given rise to the emergence of new types of black leader. As new leadership types have emerged, the old ones have been modified or completely transformed. In the Socioeconomic Transition Era, black leaders no longer deal exclusively with issues of race; they deal with issues of class among other issues as well. They no longer just represent large segments of the black community; rather, today they represent smaller subgroups in the community who often have their own agenda. In addition, black leaders today are more likely to have a significant following among whites. Attempts to create typologies of black leadership today are not without problems, and this is because there are a number of blacks who are in the public eye who would not be considered "black leaders" within the black community. Yet they are symbolically offered as representatives of (or leaders in) the black community (and thus a default community leader or representative).

With this in mind, the decision was made to use the term "public figures" instead of "leaders." Public figures in the black community were categorized based on four factors: 1) type and source of power and influence; 2) their reaction to issues confronting the black community; 3) the nature of their rhetoric regarding improving blacks' status; and 4) their commitment to Democratic Party politics as a vehicle to improve blacks' status in society. Power as a characteristic of a black public figure's status was defined as that which enables them to influence the attitudes, beliefs, feelings, and values of those seeking their guidance and direction toward achieving a common goal. The nature of their power was based on the five types of social power identified by French and Raven.[22] *Legitimate power* occurs when followers feel that an individual has the right to give orders or to demand compliance because of rank, position, or social-legal obligation. *Reward power* arises when the individual has the ability to present formal or informal rewards. *Coercive power* occurs when the individual has the ability to punish or penalize, and *expert power* is based on confidence in the leader's expertise. Finally, *referent power* is determined by friendship, liking, respect, admiration, or charisma.

The second factor used to categorize black public figures today was the way the leader chooses to respond to blacks' status in society. Some public figures are more reactive (that is, responding to events or occurrences) while others are proactive (that is, responding in anticipation of events or occurrences). Some tend to be a combination of both proactive and reactive. Third, the rhetoric of some black public figures suggests that the government has a major responsibility for addressing the status of blacks in society, while others' rhetoric advocates blacks taking total responsibility for improving their own status in society. Finally, some black public figures are more committed to Democratic Party politics as the most effective political tool to improve blacks' status in society. They feel that supporting the Democratic Party, its candidates, and its platform are the primary organizational means to improve the group's status.

Based on these four factors five types of black public figure have emerged in the Socioeconomic Transition Era: the *religious sector*, the *civic/community*, the *organization-based*, the *professional*, and the *grassroots*. The religious sector public figure has a following that varies greatly in size. Their followers can be confined to their congregation, or inclusive of other congregations in the denomination, and/or those in their immediate community who are the recipients of the congregation's community social service and outreach efforts. Although many of the religious sector public figures do not see themselves as civic or political leaders, events in the community and their positions as the heads of organized groups often draw them into leadership roles. The leadership style of the religious sector public figure tends to fluctuate between the moderate and the advocate. They often see race and racism as key factors influencing blacks' status, but most realize that other factors also have an influence. They tend to be moderate in political orientation (moderately liberal on economic and social welfare issues, but moderately conservative on social issues).

Religious sector public figures are perceived as leaders because of their positions as heads of religious congregations; therefore, legitimate power is the base for their influence. Their personal achievement is often limited to their position in the church. Their response to blacks' status is more reactive than proactive. Rarely do they offer policy solutions; rather they see their job as getting issues on the agenda. Their rhetoric is more likely to maintain that government has the primary responsibility for improving blacks' status. Their commitment to the Democratic Party as the avenue to improve blacks' status is very strong. They are quick to endorse Democratic Party candidates, and if they choose to seek public office, they are most likely to run as Democrats. Some in this group will seek controversy, but for the most part leaders in this group tend to avoid it. Their contact with the white community tends to be limited.

The second leadership type is the civic/community public figure. Although the religious sector public figure and the civic/community public figure come to their positions via different paths, their paths ultimately cross. The black church is such an influential force in black politics that it often becomes a vehicle by which civic/community public figures receive their legitimacy. The type of power and influence that civic/community public figures have is usually referent or expert. This leadership type often has moderate to high personal achievements (education, occupations, incomes, etc.). Like the religious sector public figure, the civic/ community public figure also tends to be reactive to problems in the black community. However, there are those civic/community public figures just like religious sector public figures that are proactive.

Civic/community public figures tend to seek out controversial matters more than religious sector public figures. They also tend to put the onus for improving blacks' status onto the government in most instances, but increasingly many among this leadership type are beginning to call on the black community to solve its problems with the support of the government. Civic/community public figures tend to have a strong preference for Democratic Party politics and they are more likely to run for elected office as a Democrat. They tend to have more contact with the white community than religious sector public figures.

Organization-based public figures usually head a key local or national (civic or civil rights) organization, or nonprofit organization whose goal is advancing the greater good of the black community. They may also head a social group (such as a fraternal organization, civic group, social club, etc.) whose identity is tied to the black community. Naturally they tend to have a higher personal achievement than most blacks. Their style is usually that of the moderate, and their influence is tied to their expert or referent power: expert power because of the position as the head of an organization concerned with improving the status of the black community, or referent power because of the admiration and respect due to their education or professional status, or because of contributions (often non-financial) made toward the betterment of the larger black community.

Organization-based public figures can be both proactive and reactive in their responses when addressing blacks' status; however, they tend to be more reactive than proactive even though they head or have an affiliation with an organization structured to deal with the issues influencing blacks' status. Because of their position, they tend to avoid controversy. The organization-based public figure tends to maintain that the government and the black community share responsibility for improving the status of the blacks. Their commitment to Democratic Party politics is strong but not as strong as that of religious sector or civic/community public figures. The commitment of organization-based public figures is often tied to the perception of the Democratic Party as friendly toward civil rights and social welfare issues. They tend to have more contact with the white community than religious sector or civic/community public figures.

The professional public figure has the smallest following. They are likely to be young(er), a member of the "new" black middle class and upwardly mobile. They usually have some active relationship with a black organization; however the quality of that relationship varies. They usually have the most contact of all the black public figures with the white community. As a result, professional public figures are likely to be accepted as leaders by whites and blacks. Whites often perceive them as a voice of reason. Their style can range from that of the moderate to that of the conservative. Often their position in life (because of education, income, occupation, etc.) earns these individuals their status. Their position of leadership is often tied to their jobs and their involvement in the community as a result. Thus, they have very high personal achievement and the basis for influence is expert power.

Professional public figures have the least personal contact of all the types of black public figure with the larger black community, and thus visibility in the larger black community is often low profile. Some professional public figures are closely connected to the black community, and some are marginally connected (they are physically removed via residence, employment, etc. from the community but they still have ties to the black community). Of all the leaders in the black community, the professional public figures are the most proactive because they are driven more by economic concerns than social or political concerns. They tend to promote the idea that the black community has the greatest responsibility for improving its status (and mainly via the economic system). Thus, professional public figures advocate less reliance on government to solve problems and more on using the free enterprise system. They have the weakest commitment to using Democratic Party politics as the tool to improving blacks' status. Some are actually closer to the Republican Party in their politics on matters of economic and social welfare policies. Professional public figures tend to avoid controversy at all cost.

The grassroots public figures are "the people's leaders," representing the less affluent segment of the black community and usually emerging from this popula-tion and generally have limited contacts outside the black community. They tend to have very low personal achievements. They are more likely to utilize the race-man/activist style or be very close to it. Ironically, they tend not to be very active in black betterment organizations. Referent power is the basis for their influence, and they are charismatic and widely liked by their followers. Those in the black community who are aware of this type of public figure either "really like" or "really dislike" them. Those who really like them do so because of their willing-ness to stand up and be heard. Thus, grassroots public figures are sometimes considered brazen in their activism, and ironically this is why they are disliked by some in the community. Thus, they do not shy away from controversy.

Grassroots public figures are the most reactive of any of the other leaders, and they evolved as leaders because they are very passionate about something that is happening in the community. Such leaders have limited organizational skills and rarely have an answer to the problem. As a result, they strongly believe that the government has a major responsibility to adopt policies to improve the status of blacks. Rarely do they hold the community or the people responsible for their problems. These leaders are often apolitical; nevertheless, when they are political they tend to have a strong commitment to Democratic Party politics to improve blacks' status. They tend to have little direct contact with the white community.

Blacks' Reaction to Select Black Leaders/Public Figures

As a result of changes in the demographic, geographic, and socioeconomic composition of the black community since the Civil Rights Movement, the community's reaction to certain styles and types of public figure have also changed. Community leaders and public figures come from all walks of life and the church is no longer the primary venue for ascension to that rank. Table 7.1 identifies several individuals who have emerged as black political leaders and public

TABLE 7.1 Leadership Types and Styles of Selected Black Public Figures in the Socioeconomic Transition Era

	Leadership type	Leadership style	Position held
Carol Moseley-Braun	Professional	Moderate	U.S. Senator from Illinois from 1992 to 1998
Jesse Jackson	Civic/Community/ Organization-based	Advocate	Head of Operation PUSH and Candidate for the Democratic Party Nomination 1984 and 1988
Kweisi Mfume	Organization-based/ Professional	Advocate/ Moderate	Former U.S. Representative from Maryland and head of the National Association for the Advancement of Colored People
Clarence Thomas	Professional	Conservative	Associate Justice of the U. S. Supreme Court
Louis Farrakhan	Grassroots/ Organization-based	Race-man	Leader of the Nation of Islam
Colin Powell	Professional	Moderate	Former Chairman of Joint Chiefs of Staff, National Security Advisor, and Secretary of State
Al Sharpton	Civic/community/ Grassroots	Advocate/ Race-man	Minister, Community Activist, National Action Network
Condoleezza Rice	Professional	Moderate/ Conservative	Provost Stanford University, National Security Advisor, and Secretary of State
Barack Obama	Professional	Moderate	Civil Rights Lawyer, U.S. Senator from Illinois, Presidential Nominee for the Democratic Party, and President of the United States

TABLE 7.2 Thermometer Rating of Selected Black Public Figures in the Socioeconomic Transition Era: 1996 (in percent)

	Mean score	Very warm	Warm	Chilly	Very chilly
Carol Moseley-Braun	63.8	43.9	39.4	8.1	8.6
Jesse Jackson	69.8	54.9	32.0	5.4	7.7
Kweisi Mfume	69.3	55.9	29.8	5.9	8.4
Clarence Thomas	41.6	14.5	36.8	18.9	29.9
Louis Farrakhan	51.4	28.1	36.6	12.1	23.2
Colin Powell	66.7	48.2	37.4	6.4	8.0

Source: 1996 National Black Election Study

figures since the late 1980s. As Table 7.1 suggests, black public figures today represent a variety of leadership styles and types. Some public figures utilize multiple leadership styles depending on the circumstances.[23]

Table 7.2 shows how the larger black population responded to select black leaders and public figures in the mid-1990s.[24] Blacks responding to a thermometer-rating question were asked to express their feelings on a scale of 0 to 100. Zero represented a very cold/chilly feeling toward the leader, and 100 represented very warm feelings. For our purposes the 76 to 100 was considered very warm, 51–75 was warm, 26–50 was chilly and 0–25 was very chilly. The data suggested in the 1990s that the advocate style was the most popular among blacks. Jesse Jackson and Kweisi Mfume best represent this style. Jackson had a mean thermometer rating of 69.8, and more than half of the respondents gave Jackson a thermometer rating above 75 percent (very warm). On the other hand, less than 15 percent had chilly or very chilly feelings toward Jackson. Mfume, with his overlapping leadership styles (the advocate and the moderate), had an average score of 69.3 percent. Moseley-Braun and Powell, the two most representative of the moderate style, were also well received within the black community. Although Moseley-Braun and Powell's average scores were not as high as those of Jackson or Mfume, the overall reaction to them was very positive. Powell's average rating was 66.7, and Moseley-Braun's was 63.8. While feelings toward Jackson and Mfume were skewed toward the very warm end of the thermometer, Powell and Moseley-Braun were more evenly distributed between warm and very warm.

When examining the attitudes of blacks toward leaders/public figures with peripheral styles, two things are evident. First, neither the conservative nor the race-man/activist styles was as well received as the advocate or moderate. The average thermometer rating for Louis Farrakhan (the race-man/activist style) was 51.4 compared to 41.6 for Clarence Thomas (the conservative). Second, the race-man/activist style was better received by the black community than the conservative style. Nearly half (48.8 percent) of the black respondents were chilly or very chilly toward Clarence Thomas (a score of 49.9 or less), 36.8 percent felt warm toward him, and only 14.5 percent gave him a very warm rating (a score greater

TABLE 7.3 How Blacks Rate Selected Black Public Figures in the Socioeconomic Transition Era: 2007

	Good influence	Bad influence	Not much influence	Never heard of or don't know
	%	%	%	%
Barack Obama	76	2	9	13
Colin Powell	70	3	17	10
Jesse Jackson	68	5	21	6
Al Sharpton	65	6	19	10
Condoleezza Rice	50	10	27	13
Clarence Thomas	31	18	27	24

Source: Pew Research Center 2007

than 75). On the other hand, 35.3 percent of black respondents gave Louis Farrakhan a chilly or very chilly rating, 35.6 percent a warm rating, and 29.1 percent a very warm rating. One could speculate that blacks tend to be more suspicious of the conservative leadership style than the race-man/activist style.

Table 7.3 suggests how the larger black population responds to different black public figures based on their style.[25] The pattern of support for black leadership styles in 2007 was consistent with that in 1996 with a slight modification. The two public figures with the more moderate leadership style, Barack Obama and Colin Powell, had the most favorable ratings (both above 70 percent). Jesse Jackson (advocate style) and Al Sharpton (advocate/race-man leadership style) were also perceived as having a good influence on the black community. Half (50 percent) of the black population felt that Condoleezza Rice, representing a combination of a moderate and conservative style, had good influence on the black community. Only 31 percent of the black population felt that Clarence Thomas, representing the conservative style, had a good influence on the black community. To a small degree, the data in Table 7.2 and 7.3 reaffirm what appears to be an emerging pattern in black leadership. The moderate and advocate leadership styles continue to be the most effective. However, since the 1990s, the moderate style appears to have become more effective as a leadership style than the advocate. The race-man leadership style still has more appeal among blacks than the conservative.

Individual blacks' reaction to leaders, organizations, and leadership styles varies based on a number of factors including demographics, socioeconomic characteristics, and feelings about race. In an attempt to demonstrate this point, Table 7.4 shows how blacks reacted to select black public figures based on the respondents' level of education, family income, age, racial identity, and racial consciousness. Level of education influenced blacks' reaction toward individual leaders. For the three public figures representing the moderate style (Moseley-Braun, Mfume, and Powell), level of education positively associated with influencing feelings. The data showed that increases in education resulted in an increase in warm feelings toward

TABLE 7.4 Reaction to Select Black Leaders and Leadership Groups based on Selected Characteristics of the Population in the Post-Civil Rights Era

	Education	Family income	Age	Racial identity	Racial consciousness
Carol Moseley-Braun	3.52★★★ (.582)	2.67★★★ (.389)	.066 (.074)	1.09★★ (.394)	1.75★★ (.447)
Jesse Jackson	.151 (.445)	−.551★ (.285)	−.093 (.050)	−.135 (.279)	.598★ (.325)
Kweisi Mfume	3.81★★★ (.669)	.276★★★ (.479)	.093 (.091)	1.01★ (.442)	1.61★★ (.523)
Clarence Thomas	−2.14★★★ (.511)	−1.17★★★ (.327)	.034 (.059)	−.726★ (.337)	−.537 (.372)
Louis Farrakhan	.987 (.570)	.556 (.364)	−.230★★★ (.064)	.921★★ (.367)	2.48★★★ (.413)
Colin Powell	2.59★★★ (.463)	1.35★★★ (.301)	.059 (.052)	.227 (.307)	−.089 (.343)

Source: 1996 National Black Election Study
Unstandardized regression coefficient and standard error in parentheses
Prob ★ < .05 ★★ < .01 ★★★ < .001

all three. On the other hand, the data showed that increases in a black's level of education produced negative change in attitudes toward Thomas (the conservative style). Level of education did not significantly influence feelings toward Jackson (the advocate) or Farrakhan (the race-man/activist).

Family income produced change in feelings toward black leaders/public figures similar to level of education. Like level of education, family income had no significant impact on blacks' feelings toward Farrakhan (the race-man/activist). Increases in family income were also associated with increases in warm feelings toward Moseley-Braun, Mfume, and Powell (the moderates). However, income was associated with negative change in attitudes toward Jackson (the advocate style). That is, an increase in family income was associated with a decrease in warm feelings toward Jackson. Blacks with higher family incomes were inclined to have chilly feelings toward Thomas. Age was least likely to be associated with change in feelings toward black leaders/public figures. It had no significant effect on feelings toward Moseley-Braun, Jackson, Mfume, Thomas, or Powell. It did influence attitudes toward Farrakhan suggesting that increased age resulted in decreased warm feelings for the race-man style. One could infer that the race-man/activist is more appealing to younger members of the black community than it is to older blacks.

Table 7.4 also gauges the effect of racial identity on blacks' feelings toward black leaders and public figures. For purposes here, racial identity is defined as an individual's feelings of closeness, sameness, or connectedness with the larger group.[26] The data show that identification with the racial group did not influence feelings toward Jackson (the advocate leadership style). For blacks, racial identity was associated with increased warmth toward Moseley-Braun and Mfume (representing the moderate leadership style). Support for Powell, as a representative of the moderate leadership style, was not significantly related with racial identity. Perhaps the explanation for the lack of a significant relationship between racial identity and thermometer feeling toward Powell was suspicion of his affiliation with the Republican Party. Racial consciousness was also examined as a factor producing changes in feelings toward public figures and leadership groups. Racial consciousness is a sense of racial realization, recognition of existence, or awareness.[27] Feelings of warmth or coolness toward Jackson were marginally influenced by a sense of racial consciousness.[28] Racial consciousness did not influence feelings toward Thomas or Powell. The data did show that an increase in blacks' level of racial consciousness was associated with increased warm feelings toward Farrakhan. Likewise, the level of racial consciousness was also associated with feelings of warmth toward Moseley-Braun and Mfume.

Conclusion

In the Protest Era, the leaders of the black community were more identifiable. They were unified by matters pertaining to segregation and racial inequality. Sometimes they differed in their beliefs about the best way to address the problems of segregation and racial inequality. They differed in how they became leaders. At the national level, they were identified as leaders because they headed civil rights organizations (e.g., the National Association for the Advancement of Colored People, the Urban League, and the Southern Leadership Conference) and at the local level they were prominent civic and religious leaders and the occasional businessperson. There were many "common folk" at the grassroots level who found themselves thrust into leadership positions on a very small stage because of circumstances. Some of the black leaders in the Protest Era were militant in their activity and rhetoric, and others were not. The church was perhaps the most important source of leadership during the Protest Era for several reasons. First, the church naturally provided one with an instant group of followers. Second, the church offered some degree of economic freedom and protection from retaliation and intimidation.

During the Politics Era problems of segregation and racial inequality were still evident; however their effects on the black community began to differ increasingly based on factors such as class, demographics, and geography. Black leadership styles and types during the Politics Era were very similar to those of the Protest Era. Yet black leaders in the Politics Era differed from those in the Protest Era in one major way. The message and actions of black leaders in the Politics Era shifted from protesting against social injustices to the dismantling of America's system of apartheid and overcoming its effects on the black population. In the Politics Era, black leaders' messages were increasingly about addressing the institutional factors that continued to deny blacks social and economic opportunities.

Interestingly though, after passage of the civil rights legislation and the deaths of several key black leaders of the Civil Rights Era, black leaders in the Politics

Era had difficulty finding their way. The lack of a common point of focus (i.e., dismantling of racial segregation) led to increased competition among black leaders, both locally and nationally, giving rise to what Norman Kelly termed "The Head Negro in Charge Syndrome."[29] This syndrome was described as "a condition in which self-appointed 'leaders' hijack the political process by somehow appealing to blacks' sense of collectivity, while having an agenda that is mostly about them, making them the leader."[30] Thus, the message of seeking opportunity though desegregation in the Protest Era did not carry over to the Politics Era for several reasons. First, changing times made it difficult to appeal to the collective black population based on creating opportunities because the civil rights legislation had opened the doors to new opportunities among blacks in education, employment, and housing. Second, changes in the characteristics of the black community made it more difficult for black leaders to "appeal" to the emerging black community using the leadership styles of the Protest Era. During the Politics Era, the emergence of a more educated black population meant the leaders had to develop leadership styles that appealed to a changing population. Black leaders during this period never came to a consensus about what the focus of the new movement should be and this became problematic in this new era of black politics. Walters and Smith described what emerged as a "black leadership conundrum."[31]

During the Socioeconomic Transition Era, changes in the social and economic composition of the black community gave rise to a different leadership structure. Smith suggested that this transformation was an inevitable consequence of the civil rights revolution[32] because the leadership structure reflected the changes in the socioeconomic, demographic, and geographic composition of the black community. More importantly, these changes made it difficult for a few individuals or organizations to speak to the needs of the larger community. Instead, politics within the black community became pluralistic. Multiple competition groups (much smaller than the traditional groups) emerged, and the focus of these groups and their leaders reflected interests ranging from social, to political, to economic. As a result, black leaders have begun to emerge via nontraditional organizations outside the black community itself and focus on issues extending beyond the traditional civil rights and social welfare concerns.

Smith spoke of a process of cooptation and institutionalization of black leaders that accompanied the civil rights revolution and suggested there were advantages and disadvantages for the black community. One such consequence he concluded was that:

> the incipient incorporation of black leadership into systemic institutions and processes has had the perhaps predictable consequence of further isolating black leadership from the community it would purport to lead. . . . The consequences . . . can only bode conflict and confusion in the future and the further eroding of the much talked about leadership solidarity.[33]

Then there are black leaders who wanted their message to transcend race. However, other blacks frequently accuse black leaders who transcend race as "selling out" or betraying the race.[34] This factor has led many to suggest that black politics is faced with a leadership conundrum.[35] Robert Smith wrote:

> analysis ... of the black freedom struggle leads me to conclude that the results of incorporation are that blacks have lost the capacity to effectively press their demands on the system and that the system has consequently responded to their demands with symbolism, neglect and an ongoing pattern of cooptation. Consequently, black politics has become largely irrelevant in terms of a politics and policies that would address effectively the problems of the race in the post-civil rights era.[36]

The black leadership conundrum continued into the Socioeconomic Transition Era. Perhaps the reasons for the description of black leadership are the unique problems that they must overcome. For one, there is constant tension between the black perspective and the dominant perspective.[37] Blacks and whites still differ significantly in their thinking on many issues, especially on matters pertaining to race and social welfare policy. Black leaders also have to effectively deal with the problem of being in the minority in the decision-making process. According to Covin, even "legitimate black leadership must operate in a context that is controlled by others, a context where the interests of blacks are at odds with that of the larger white society."[38] When black leaders are in positions of political power, their ability to govern can be curtailed by barriers such as contending with other elected officials who are hostile to black interests.[39] Lawson suggested that black leaders' power is limited because they cannot deliver political dividends without the cooperation of their white colleagues.[40] Limited economic resources among their constituents, and often the ability to garner those resources, also hamper black leaders. Black leaders who are effective in utilizing the resources of the black community are likely to arouse antagonisms in the larger community.[41]

The future of black politics in the Socioeconomic Transition Era depends on the community's leadership and ability to establish a common agenda. The leadership problems are partially responsible for the failure of the black community to develop a meaningful agenda. This failure to agree on both a black agenda and ways to advance the black community as a collective political entity occurred for several reasons. First was the inability of black leadership in the Politics Era to establish an agenda beyond the civil rights agenda. The problem here was that the civil rights agenda had been fulfilled, at least legislatively. Second, beyond a few prominent organizations to promote civil rights, there were few organizations in place to organize the populace. Furthermore, the civil rights organizations that existed were most effective in identifying problems and not in formulating and implementing solutions. Third, the lack of organizations to effectively compete with the civil rights organizations in the black community left the door open for the more flamboyant charismatic individual leaders.

Thus, during the Politics Era, the black community lacked effective competition among individual leaders and/or leadership organizations.

Finally, the political leaders that did emerge were the protégés of the Protest Era. In other words, many were mesmerized by the political styles of the Protest Era leaders and sought to emulate their mentors' style and did not build their own ideas or legacy. In the process, many leaders in the Politics Era ended up perfecting the leadership styles of their mentors; as a result, their politics were more about rhetoric than substance. Also important to the future of black politics in the Socioeconomic Transition Era is blacks' ability to mobilize as an electorate and develop and maintain coalitions with other minorities and progressive whites.[42] Smith claims that blacks have not moved forward politically because they have not effectively mobilized, formed coalitions with other minorities, and become part of the government majority group.[43] This too may be a consequence of the leadership conundrum.

8

BEYOND SOCIOECONOMIC STATUS

Other Factors Influencing Black Politics Today

One of the underlying arguments to the point in this is that growing socioeconomic divisions within the black community are increasingly posing a threat to black politics as we knew it. Social, political, and economic interests within the black community are more diverse today than they were in either the Protest or Politics Eras. Furthermore, social and economic changes in society have created an environment that makes the ability to forge a common "black" political agenda increasingly more difficult to achieve. In a strange twist of faith, the same civil rights legislation that was to empower and liberate black people as a community in the United States has created an environment in which the black community now comprises a collection of political sub-communities that are divided by socioeconomic and geographic factors and driven increasingly by individual interests. The social and economic changes in society during the Protest and Politics Eras have set the stage for a shift in the dynamics of black politics today. Because of these changes, black politics today has become more complex than it was in the Protest or Politics Eras. This third era of black politics is one in which blacks' struggle for social and economic significance at the sub-population and individual levels is becoming just as important as blacks' struggle for collective political significance in the Politics Era.

There are several key points to be made about the dynamics of the black community in the Socioeconomic Transition Era that contribute to the complexity of black politics. First, the rise of a new black middle class symbolizes a community in transition and this transition is driven in part by improved social and economic opportunities at the individual level. In the Socioeconomic Transition Era, a significant number of blacks are living a relatively affluent lifestyle. As time passes and we get further away from the Civil Rights Era itself, many blacks will find themselves physically detached from the "black community."

Likewise, many (especially the younger generations) will find themselves mentally detached from the actual social and political struggles of the previous eras of black politics. A consequence of these developments is the potential for a decline of shared aspirations, social bonds, and values among various segments of the community.

Another factor that has contributed to the complexity of black politics today is the emergence of class-based politics as an aspect of black politics. No longer is black politics driven almost exclusively by race. Class has always played a role in black politics, but its role was less defined and less prominent in the past eras of black politics. Class concerns did not drive blacks' political agenda or their behavior in the past. In the Politics and Protest Eras, the influence of class on blacks' political behavior wasn't much greater than that of age, religion, or region. The importance of class to black politics during the Protest and Politics Eras was limited to its role in providing political and social leadership. Despite this role of class in providing leaders in the previous eras of black politics, the group's racial interests were clearly more dominant than the class interests of these leaders in shaping the political agenda. In contrast, today class is becoming a factor within the black community and the foundation upon which subpopulations began to build individualized political agendas.

The changing social and economic dynamics of the black community have contributed to the development of a more complex black politics today. Today's black politics has two dimensions: one external and one internal. Race is still factored as it relates to the external dynamics of black politics today. That is, race matters most in defining blacks' political activity and behavior aimed at those entities outside of the black community. It is in the external dimensions of black politics where blacks show a great deal of political solidarity. The circling of the wagons has remained a fairly consistent characteristic in blacks' political behavior across the three eras of black politics. If anything, the previous findings in this book suggests that the influence of race in American politics has changed more among whites than blacks. This isn't to say that race no longer matters in the politics of white America; rather it is to say that race has been and remains a more stable force in the politics of blacks than in the politics of whites. As a result, when it comes to blacks' politics and political activity in the external context blacks are still rather harmonious in their collective behavior and unified race.

Although class does not factor much in the external politics of the black community, it is a factor in the internal politics of the black community. In the previous eras of black politics, class did not matter because blacks did not differ much over where they thought the group needed to go. Today, there is increasing disagreement over political and policy direction within the group. The increasing socioeconomic divisions within the black community are leading to a lack of consistency in political aspirations, bonds, and values. For example, socioeconomic divisions within the community are, in part, a key contributor to the leadership crisis in the black community. In the Protest and early stage of the Politics Eras of black politics, there was no question about who the black leaders were and who they represented. Black leaders emerged through the same channels regardless of their socioeconomic standing. In the Socioeconomic Transition Era, it is more difficult to identify black leaders and who they speak for within the population because of the diversity within the population and the changes in political tactics (i.e., deracialization). Although the focus to this point has been on the relationship between black politics and the growing socioeconomic divisions within the black community, there are other factors that also serve to define black politics today. To follow are brief discussions of a few of the factors that will also influence black politics as the Socioeconomic Transition Era evolves.

The Changing Nature of Minority Group Politics

Minority politics, in general, embraces those efforts by underrepresented political groups to influence the allocation of society's social, political, and economic resources and determine what the prevailing ideals and values of society will be. It also involves those activities engaged in by minority groups to influence the political conduct of others: namely the majority (or dominant) group. In majority/ minority political relationships, the majority group has a greater capacity to control and influence the allocation of society's social, political, and economic resources and values because of its dominance of the political institutions that allocate these resources. The minority group has a limited capacity to influence the allocation of society's resources, and thus they must depend on a substantial contingent of the majority group to help advance their agenda or form coalitions with other minority groups. The struggle for power (or at least power sharing) can be the foundation for the political relationship between the majority and minority. However, not all minority groups choose to challenge the actions or positions of the majority, nor do they choose to engage in a struggle to share power. Thus, some minority groups choose not to be political. They choose to use their resources to gain influence and power in other arenas (i.e., cultural, social, economic). The minority group in the political process is often marginalized because of social characteristics (such as ethnicity, gender, sexual preference or religion), while others are marginalized because of their size and/or the nature of their agenda among other things. The nature of a minority group's political relationship with the majority can affect their social and economic development, because the attainment of power in one arena can give rise to the gaining of power in another.[1]

Minority group politics has changed considerably since the end of the Protest Era of black politics. In the Protest Era and the first half of the Politics Era, blacks were the principal minority group in the political arena. The political agenda and struggles as they pertained to minority groups were largely tied to the plight of black Americans. Not only was the agenda for minority group politics largely centered on issues pertaining to blacks, but blacks were very influential in forging the political agenda as it related to minorities. It was the protest actions and political activity of blacks that forced the "minority political agenda" onto mainstream politics. During the latter phase of the Protest Era (late 1960s) and initial phase of the Politics Era (early 1970s), blacks began to seek ways to influence the agenda via means such as voting and holding political office. It was the political success of blacks that energized and inspired other political minority groups to flex their social, political, and economic muscles. The young people's protest movement brought an end to the Vietnam War and women were leading the charge for equal rights legislation.

In the latter part of the Politics Era, new minority groups began to move into the political picture. The vast majority of these groups began to emerge because of their plight as ethnic or racial minorities and the awareness and sensitivity that were indirectly brought to their plight by the Civil Rights Movement. These groups became players in the political arena because of their increased activism. Women, whether through the actions of the feminist movement or the changing economic and social dynamics of society, became a major group in the struggle for equal rights and equality. Hispanic and Latino populations also became more influential as economic and political actors. They became key players in the political arena as a minority group because of population growth and the political issues specific to them as an ethnic group (language-related issues, their economic plight, issues surrounding legal and illegal immigration, employment, etc.). As we moved into the Socioeconomic Transition Era, gender-based groups became increasing effective in placing their cause onto the political agenda. Gays (via the Gay Rights Movements) came out of the closet and started to demand equal rights. As a result of the diversity and multicultural movements in society, Asians and other immigrant groups began to emerge as a force in the political arena because of population growth, economic influence, and globalization issues.

It is debatable whether blacks' political status as the principal minority group has been altered by the emergence of new minority groups onto the political scene. Nevertheless, blacks' position as the pre-eminent minority group has been challenged in the Socioeconomic Transition Era by several factors. First, as a political minority the black community has not been able to put forth a solid political agenda beyond the civil rights agenda. Although the black community continues to have social, political, and economic concerns beyond those of the Civil Rights Era, these issues continue to be framed within the civil rights context. Second, the political tactics used by blacks as a political minority in the Socioeconomic Transition Era have not changed since the Protest Era, nor has the black community effectively used their vote to influence the national political agenda. Third, since the end of the Protest Era of black politics, there has been a leadership crisis in the black community. The leaders that emerged in the Politics Era of black politics were closely tied to the Protest Era leadership, and they failed to transition with the changing nature of minority politics. Fourth, the white community found itself at odds over "the African-American Problem." Some whites felt that enough has been done for the black community and it is time to move on. Others acknowledge a problem continues to exist but they are without any clue as to what should be done next. Finally, the nation's focus has moved from issues concerning the larger society to issues concerning the individual. As a consequence Americans in general are not giving much thought to the issues concerning larger society, let alone those affecting groups beyond their own.

Black Organizations Struggle for Influence

A large part of the black community's political success in the Protest Era can be attributed to the presence of strong and viable institutions and organizations. Segregation, as a way of existence, created an environment for black organizations to flourish. Furthermore, segregation forced the development of strong institutions within the black community. The institutions and organizations that emerged during the Protest Era of black politics served two basic functions in the black segregated society. First, they served as a basis for organizing and the establishment of a civil society within the context of a larger society. That is, the act of segregation itself made it necessary for the black community to function as a "society within a society." Many institutions in the black community mirrored those in the larger society, and they were vital to the black community's social, political, and economic development. Rarely did these institutions have much significance outside of the black community. Nevertheless, within the black community they were instrumental in the functioning of the segregated black society. Black organizations and institutions in the Protest Era served to inform, to build social capital, and to give meaning to black life and culture. Second, as the result of an evolutionary process, many of these institutions ultimately came to function as vehicles to challenge segregation and combat the consequences thereof. As a result, many of these institutions were closely involved in politics either directly or indirectly.

During the Protest Era of black politics, there were four major categories of institutions within the black community that were instrumental in the community's social, political, and economic development. First, there were social clubs/organizations that were generally formed around a common interest or recreational activity. Membership of these social clubs/organizations tended to consist of the better informed. As a result, they informally disseminated a lot of information. Because of the nature of the black community's struggle for civil rights, many of these institutions were forced into political action. The second category was civil rights organizations that were formed to address issues of public concern regarding the black community. By their very nature they were active in politics and the composition of these groups cut across all socioeconomic groups in the community. The third category included religious institutions and groups that got their start in churches. Organizations in this category were the least political in the structure, but they played a major role in black politics during the Protest Era. Religious organizations' role in politics was augmented because they constituted a critical mass and because the leader of the group was often very charismatic. Many religious leaders were prominent figures in local politics because of their position. They were also leaders in protest movements because their positions as spiritual leaders give them a level of economic and personal protection. Finally, there were academic institutions. Academic institutions' role in the civil rights movement was very peculiar. On one hand, they were a hotbed for stimulating student activity and involvement in the protest movements. On the other hand, these institutions were very low-key in serving as leadership organizations in the movement itself.

Whereas many black institutions and organizations flourished in segregated society, their existence in the post-segregated society has deteriorated. As the black community transitioned from protest to politics, black organizations' and institutions' involvement in politics began to diminish. During the Politics Era, the struggle to end segregation in the formal sense was over and attention had turned to desegregation of the institutions in larger society. The initial phase of desegregation involved a group-level effort. That is, it involved the racial integration of large institutions such as schools, public accommodations, public facilities and the like. In many cases, mass political actions or protests were preceded by the act of integrating. In the latter phase of the Politics Era, the act of desegregating became an event that occurred at the individual level. Acts of breaking down barriers were very individualized as they occurred in employment, housing, civic, and social organizations.

In the Politics Era, the role that black institutions and organizations played in politics gradually began to change. The role social organizations and academic institutions played in politics, for the most part, was gradually phased out. The dynamics of social organizations changed considerably, and during the Politics Era blacks' membership of social organizations began to change. They began to change in part because of changing demographics and geographic patterns within the black community. Blacks became truly diverse in their social and economic characteristics and where they lived, but perhaps most importantly membership opportunities were not limited to black social clubs nor where there were limitations in the scope and type of social club and organization available for them to join. This was also true in academic institutions. In the late 1960s and early 1970s, many blacks began to attend white institutions of higher education in significant numbers. At most of these white institutions of higher learning, the political activity of blacks began to turn inward. That is, the attention of blacks at these institutions turned away from the politics of the larger society to address the politics and racism that existed at these institutions. Simultaneously, many black institutions of higher learning found themselves engaging in the politics of survival. Questions began to arise about the role and need for black academic institutions in an integrated society. Not to mention that black institutions of higher education found themselves engaged in the politics of resources seeking. As a result the energies and activities of many black students during the Politics Era were focused on the politics within the academic institutions.

The role of black religious institutions in black politics has been rather peculiar. On one hand, they have been reluctant participants in black politics. On the other hand, religious institutions played a vital role in black politics (especially) during the Protest Era and this carried over into the Politics Era. Black churches have a very loyal constituency and they are the only institutions in the black community with a diverse mass following. The black church is the only institution in the black community that brings blacks together for a common purpose regardless of their socioeconomic status. The black church was for a long time the kingmaker in the black community. The black church during the Protest and Politics Eras was a platform to gain influence and to propel one's self into the political arena. Many in the black community who sought leadership positions (whether political or nonpolitical) understood the importance of the black church in achieving that goal. Similarly, many outside of the black community who wanted to get elected also understood the importance of the black church in delivering black votes to a candidate. In the Socioeconomic Transition Era of black politics, the black church's role as the selector of black leadership is weakening, but its role as the anointer of black political leadership is still prevalent. However, the increase in the use of technology and changing demographics and geographic will cause the role of the black church as a selector and screener of black leaders to diminish.

The problems with the role of black civil rights organizations in the Politics Era were twofold. First they failed to adjust to a post-civil rights politics. For the most part, most civil rights organizations remained in protest mode when the general aims of black politics had changed to electoral politics. As a result, most of the civil rights organizations became highly ineffective because they failed to change with the times. Many of these organizations failed to find their niche within the community and they were ineffective in helping to forge a new agenda for the black community. Civil rights organizations at the national, state, and local levels seemed to have difficulty deciding what the focus of the post-Civil Rights Era would be. At the same time, there were challenges being posed to the traditional civil rights organizations from more radical groups on the left. These groups had great appeal among younger blacks. Because of the difficulty black civic organizations had finding their post-civil rights movement niche and purpose, they were slow in determining the Politics Era agenda and they were unable to contribute to the forging of a political agenda for the larger black community.

Many black organizations and institutions in the Socioeconomic Transition Era are struggling for significance within the black community and the larger political arena. Demographic and geographic changes among blacks since the 1980s have made it hard for black organizations to mobilize the masses and this has led to a decline in the role of black institutions in the political arena. Traditional black institutions have had a hard time appealing to and attracting younger generations of blacks who often were not exposed to such organizations, their history, and their purpose. The greatest membership appeal is found among those who remain in (or have very close interaction with) the mainstream black community. In addition, black institutions have not been successful appealing to other groups outside of the black community. In many instances, groups outside of the black community and parallel institutions have chosen to address related political issues on their own terms and often without joining in coalition with black organizations or institutions.

Organizationally, there are several factors that have impeded the ability of black organizations (especially the civic and social-based organizations) from becoming more effective politically today. First, the political prominence of black organizations and institutions has been replaced by "individuals" and "personalities." In black politics, dynamic personalities have always been key components in organizational leadership. However, in the Protest Era of black politics, these dynamic personalities were those of leaders who were linked to well organized and structurally sound organizations. Black cultural values, exceptional oratory skills, and a strong personal presence could quickly propel one to a position of leadership within the black community. This pattern continued into the Politics Era. However in the Socioeconomic Transition Era, the leaders of black political organizations are often better known than the organizations they represent. In many instances, the organizations they represent are merely shadow organizations.

Second, the decentralized nature of national black organizations makes them structurally weak as a political entity. The decentralized nature of many of the black national organizations makes them dependent on the local organization for financial resources. Often leaders in black national organizations are upstaged by local organizational leaders; as a result, they are not as influential in the local community as the local organizations' leader. The strength of the national organization usually lay in its ability to call national attention to local crisis and issues. Today, in times of crisis, national organizations are limited in their ability to offer financial or technical resources to help resolve the problem at hand. Furthermore, the decentralized nature of black organizations tends to make them more reactive than proactive. Finally, while black political organizations have been progressive in their rhetoric, their tactics have not changed with the times. Many black organizations are still in the Protest Era mode of political operations. They have not adjusted their tactics to take advantage of the social and technological changes that have occurred in society. In the Socioeconomic Transition Era of black politics, use of the internet for funding, organizing, and disseminating information are far more effective in getting the message out than many of the tactics used during the Protest Era of black politics.

In Search of a Political Agenda

Cobb and Elder defined agenda setting as a process by which issues are identified and exposure is sought to bring the issue into the public arena for a debate and potential governmental action.[2] A political agenda is a list of issues that a group wishes to have dealt with via the political process. Yvonne Bynoe describes the black political agenda(s) as "status reports" that set out recommendations for actions.[3] Walton and Smith describe it as a broad-based policy agenda that has two primary components: the *rights* and *materials*. The *rights* component is racial in that it focuses primarily on issues specifically related to the plight of blacks as a racial group in America. The *materials* component covers non-racial issues and is intended to benefit the greater society. They conclude, "the black agenda is not really black, but is rather a broad-based liberal reform agenda."[4] The fact that the black community's agenda has become a broad-based liberal reform agenda makes it increasingly difficult to speak of a "black political agenda." There was a time, however, when the pursuit of a black agenda was more than the pursuit of a "liberal reform agenda." Pursuit of a black agenda was a legitimate effort to "set out a course of recommendations" to improve the social, political, and economic quality of life for blacks.

During the Protest Era and the early phase of the Politics Era of black politics, the black community did not have trouble articulating the problems of the "community" and thus the need for an agenda. For the most part, the social, political, and economic conditions and plight of the collective group made it rather easy to identify the concerns of the community. Countless attempts to forge a "black agenda" would be undertaken on many levels. The success of these undertakings varied from place to place. However, as we moved from one era of black politics to another, it became even more of a daunting task to forge a unified black political agenda. Bynoe posits that black agendas failed in the past for two reasons. First, they have failed to bring about change because the support and/or input of the masses were not sought when these agendas were formulated. Second, black political agendas have not met with success because the masses were not provided with specific information about what was needed from them to make the plan work.[5] An alternative explanation is that the failure to forge a black political agenda is the outcome of politics within the black community itself (thus internal politics). The inability to forge a unified black political agenda is the result of growing ideological differences within the black community about how best to address the issues/problems facing the black community.

In the Protest Era, the black agenda was more of a spontaneous reaction to blacks' social, political, and economic conditions of the time. The agenda wasn't so much about planning for future action; rather it was about dealing with the urgency of now. Race and matters of race almost exclusively drove the black agenda. The black agenda that evolved was an immediate reaction to the prejudice, discrimination, and racism of the day that were having a negative impact on the quality of life of blacks regardless of their socioeconomic standing in the community. The issues facing blacks were the same no matter where they were in the U.S., and thus the national issues were the basis for a black political agenda. Consequently the collective necessity of the population (or the notion of for the good of the total population) was the force steering the black political agenda. The major issues that constituted the black political agenda were related to matters of civil rights and desegregation. For the most part, there were no secondary agendas because most blacks felt their socioeconomic status was largely tied to structural discrimination and racism. The circumstances made it easier for blacks (from all walks of life) to pull together to support a common political agenda. The disagreement that existed within the community was largely over how best to address the issues of structural discrimination and racism. The political conditions of the day drove blacks, regardless of their ideology or political orientation, to work together to promote a common agenda.

At the start of the Politics Era, race and racial issues would continue to drive the black political agenda. However, as we got further into the Politics Era, other factors, mainly those related to addressing social welfare and public safety, would begin to influence the community's political agenda. Early on in the Politics Era, there was an attempt to develop a post–civil rights black political agenda via the Gary Declaration as presented to the National Black Political Convention in 1972:

> The Black Agenda is addressed primarily to Black people in America. It is our attempt to define some of the essential changes that must take place in this land as we and our children move to self-determination and true independence. It assumes that no truly basic change for our benefit takes place in Black or White America unless we Black people organize to initiate that change. It assumes that we must have some essential agreement on overall goals, even though we may differ on many specific strategies.[6]

The National Black Political Convention called for actions in the areas of economic and political empowerment, community and human development, and self-determination. The ultimate aim was to define the future path for black political efforts. Among the reasoning behind the Gary Convention was the creation of a national political agenda for the black community. The general feelings were that the American system wasn't working for black people and could not work without fundamental change. The Convention declared that both political parties had betrayed blacks whenever their interests conflicted with that of blacks. It was important for black people to move toward a struggle for fundamental social transformation. Finally, the Convention declared that the blacks in Africa, throughout the Diaspora and people in the third world had fallen prey to the same exploitation and deceit that blacks in America had.[7] There was much discussion at the Gary Convention about the establishment of an independent black political party, but delegates were unable to come to an agreement among the various ideologies to advance this plan and other provisions.[8]

The inability of the Gary Convention delegates to put together a black political agenda because of ideological differences was characteristic of what was happening in the larger community. There was agreement for the most part among the black political community about where the group wanted to go; however, there was significant disagreement about how best to get there. There appeared to be two prevailing beliefs within the black community with regards to this question. One ideology embraced the idea of black independence. There were those advocating that blacks remained culturally and racially independent. This group did not necessarily endorse independence in a physical sense. They certainly supported and valued the premises of the struggle for equal opportunity and equal protection of the law that had occurred during the Protest Era. However, they felt it was important to elevate blackness to the same level as whiteness. This ideology strongly endorsed a pro-black political agenda, and the more extreme elements embraced an anti-white element. Thus, this ideology embraced the promotion of an agenda that enhanced and promoted the social, political, and economic development of race (which included black people in Africa and in the Diaspora).

The other prevailing ideology embraced the idea of interdependence. This ideology supported the notion of blacks merging into the mainstream of America. After all, much of the political efforts of the civil rights movement resulted in calls for desegregation and for blacks to have the opportunity to take advantage of the social, political, and economic opportunities of America that were once denied them. This ideology did not necessarily mean that blacks were willing to abandon their racial and cultural traditions or give up their "blackness." However, it did mean the acceptance of the idea of blacks and whites living in a society in which people "were judged by the content of their character and not the color of their skin." This ideology was one in which greater focus was placed on improving the life chances for blacks at the individual level rather than at the group level.

Later in the Politics Era, collective necessity and political activism started to give way as the main factors steering the black political agenda. Although the black community felt empowered and they were anxious to flex their political muscles, large segments of the community continued to be plagued by an economic despair that required solutions beyond the political arena. Likewise, there were segments of the emerging black middle class that embraced an agenda grounded in improving and increasing blacks' economic opportunities. As a result, the call for economic empowerment began emerging in some quarters as a factor steering the black agenda. As race relations began to falter as one of the most important issues facing America among the vast majority of blacks during the Politics Era, social welfare concerns became the main political issue that galvanized the black community. Into the Socioeconomic Transition Era, social welfare concerns (and public safety) continue to be the common issues upon which blacks are most likely to build a collective agenda. In the Socioeconomic Transition Era, economic empowerment has replaced political empowerment as the preferred activity to improve blacks', as a group, quality of life. Political activism, except in the 2008 presidential, had leveled off and individual or subgroup politics is replacing community-based politics.

The Future of Black Politics

In 2008, Barack Obama became the first U.S. president of African ancestry. Obama, a civil rights lawyer and law professor, cut his teeth in national politics by working on then presidential candidate Bill Clinton's election. Obama was a community advocate and organizer in Chicago and this work led him to run for the Illinois State Senate in 1996. He won the senate election and set his sights on a national legislative position.[9] In 2000, Obama challenged incumbent Bobby Rush, a political icon in Chicago politics and a former member of the Student Non-Violent Coordinating Committee (SNCC) in the mid-1960s and co-founder of the Illinois Black Panther Party.[10] Despite his defeat for the First Congressional House Seat in Illinois, Obama decided to run for the open Illinois U.S. Senate seat in 2004 and he won. Obama defeated his Republican opponent by 43 percentage points. In February of 2007, Obama announced his plans to run for the Office of President of the United States. After a hard-fought primary against Hillary Clinton, the then Senator from New York and former first lady, Obama won the nomination to be the Democratic Party's candidate.[11] In November 2008, Obama defeated Arizona Senator John McCain, receiving 52.9 percent of the votes cast.[12]

Despite Obama holding the highest office in the land, black politics still has not come of age. The black vote contributed greatly to the election of Barack Obama to the office of president of the United States. Obama received 95 percent of the black vote.[13] The white vote divided enough in the 2008 election (55 percent for McCain to 43 percent Obama)[14] and blacks' level of participation increased enough between 2004 and 2008 to give greater influence to the black vote. Voter turnout among blacks was 4.9 percent higher in 2008 than it was 2004. This increase was largely attributed to increased voter participation among young voters (18–29 years of age) and black women. Between 2004 and 2008, the voter turnout rate among young voters increased by 8.7 percent and it increased 5.1 percent among black females. However, the significant increase in the percentage (4.6) of black males voting between the 2004 and 2008 elections should not be devalued. Between 2004 and 2008, the number of blacks voting went from 13.8 million to 15.9 million, an increase of 2.1 million votes. The number of whites voting in the 2008 election was down by 400,000. Blacks increased their share of the electorate from 11.0 percent in 2004 to 12.1 percent in 2008.[15]

Obama's election has several implications for black politics today. Since Obama's election, the notion of America as a post-racial society has been advanced among some quarters of the media. The central idea of America as a post-racial society rests on the notion that the election of Barack Obama is evidence that race has become a non-issue and signifies a society where people are judged by the character and not by the color of their skin. However, this view is not universally shared by all racial groups. For example, in a recent study, 43 percent of blacks said there was "a lot" of discrimination against blacks and 39 percent said there was "some" discrimination against blacks. Over 80 percent of blacks, despite being optimistic about the future, felt there was at least some continuing discrimination against blacks. On the other hand, only 10 percent of white Americans felt there was a "lot" of discrimination against blacks and 31 percent felt there was only "some" discrimination. Hence, roughly 56 percent of whites felt there was only a "little" discrimination against blacks or "none at all."[16]

So, why do most whites feel that racial discrimination is a thing of the past and talk of a post-racial society, while most blacks feel that racial discrimination continues and that we are not in a post-racial society? Both groups would agree that since the end of the Protest Era of black politics, there has been a great deal of progress in our society. Overall, public perceptions of widespread discrimination against blacks has declined since 2001.[17] However, the difference might be in how both define and measure progress. It appears that whites in general define and measure racial progress in a social context, while blacks are more likely to define racial progress in an economic context. The fact that blacks are no longer confined to segregated facilities and the absence of overt discrimination is evidence for many whites of racial progress and thus of a post-racial society. Similarly, whites are increasingly comfortable in their social interaction and relationships with individual blacks even though they may not be comfortable with the larger group. Blacks on the other hand, especially in the Socioeconomic Transition Era, tend to refer to their individual economic well-being or the economic well-being of the group as the measure of progress. While most blacks would agree that there has been much improvement in the social interaction and relationships between blacks and whites, they would also agree that blacks are still more likely to experience discrimination and racism in an economic context than in a social context.

The election of Barack Obama sent different messages to blacks and whites about the future of black politics. For whites, the fact that a large proportion of whites voted for a black presidential candidate is validation for many of them of a post-racial society. Their willingness to support a black candidate demonstrates that whites can be race free in their judgments about blacks and who will lead this nation. In a 2009 Gallup poll, 59 percent of the white respondents felt that relations between blacks and whites would eventually be worked out.[18] The implications are that from a post-racial perspective, black politics would have no future because issues of race no longer matter and when they do matter it is at the individual level and not at the group level. For blacks, Obama's election breathed life into black politics (if only symbolically). It provided blacks with a reason to continue placing demands on the political system from a group perceptive. Ironically, in the first year of Obama's term, the percentage of blacks stating that the relations between blacks and whites will always be a problem rose from 30 to 40 percent. Obama's election unified blacks in ways not seen since the early Politics Era of black politics. It provided blacks (at the group level) with a sense of self-pride and sense of hope. The question now is whether black politics will be able to capitalize on this momentum.

In the same way that Obama's election symbolized "change and hope" for blacks, it also highlighted the transitional nature of black politics today. Obama's campaign and ascendency to the office of president of the United States was a contrast between old-style black politics with that of new-style black politics. The focal point of old-style politics was the political and economic advancement and well-being of the black community. Old-style black politics was largely tied to blacks' racial experiences and a history of subjugation, discrimination, and segregation. Old-style black politicians had a political agenda that was centered on civil rights and improving blacks' social well-being in society. Old-style black politics largely appealed to the black community and liberal whites. Old-style black politicians were less likely to have the political bargaining and negotiation process starting behind closed doors (although it did happen); negotiations often started out in a public arena in the form of protest marches, sit-ins, and public rallies. Old-style black politicians' inner circle was largely made of other blacks. Old-style black politicians saw the black community as their primary constituents. Today's black politician is increasingly adopting a style of politics that is the polar opposite of that of the previous generations of black politicians. This politician is more inclined to focus on the social and economic development of the larger society. The general belief is that emphasis should be placed on improving the quality of life for all groups in society with no special consideration given to race or ethnicity. Thus, the emerging political tactic of black politicians in the Socioeconomic Transition Era is one of deracialized politics. The emerging generation of black politicians is adopting a broad-based agenda where race-specific issues are de-emphasized in favor of race-neutral issues. It is argued that these race-neutral issues would augment opportunity for blacks by creating opportunity for everybody.

The future of black politics today depends on the answer to two questions. First, can black politics survive in the absence of a racialized agenda? Second, does new-style black politics pose a threat to black politics in general? The future of black politics lies somewhere between the extremes of old-style black politics and the emerging style that de-emphasizes race. On one hand, no longer can black politics be driven exclusively by race and the socioeconomic plight of blacks. On the other hand, the political strategy of de-emphasizing race gives legitimacy to those who believe that we have moved into a post-racial society. There can be no black politics in the absence of "racial politics," but "race" does not have to be the primary driving force behind black politics.

NOTES

1 BLACK POLITICS TODAY: THE EVOLUTION

1 King, Kendra, *African-American Politics* (Cambridge, UK: Polity Press, 2010), 219.
2 Gray, Kevin Alexander, *Waiting for Lighting to Strike: The Fundamentals of Black Politics* (Oakland, CA: AK Press, 2008).
3 Kelly, Norman, *Head Negro in Charge Syndrome: The Dead End of Black Politics* (New York: Nation Books, 2004).
4 Bia, Matt, "Is Obama the End of Black Politics?" *The New York Times Magazine* (August 10, 2008).
5 The Frederick Douglas Foundation, "2010 Black Republican Candidates," www.frederickdouglasfoundation.com/2010Candidates.html.
6 Cohen, Cathy, *Democracy Remixed* (New York: Oxford University Press, 2010); Thompson III, J. Phillip, *Double Trouble: Black Mayors, Black Communities, and the Call for a Deep Democracy* (New York: Oxford University Press, 2006).
7 Thompson III, J. Phillip, *Double Trouble: Black Mayors, Black Communities, and the Call for a Deep Democracy* (New York: Oxford University Press, 2006).
8 Lawson, Steven, *Running for Freedom: Civil Rights and Black Politics in America Since 1941* (Oxford, UK: Wiley-Blackwell, 2009).
9 Cohen, Cathy, *Democracy Remixed* (New York: Oxford University Press, 2010); Thompson III, J. Phillip, *Double Trouble: Black Mayors, Black Communities, and the Call for a Deep Democracy* (New York: Oxford University Press, 2006).
10 Ibid.
11 Marable, Manning, *Beyond Black and White: Transforming African-American Politics* (New York: Verso, 1995), 203.
12 Fraser, Carly, "Race, Post-Black Politics, and the Democratic Presidential Candidacy of Barack Obama," in *Barack Obama and African American Empowerment: The Rise of Black America's New Leadership,* edited by Manning Marable and Kristin Clarke (New York: Palgrave Macmillan, 2009).
13 Ali, Omar H., "Black Politics," in *Encyclopedia of African American History, 1986 to the Present: From the Age of Segregation to the Twenty-first Century*, edited by Paul Finkelman (New York: Oxford University Press, 2008).
14 Harris, Frederick, "Toward a Pragmatic Black Politics," in *Barack Obama and African American Empowerment: The Rise of Black America's New Leadership,*

edited by Manning Marable and Kristen Clarke (New York: Palgrave Macmillan, 2010).

15 Ibid.

16 Pohlmann, Marcus, *Black Politics in Conservative America*, second edition (New York: Addison Wesley Longman, Inc., 1999), 10.

17 Hill, Rickey, "The Study of Black Politics: Notes on Rethinking the Paradigm," in *Black Politics and Black Political Behavior: A Linkage Analysis*, edited by Hanes Walton, Jr. (Westport, CT: Praeger, 1994), 11.

18 Hanks, Lawrence, *The Struggle for Black Political Empowerment in Three Georgia Counties* (Knoxville: University of Tennessee Press, 1987), preface.

19 Jordan, Kenneth A. and Modibo M. Kadlie, "Black Politics During the Era of Presidents Reagan and Bush," in *Black Politics and Black Political Behavior: A Linkage Analysis*, edited by Hanes Walton, Jr. (Westport, CT: Praeger, 1994), xxxvi.

20 Hill, Rickey, "The Study of Black Politics: Notes on Rethinking the Paradigm," in *Black Politics and Black Political Behavior: A Linkage Analysis*, edited by Hanes Walton, Jr. (Westport, CT: Praeger, 1994), 11.

21 Winant, H., *Racial Conditions: Politics, Theory and Comparisons* (Minneapolis: University of Minnesota Press, 1994).

22 Harry S. Truman Library and Museum, "Desegregation of the Armed Forces: Chronology," http://www.trumanlibrary.org/whistestop/study_collections/desegregation/large/#1947

23 Pub L. 88–352, 78 Stat. 241, July 2, 1964.

24 "Fair Housing Act". Sec. 801. [42 U.S.C. 3601].

25 "Voting Rights Act of 1965," Pub L. No 89–110, 79 Stat. 445 (current version at 42 U.S.C. 1971gg-8 2003).

26 Horton, Carrel and Jessie Carney Smith, *Statistical Record of Black America* (New York: Gale Research Inc., 1990), 479–480.

27 U.S. Census Bureau, Current Population Survey, November 2008 and earlier reports, Internet Release date: July 2009.

28 Rustin, Bayard, "From Protest to Politics: The Future of the Civil Rights Movement," *Commentary*, 39, no. 2 (1965): 25–31.

29 Tate, Katherine, *From Protest to Politics: The New Black Voters in American Elections*, enlarged edition (New York: Russell Sage Foundation, 1994).

30 Dawson, Michael, *Behind The Mule: Race and Class in African-American Politics* (Princeton, NJ: Princeton University Press, 1994), chapter 1, 4.

31 Marable, Manning, *Race, Reform, and Rebellion: The Second Reconstruction and Beyond in Black America, 1945–2004*, third edition (Jackson: The University Press of Mississippi, 2007), chapters 5 and 6.

32 Dawson, Michael, *Behind The Mule: Race and Class in African-American Politics* (Princeton, NJ: Princeton University Press, 1994), chapter 1, p.4.

33 The original Reconstruction Period, the late 1860s to the late 1870s, was a period in American history in which attempts were made to rebuild the Southern social, political, and economic systems that had been disrupted as a result of the Civil War. One of the aims of the Reconstruction Period was to include and make blacks (as former slaves) an integral and equal part of these systems.

34 Marable, Manning, *Race, Reform, and Rebellion: The Second Reconstruction and Beyond in Black America, 1945–2004*, third edition (Jackson: The University Press of Mississippi, 2007), chapter 7.

35 Engstrom, R. F. and M. D. McDonald, "The Elections of Blacks to City Councils: Clarifying the Impact of Electoral Arrangements on the Seats Population Relationship," *American Political Science Review*, 75 (1981): 344–354; Zax, J. S., "Election Methods and Black and Hispanic City Council Membership," *Social Science Quarterly*, 71 (1990): 339–355; Welch. S., "The Impact of At-large Elections on the Representation of Blacks and Hispanics," *Journal of Politics*, 52 (1990): 1050–1076; Bullock, C. and S.A. McManus,

"Black and Hispanic Council Representatives: Does Council Size Matter?," *Urban Affairs Quarterly*, 29 (1993): 276–298.

36 Lichter, Daniel T., Domenico Parisi, Steven Grice, and Michael Taquino, "Municipal Under Bounding: Annexation and Racial Exclusion in Small Southern Towns," *Rural Sociology*, 72 (2007): 47–69.

37 Horton, Carrel and Jessie Smith, *Statistical Record of Black America* (New York: Gale Research Inc., 1990), 489–490; David Bositis, *Black Elected Officials: A Statistical Summary* (Washington, DC: Joint Center for Political Studies Press, 2001).

38 U.S. Bureau of Census, *Current Population Reports*, P20-504, P20-524, and P20-542.

39 Hamilton, Charles V., "Political Access, Minority Participation, and The New Normalcy," in *Minority Report*, edited by L. W. Dunbar (New York: Pantheon Books, 1982), 3–25.

40 Jynes, Gerald and Robin Williams, A *Common Destiny: Blacks and American Society* (Washington, DC: National Academy Press, 1989), 251.

41 Durant, Thomas J. and Kathleen Sparrow, "Race and Class Consciousness Among Lower and Middle-Class Blacks," *Journal of Black Studies*, 27, no. 3 (January 1997): 334.

42 Marable, Manning, *Race, Reform, and Rebellion: The Second Reconstruction and Beyond in Black America, 1945 to 2006*, third edition (Jackson: University Press of Mississippi, 2007), chapter 9.

43 Ibid.

44 Kilson, Martin, "The New Black Political Class," in *Dilemmas of the New Black Middle Class*, edited by Joseph Washington, Jr. ("The edited writings in this volume . . . were developed for a two-day symposium in the Spring of 1980, sponsored by the University of Pennsylvania's Afro-American Studies Program, entitled 'New Black Middle-Class Prospects.'")

45 Young, I. M., *Justice and the Politics of Difference* (Princeton, NJ: Princeton University Press, 1990), 191.

46 Smith, Robert C., "Black Power and the Transformation from Protest to Politics," *Political Science Quarterly*, 96, no. 3 (1981): 431–443.

47 Ibid.

48 Reference to the lyrics of musical performer James Brown's song "Say it Loud."

49 Hofstede, Geert H., *Culture's Consequences: Comparing Values, Behaviors, Institutions, and Organizations Across Nations* (Thousand Oaks, CA: Sage Publications, 2001), 225.

50 Story, Ronald and Bruce Laurie, *The Rise of Conservatism in America, 1945–2000: A Brief History with Documents* (Boston, MA: Bedford/St. Martins Books, 2007); Schoenwald, Jonathan, *A Time for Choosing: The Rise of Modern American Conservatism* (New York: Oxford University Press, 2001).

51 Marable Manning, *Beyond Black and White: Transforming African-American Politics* (New York: Verso, 1995).

52 Marable, Manning, *Race, Reform, and Rebellion: The Second Reconstruction and Beyond in Black America, 1945–2004*, third edition (Jackson: The University Press of Mississippi, 2007), chapters 6 and 7.

53 DuBois, W. E. B., *The Philadelphia Negro: A Social Study* (Philadelphia: University of Pennsylvania Press, originally printed in 1899 and reprinted in 1996).

54 Michael Dawson, *Behind the Mule: Race and Class in African-American Politics* (Princeton, NJ: Princeton University Press, 1994), 4.

55 Davis, James A., Tom W. Smith, and Peter V. Marsden, *General Social Surveys*, 1972–2006 [CUMULATIVE FILE]. ICPSR04697-v2. (Chicago, IL: National Opinion Research Center [producer], 2007. Storrs, CT: Roper Center for Public Opinion Research, University of Connecticut/Ann Arbor, MI: Inter-university Consortium for Political and Social Research [distributors]), 2007-09-10. doi:10.3886/ICPSR04697.

56 The American National Election Studies (www.electionstudies.org). *The ANES Guide*

to Public Opinion and Electoral Behavior (Ann Arbor: University of Michigan, Center for Political Studies [producer and distributor]).

57 Tate, Katherine, *National Black Election Study* (1996) ICPSR version. Columbus: Ohio State University [producer], 1997; Ann Arbor, MI: Inter-University Consortium for Political and Social Research [distributor], 1998.

58 CBS New/Black Entertainment Television (BET) Monthly Poll, July 2004. ICPSR version. New York: CBS News [producer], 2004; Ann Arbor, MI: Inter-University Consortium for Political and Social Research [distributor], 2005.

59 Jackson, James S., Vincent L. Hutchings, Ronald Brown, and Cara Wong. *National Politics Study, 2004.* ICPSR24483-v1. (Ann Arbor, MI: Inter-University Consortium for Political and Social Research) [distributor], 2009-03-23. doi:10.3886/ICPSR24483.

60 Pew Research Center for Social and Demographic Trends. *Oct 2007 Race Survey* (Sept 5-Oct 5).

61 GSS provides useful information regarding socioeconomic status and opinions on a host of social, political and economic issues. The ANES provides quality data on political participation, public opinions, and voting behavior since 1948. The small black sample size in the yearly studies means there are limitations with using GSS and ANES to draw definitive conclusions about blacks' political behavior and public opinion. Furthermore, it limits the ability to break the samples down into smaller units for purposes of analysis. To overcome this limitation, several study years will be pooled for purposes of analysis. The NBES includes a random sample of the black electorate taken in 1996 and provides information about basic political, social and demographic factors. The 2004 National Political Study provides data about individuals' political attitudes, beliefs, aspirations, and behavior at the turn of the millennium. The CBS/BET Monthly Poll was part of a series that solicited the opinions of only black respondents on a number of issues including the presidency and other political and social issues. The Pew Research Center data will provide information on the issues, attitudes and trends shaping America and the world that included an oversample of blacks.

2 A COMMUNITY IN TRANSITION AND DIVIDING BY CLASS

1 Frazier, E. Franklin, *Black Bourgeoisie: The Rise of a New Middle-Class* (New York: Free Press, 1957), 22–23.

2 Lowery, Mark, "The Rise of the Black Professional Class," *Black Enterprise*, 26, no. 1 (August 1995), 43; Blackwell, James E., *Mainstreaming Outsiders: The Production of Black Professionals* (Dix Hills, NY: General Hall, 1987).

3 Gates Jr., Henry Louis, "The Two Nations of Black America: The Best of Times and Worst of Times," *Brooking Review*, 16, no. 2 (Spring 1998): 4 (4).

4 For our purposes, the terms upper socioeconomic status group and middle class are interchangeable unless otherwise stated.

5 Gilbert, Dennis and Joseph A. Kahl, *The American Class Structure: A New Synthesis* (Belmont, CA: Wadsworth Publishing Company, 1987), chapter 1.

6 Landry, Bart, *Black Working Wives: Pioneers of the American Family Revolution* (Berkeley: University of California Press, 2000), 10.

7 Frazier, E. Franklin, *Black Bourgeoisie: The Rise of A New Middle-Class* (New York: Free Press, 1957); Wilson, William Julius, *The Declining Significance of Race: Blacks and Changing American Institutions* (Chicago, IL: University of Chicago Press, 1978); Landry, Bart, *The New Black Middle Class* (Berkeley: University of California Press, 1987).

8 McAdoo, Harriette P. "Factors Related to Stability in Upwardly Mobile Black Families," *Journal of Marriage and the Family*, 40, no. 4 (1978): 762–778; Bowser, Benjamin P., *The Black Middle-Class: Social Mobility and Vulnerability* (Boulder, CO: Lynne Rienner Publishers, 2007).

9 Collins, Sharon, "The Making of the Black Middle-Class," *Social Problems*, 30, no. 4 (1983): 369–382.

10 Oliver, Melvin L. and Thomas M. Shapiro, *Black Wealth/White Wealth: A New Perspective on Racial Inequality* (New York: Routledge Press, 1997).

11 Billingsley, Andrew, *Black Families in White America* (Englewood Cliffs, NJ: Prentice-Hall, 1968); Pattillo-McCoy, Mary, *Black Picket Fences: Privilege and Peril in the Black Middle-Class Neighborhood* (Chicago, IL: University of Chicago Press, 1999).

12 Marsh, Kris, William Darity, Philip Cohen, Lynne Casper, and Danielle Salters, "The Emerging Black Middle-Class: Single and Living Alone," *Social Forces*, 86, no. 2 (December 2007): 735–762.

13 Levine, Chester, Laurie Salmon, and Daniel Weinberg, "Revising the Standard Occupational Classification System," *Monthly Labor Review Online*, Bureau of Labor Statistics, May 1999, 122, no. 5.

14 The data source used to examine changes in blacks' occupation classification was the 1972–2006 General Social Surveys.

15 Upper white-collar workers included those employed in professional or managerial positions, while lower white-collar workers included those employed in technical, sales, clerical, and other administrative support jobs.

16 1972 to 2006 General Social Surveys.

17 E. Franklin Frazier, *Black Bourgeoisie: The Rise of a New Middle-Class* (New York: Free Press, 1957), 50–51, 52.

18 Table F-23. Families by Total Money Income, Race and Hispanics Origin Households: 1967 to 2008. *Current Population Survey, Social and Economic Supplement*, U.S. Census Bureau.

19 For the purposes of this study, black families were divided into three income groups based on constant 2008 dollars. The lower-income group consisted of families with incomes under $49,999, which was $11,522 under the national median or 81 percent of the national median. The moderate-income group consisted of families with incomes between $50,000 and $99,999 annually, and the upper-income group included families with incomes above $100,000.

20 Frazier, E. Franklin, *Black Bourgeoisie: The Rise of a New Middle-Class* (New York: Free Press, 1957), 22–23.

21 Table A-2 Percent of People 25 Years Old and Over Who Have Completed High School by Race, Hispanic Origin Years 1940 to 2000. U.S. Census Bureau.

22 U.S. Census Bureau, *Statistical Abstract of the U.S.: 1986, 1991, and 2001.*

23 Blackwell, James, *Mainstreaming Outsiders: The Production of Black Professionals* (Dix Hills, NY: General Hall, 1987).

24 The moderate status/education-based group included those individuals with 12 to 15 years of school and the moderate economic-/income-based group included those individuals with a family income between $50,000 and $100,000.

25 The upper status-based group included those individuals with 16 or more years of school and the upper economic-based group included those individuals with a family income above $100,000.

26 The size of the black middle class was tabulated by using the average of the percentage of black families in the upper-income group and the percentage of blacks with 16 or more years of college.

27 Day-Vines, N. L., J. Patton, and J. Baytops, "Counseling African American Adolescents: The Impact of Race and Middle Class Status" *Professional School Counseling*, 7 (2003): 40–51.

28 Hacker, Andrew, *Two Nations: Black and White, Separate, Hostile, Unequal* (New York: Ballantine Books, 1992).

29 Sigelman, Lee and Susan Welch, *Black Americans' Views of Racial Inequality: A Dream Deferred* (Cambridge: Cambridge University Press, 1991).

30 Thernstrom, Stephan and Abigail Thernstrom, "We Have Overcome," *The New Republic*, 217, no. 15 (October 1997): 23 (5).

31 Ibid.

32 "Up From Separatism," *The Economist* (US), 337, no. 7937 (October 21, 1995) 30 (1).

33 Loury, Glenn, "American Tragedy: The Legacy of Slavery in our Cities and Ghettos," *Brooking Review*, 16, no. 2 (Spring, 1998): 36 (5).

34 Manning, Marable, "Beyond Color-Blindness," *The Nation*, 267, no. 20 (December 14, 1998): 29 (1).

35 Sigelman, Lee and Susan Welch, *Black Americans' View of Racial Inequality: The Dream Deferred* (Cambridge: Cambridge University Press, 1991).

36 Hacker, Andrew, *Two Nations: Black and White, Separate, Hostile, Unequal* (New York: Ballantine Books, 1992), 219.

37 Results are based on data found in the General Social Survey (combined 2002–2006) and the 2004 National Politics Study.

38 Wilson, William Julius, *The Declining Significance of Race* (Chicago, IL: University of Chicago Press, 1980).

39 Ibid., 2.

40 Hughes, Michael and Melvin Thomas, "The Continuing Significance of Race Revisited: A Study of Race, Class, and Quality of Life in America, 1972 to 1996," *American Sociological Review*, 63, no. 6 (December 1998): 785–795.

41 Wilson, George and Ian Sakura-Lemessy, "Earning over the Early Work Career Among Males in the Middle-class: Has Race Declined in Its Significance?" *Sociological Perspectives*, 43, no. 1 (2000): 159–171.

42 Wilson, George, "Income in Upper-Tier Occupations Among Males over the First Decade of the Work-Career: Is Race Declining in Its Significance?" *National Journal of Sociology*, 12, no. 1 (Winter 2000): 105–107.

43 D'Amico, Ronald and Nan Maxwell, "The Continuing Significance of Race in Minority Male Joblessness," *Social Forces*, 73, no. 3 (March 1995): 969–991.

44 Steffensmier, Darrel and Stephen DeMuth, "Ethnicity and Sentencing Outcomes in the U.S. Federal Courts: Who is Punished more Harshly?" *American Sociological Review*, 65, no. 5 (October 2000): 705–729.

45 Willie, Charles, "The Inclining Significance of Race," in *Caste and Class Controversy on Race and Poverty: Round Two of the Willie/Wilson Debate*, second edition (New York; General Hall, Inc., 1989), chapter 1.

46 West, Cornel, *Race Matters* (Boston, MA: Beacon Press, 1993), chapter 1.

47 Ibid.

48 Hacker, Andrew, *Two Nations: Black and White, Separate, Hostile, Unequal* (New York: Ballantine Books, 1992), 219.

49 Jones, James M., *Prejudice and Racism*, second edition (New York: The McGraw-Hill Company, 1997), chapter 1.

50 Smith, Robert C., *Racism in the Post-Civil Rights Era* (Albany: State University of New York Press, 1995), chapter 3.

51 Ibid., chapter 4.

52 Tate, Katherine, *From Protest to Politics: The New Black Voters in American Elections* (New York: Russell Sage Foundation, 1993), 23–25.

53 Park, Robert and Ernest W. Burgess, *Introduction to the Science of Sociology*, first edition (Chicago, IL: University of Chicago Press, 1921).

54 Park, Robert, *Race and Culture* (New York: Free Press, 1950), 149–150.

55 Frazier, E. Franklin, *The Negro in the United States* (New York: MacMillan Company, 1949).

56 Frazier, E. Franklin, *Black Bourgeoisie; The Rise of a New Middle-Class* (Glencoe, IL: Free Press, 1957), 191.

57 Bell, Derrick, *Faces at the Bottom of the Well: The Permanence of Racism* (New York: Basic Books, 1992).

58 Swain, Carol, "Affirmative Action: Legislative History, Judicial Interpretations, Public Consensus," in *American Becoming: Racial Trends and Their Consequence*, Volume 1, edited by Neil J. Smelser, William Julius Wilson, and Faith Mitchell (Washington, DC: National Academy Press, 2001), 344.

59 Handy, K., "Race and Class Consciousness among Southern Blacks," *Sociological Spectrum*, 4 (1984): 383–403.

60 Hacker, Andrew, *Two Nations: Separate, Hostile, Unequal* (New York: Ballantine Books, 1992); Thernstrom, Stephan and Abigail Thernstrom, *America in Black and White* (New York: Simon & Schuster, 1997).

61 Pew Research Center's Social and Demographic Trends, "Blacks See Growing Gap Between Poor and Middle Class," Nov. 13, 2007.

62 Fraser, Edward and Edward Kick, "The Interpretive Repertoires of Whites on Race-Targeted Policies: Claims Making of Reverse Discrimination," *Sociological Perspective*, 43 (Spring 2000): 13–27.

63 Kluegel, James and Eliot Smith, *Beliefs About Inequality* (New York: Aldine de Gruyter, 1986).

64 Williams, David, James Jackson, Tony Brown, Myriam Torres, Tyrone Forman, and Kendrick Brown, "Traditional and Contemporary Prejudice and Urban Whites' Support for Affirmative Action and Government Help," *Social Problems*, 46 (November 1999): 503–537.

65 Tuch, Steven and Michael Hughes, "White Racial Policy Attitudes," *Social Science Quarterly*, 77, no. 4 (1996): 711 (23).

3 THE FOUNDATIONS FOR A POLITICAL DIVIDE

1 For purposes of this study, the Baby–Boomer cohort is made up of those individuals born between 1946 and 1964. The pre-Baby-Boomer generations were born before 1946 and those born after 1964 will be referred to as the post-Baby-Boomer generations.

2 U.S. Census Bureau, 1990. Census of Population, *General Population Characteristics*, Table 12.

3 U.S. Census Bureau, "Monthly Postcensal Resident Population, by Single Year of Age, Sex, Race and Hispanic Origin," published June 2000; "Annual Population Estimates by Sex, Race, and Hispanic Origin, selected years from 1990 to 2000," published 26 May 2000; "Projections of the Total Resident Population by 5-year Age Groups, Race, and Hispanic Origin with Special Age Categories: Middle Series, 1999 to 2100," published 13 January 2000 (http://www.census.gov/population/).

4 Ibid.

5 Since 1987, the General Social Survey has included a variable that gives the respondents a socioeconomic index score (SEI). This score, ranging between 17.1 and 97.4, is calculated by using a number of the measures used to determine one's socioeconomic standing. For our purpose here, 17.1 to 43.8 was considered low, 43.9 to 70.6 moderate, and above 70.7 high.

6 Moderate income, based on 2006 dollars, was between $40,000 and $89,000, and a high income for our purposes was greater than $90,000.

7 Wilson, William Julius, *The Declining Significance of Race: Blacks and Changing Americans Institutions* (Chicago, IL: University of Chicago Press, 1978); Smith, James P. and Finis Welch, "Black Economic Progress after Myrdal," *Journal of Economic Literature*, 27 (1989): 519–564; Jaynce, Gerald David and Robin Williams, Jr., *A Common Destiny: Blacks and American Society* (Washington, DC: National Academy Press, 1989).

8 Dawson, Michael, *Behind the Mule: Race and Class in African-American Politics* (Princeton, NJ: Princeton University Press, 1994), 15–16.

9 Those with incomes above $100,000 (based on 2007 dollars).

10 U.S. Census Bureau, *Current Population Survey, Annual Social and Economic Supplements*. Poverty and Health Statistics Branch/HHES Division. Table 2. Poverty Status of People by Family Relationship, Race, and Hispanic Origin: 1959–2006.

11 U.S. Census Bureau, *Current Population Survey, Annual Social and Economic Supplements*. Table H-1. Income Limits for Each Fifth and Top 5 Percent of Black Household: 1967 to 2006.

12 Mazumder, Bhashkar, "Upward Intergenerational Economic Mobility in the United States." Economic Mobility Project. An Initiative of the Pew Charitable Trusts 2008.

13 McBrier, D. B. and G. Wilson, "Going Down? Race and Downward Occupational Mobility for White Collar Workers in the 1990s," *Work and Occupation*, 31, no. 3 (August 2004): 283–322; Hertz, T., "Rags, Riches and Race: The Intergenerational Economic Mobility of Black and White Families in the U.S.," in *Unequal Chances: Family Background and Economic Success*, edited by S. Bowles, H. Gintis, and M. Osborne (New York: Russell Sage Foundation/Princeton, NJ: Princeton University Press, 2005), 165–191; Isaacs, J. B., *Economic Mobility of Black and White Families* (Washington, DC: The Pew Charitable Trusts/Brooking Institution, 2007).

14 McBrier, D. B. and G. Wilson, "Going Down? Race and Downward Occupational Mobility for White Collar Workers in the 1990s," *Work and Occupation,* 31, no. 3 (August 2004): 283–322.

15 Yamaguchi, Kazuo, "Black White Differences in Social Mobility in the Past 30 Years: A Latent-Class Regression Analysis," *Research in Social Stratification and Mobility,* 27 (2009): 65–78.

16 Smith, J. C. and C. Horton, *Statistical Record of Black America,* fourth edition (Detroit, MI: Gail Research Press, 1997); Wilson, F. H., "Rising Tide or Ebb Tide? Recent Changes in the Black Middle Class in the U.S. 1980–1990," *Research in Race and Ethnic Relations,* 8 (1995): 21–55.

17 Wheary, J., *The Future Middle-Class: African Americans, Latinos and Economic Opportunity* (New York: Demos: A Network of Ideas and Action, 2006).

18 Heflin, C. M. and M. Pattillo, "Poverty in the Family: Race, Siblings, and Socioeconomic Heterogeneity," *Social Science Research,* 35, no. 4 (2006): 804–822; Chiteji, N.S. and D. Hamilton, "Family Connections and the Black-White Wealth Gap Among Middle-Class Families," *The Review of Black Political Economy*, 30, no. 1 (2002): 8–28.

19 Charles, C. Z., G. Dinwiddie and D. Massey, "The Continuing Consequences of Segregation: Family Stress and College Academic Performance," *Social Science Quarterly*, 85, no. 5 (2004): 1353–1373; Heflin, C. M. and M. Pattillo, "Poverty in the Family: Race, Siblings, and Socioeconomic Heterogeneity," *Social Science Research,* 35, no. 4 (2006): 804–822; Chiteji, N.S. and D. Hamilton, "Family Connections and the Black-White Wealth Gap Among Middle-Class Families," *The Review of Black Political Economy*, 30, no. 1 (2002): 8–28. Wheary, J., *The Future Middle-Class: African Americans, Latinos and Economic Opportunity* (New York: Demos: A Network of Ideas and Action, 2006).

20 Jargowshy, P. A., "Take the Money and Run: Economic Segregation in the U.S. Metropolitan Areas," *American Sociological Review*, 61 (1996): 984–998; Massey, Douglas and M. Evers, "The Ecology in Inequality: Minorities and the Concentration of Poverty 1970–1980," *American Journal of Sociology*, 95 (1990): 1153–1188.

21 Pattillo-McCoy, M., "The Limits of Out-Migration for the Black Middle-Class," *Journal of Urban Affairs*, 22, no. 3 (2000): 225–241.

22 Adelman, R. M., "Neighborhood Opportunities, Race, and Class: The Black Middle-Class and Segregation," *City and Community*, 3, no. 1 (2004): 43–63.

23 Pattillo-McCoy, M., "The Limits of Out-Migration for the Black Middle-Class," *Journal of Urban Affairs*, 22, no. 3 (2000): 225–241.

24 Hope, J., "The Price They Pay for the Places They Live," in *American Families: Issues in Race and Ethnicity*, edited by C. K. Jacobson (New York: Garland Publishers, 1995), 407–427.

25 Iceland, John, Cicely Sharpe, and Erika Steinmetz, "Class Differences in African-American Residential Patterns in U.S. Metropolitan Areas: 1990–2000," *Social Science Research,* 34 (2005): 252–266.

26 Freeman, Lance, "Is Class Becoming a More Important Determinant of Neighborhood Attainment for African-Americans?" *Urban Affairs Review*, 44, no. 1 (September 2008): 3–26.

27 Park, Robert, *Race and Culture* (New York: Free Press, 1950), 149–150.

28 Gordon, Milton, *Assimilation in American Life: The Role of Race, Religion, and National Origins* (New York: Oxford University Press, 1964).
29 Portes, Alejandro and Min Zhou, "The New Second Generation: Segmented Assimilation and Its Variants," *Annals, AAPSS*, 530 (November 1993): 74–96.
30 Frazier, E. Franklin, *The Negro in the United States* (New York: MacMillan Company, 1949).
31 Frazier, E. Franklin, *Black Bourgeoisie: The Rise of A New Middle-Class* (New York: Free Press, 1957), 191.
32 Smith, Sandra and Mignon R. Moore, "Intraracial Diversity and Relations among African-Americans: Closeness among Black Students at a Predominately White University," *American Journal of Sociology*, 16, no. 1 (July 2000): 1–38.

4 ATTITUDES AND PERCEPTIONS IN BLACK AND WHITE: WHAT THEY SUGGEST ABOUT RACE AND POLITICS

1 Hacker, Andrew, *Two Nations: Black and Whites, Separate, Hostile, Unequal* (New York: Ballantine Books, 1992), chapter 1.
2 Parent, Wayne and Paul Stekler, "Black Political Attitudes and Behavior in the 1990s," in *Blacks and the American Political System*, edited by Huey Perry and Wayne Parent (Gainesville: University Press of Florida, 1995), chapter 3.
3 Schuman, Howard, Charlotte Stech, and Lawrence Bobo, *Racial Attitudes in America: Trends and Interpretations* (Cambridge, MA: Harvard University Press, 1997).
4 Data for the Politics Era were the combined 1985, 1986 and 1987 General Social Surveys.
5 Upper socioeconomic status group for purposes here included all individuals with a junior college degree or higher.
6 Findings based on the combined 2004/2006 General Social Surveys.
7 Data source for Table 4.2c was the combined 1996, 1998 and 2000 American National Election Studies.
8 Source was the combined 1996, 1998 and 2000 American National Election Studies.
9 Jackson, James S., Vincent L. Hutchings, Ronald Brown, and Cara Wong. *National Politics Study, 2004* [Computer file]. ICPSR24483-v1. Ann Arbor, MI: Inter-university Consortium for Political and Social Research [distributor], 2009-03-23. doi:10.3886/ICPSR24483.
10 See General Social Surveys.
11 Bennett, Stephen Earl, "'Know-Nothings' Revisited Again," *Political Behavior*, 18, no. 3 (September 1996): 213–233.
12 Key, V. O., *Southern Politics in State and Nation*, reprint (Knoxville: The University of Tennessee Press, 1949).

5 BLACKS' PUBLIC OPINION TODAY: A QUESTION OF CONSENSUS

1 Welch, Susan and Micheal W. Combs, "Intra-racial Differences in Attitudes of Blacks: Class cleavages or Consensus?" *Phylon*, 46 (2) (Summer 1985): 91–97.
2 Hamilton, Charles V., "Public Policy and Some Political Consequences," in *Public Policy for the Black Community,* edited by Marguerite Ross Barnett and James A. Hefner (New York: Alfred Publishing, Co., 1976).
3 Hamilton, Charles V., "Public Policy and Some Political Consequences," in *Public Policy for the Black Community,* edited by Marguerite Ross Barnett and James A. Hefner (New York: Alfred Publishing, Co., 1976); Dawson, M. C., "A Black Counterpublic?: Economic Earthquakes, Racial Agenda(s), and Black Politics," *Public Culture*, 7, no. 1 (1994): 195–223.
4 Gilliam, Jr., Franklin D., "Black America: Divided by Class?" *Public Opinion*, 9 (February/March 1986): 53–57.

5 Inniss, Leslie Baham and Jeralynn Sittig, "Race, Class, and Support for the Welfare State," *Sociological Inquiry*, 66, no. 2 (Spring 1996): 175–196.
6 Jennings, James, "Race, Class, and Politics in the Black Community of Boston," *The Review of Black Political Economy*, 11 (Fall 1982): 47–63.
7 Gilliam, Jr., Franklin D., "Black America: Divided by Class?" *Public Opinion*, 9 (February/March, 1986): 53–57.
8 Welch, Susan and Lorn Foster, "Class and Conservatism in the Black Community," *American Politics Quarterly*, 15, no. 4 (October 1987): 445–470.
9 Dawson, Michael, *Behind the Mule: Race and Class in African-American Politics* (Princeton, NJ: Princeton University Press, 1994), 72.
10 Allen, Richard, Michael Dawson, and Ronald Brown, "A Schema-Based Approach to Modeling an African-American Racial Belief System," *American Political Science Review*, 83, no. 2 (June 1989): 421–441.
11 Wilson, William, *Declining Significance of Race* (Chicago, IL: University of Chicago Press, 1980).
12 Billings, Charles, "Racial Identity and the Politics of Place: Collectivized Rights and American Democratic Theory," *International Journal of Contemporary Sociology*, 31, no. 2 (October 1994): 297–310.
13 Allen, Richard, Michael Dawson, and Ronald Brown, "A Schema-Based Approach to Modeling an African-American Racial Belief System," *American Political Science Review*, 83, no. 2 (June 1989): 421–441.
14 The American National Election Studies (www.electionstudies.org). *THE ANES GUIDE TO PUBLIC OPINION AND ELECTORAL BEHAVIOR*. Ann Arbor: University of Michigan, Center for Political Studies [producer and distributor].
15 The "other problems" included responses that identified agricultural, governmental functioning, natural resources, and labor issues.
16 National Bureau of Economic Research, Inc., U.S. Census Bureau, Housing and Household Economic Statistics Division, http://www.census.gov/hhes/www/poverty/history/recessn.html.
17 The lower-educated category included individuals with less than a high school education, the moderate-educated group included individuals with a high school education and/or some college, and the higher-educated included individuals with at least a bachelor's degree.
18 Newport, Frank, "Blacks as Conservative as Republicans on Some Moral Issues," Gallup. December 3, 2008.

6 BLACK POLITICS AND THE CONTINUING STRUGGLE FOR POLITICAL INFLUENCE IN THE SOCIOECONOMIC TRANSITION ERA

1 Stone, Chuck, "The Negro Vote: Ceteris Paribus," *Black Political Power in America* (New York: The Bobbs-Merrill Company, 1968).
2 Ibid., chapter 4.
3 Dorn, Edwin, "Rules of Suffrage and Political Equality," *Rules and Racial Equality* (New Haven, CT: Yale University Press, 1979).
4 Ibid. chapter 3.
5 Civil Rights Act of 1964, Public Law 88–352, 78, Statue 241.
6 In 1978, the U.S. Census Bureau began to report voter registration and turnout numbers for the total population (this case would include all blacks over the age of 18) and the citizen population (which included only blacks who were legal residents and qualified to vote). Thus, the total population numbers are generally lower than the citizen population numbers. The numbers used here are based on the average citizen population figures (1978 to 2008) minus total population figures (1978 to 2008) plus the total population for the respective years (1968, 1972 and 1976). This amounts to adding 4 percentage points to the data presented in Table A1. Reported Voting and Registration, by Race,

Hispanic Origin, Sex and Age for Groups: November 1964 to 2008, U.S. Census Bureau, Current Population November 2008 and earlier reports: Internet release date: July 2009.

7 Voter registration and turnout tend to be the lower for the 18-to-21 age group.

8 U.S. Census Bureau, Table A1. Reported Voting and Registration, by Race, Hispanic Origin, Sex and Age for Groups: November 1964 to 2008, Current Population November 2008 and earlier reports: Internet release date: July 2009.

9 Five age groups: 18 to 24; 25 to 44; 45 to 64, 65 to 74; and 75 plus.

10 U.S. Census Bureau, Reported Voting and Registration, by Race, Hispanic Origin, Sex and Age for the U.S., November 2000, Internet release date, May 2002, and November 2004, Internet release date: May 25, 2005.

11 Table A1. Reported Voting and Registration, by Race, Hispanic Origin, Sex and Age for Groups: November 1964 to 2008, U.S. Census Bureau, Current Population November 2008 and earlier reports: Internet release date: July 2009. Table A1 did not provide "citizen population" data for the 1964 through 1976 election years. The figures provided for elections between 1964 and 1976 are an estimate based on the "citizen population" average for the presidential elections between 1980 to 2008 minus the average total population figures for presidential elections (1980 to 2008). This figure was then added to the total population voter registration for the respective presidential election years of 1964, 1968, 1972 and 1976. Overall, this formula amounted to 3.8 percentage points being added to the data presented in Table A1 for the 1964, 1968, 1970, 1972, 1974 and 1976 election years.

12 Grant, Moyra, *Key Ideas in Politics* (Cheltenham, UK: Nelson Thornes, 2003), 21.

13 The information is based on data found in the 1948 to 2002 and 2004 American National Election Studies. For purposes of analysis, the presidential election year and the previous off-year election were combined to produce the results. Reference in the text will be made only to the presidential election year.

14 These figures are based on the averages derived from the responses to the party identification questions in the General Social Survey and American National Election Studies for the respective years.

15 Reeves, Keith, *Voting Hopes or Fears?: White Voters, Black Candidates and Racial Politics in America* (New York: Oxford University Press, 1997), chapter 1.

16 Lamis, Alexander, *Southern Politics in the 1990s* (Baton Rouge: Louisiana State University Press, 1999), chapter 1, 8.

17 Rhodes, Terrel, *Republicans in the South: Voting for the State House, Voting for the White House* (Westport, CT: Praeger Publishers, 2000), chapter 6.

18 Key, V. O., *Southern Politics in States and Nations* (New York: Knopf, 1949), 227.

19 Rhodes, Terrel, *Republicans in the South: Voting for the State House, Voting for the White House* (Westport, CT: Praeger Publishers, 2000), chapter 6.

20 Carmines, Edward G. and James Stimson, *Issue Evolution: Race and the Transformation of American Politics* (Princeton, NJ: Princeton University Press, 1989).

21 Lublin, David, *The Republican South: Democratization and Partisan Change* (Princeton, NJ: Princeton University Press, 2004).

22 Lamis, Alexander, *Southern Politics in the 1990s* (Baton Rouge: Louisiana State University Press, 1999), chapter 13, 384.

23 Murphy, Reg and Hal Gulliver, *The Southern Strategy* (New York: Charles Scribner's Sons, 1971), chapter 1.

24 Black, Earl and Merle Black, *The Rise of Southern Republicans* (Cambridge, MA: The Belknap Press of Harvard University Press, 2002).

25 Lamis, Alexander, *Southern Politics in the 1990s* (Baton Rouge: Louisiana State University Press, 1999), chapter 1.

26 Goodman, Walter, "Brown versus Board of Education: Uneven Results 30 Years Later," *New York Times*, May 17, 1984: ProQuest Historical Newspaper *The New York Times* (1951–2004).

27 Reeves, Keith, *Voting Hopes and Fears?: White Voters, Black Candidates and Racial Politics in America* (New York: Oxford University Press, 1997), 29.

28 Walton, Hanes, Jr. and Robert Smith, *American Politics and the African American Quest for Universal Freedom* (New York: Longman Press, 2000), chapter 7.
29 Source for data was *New York Times, Week in Review, The Electorate: A Political Portrait, November 6, 2004* http://www.nytimes.com/packages/pdf/politics/20041107/_px_ELECTORATE.xls.
30 Data for Asians' support of Democratic candidates before 1992 were not available.
31 Local Exit Polls—Election Center 2008—Elections & Politics from CNN.com, http://www.cnn.com/ELECTION/2008/results/polls.
32 Alabama, Arkansas, Delaware, Florida, Georgia, Kentucky, Louisiana, Maryland, Mississippi, North Carolina, Oklahoma, South Carolina, Tennessee, Texas, Virginia, and West Virginia.
33 Tate, Katherine. NATIONAL BLACK ELECTION STUDY, 1996 [Computer file]. ICPSR version. Columbus: Ohio State University [producer], 1997. Ann Arbor, MI: Inter-university Consortium for Political and Social Research [distributor], 2004. doi:10.3886/ICPSR02029.

7 BLACK POLITICAL LEADERSHIP TODAY

1 Bass, Bernard, *Stogdill's Handbook of Leadership: A Survey of Theory and Research* (New York: Free Press, 1989); Bass, Bernard, "From Transactional to Transformational Leadership: Learning to Share the Vision," *Organizational Dynamics*, 18, no. 3 (Winter, 1990): 19–31.
2 Smith, Robert C., *We Have No Leaders: African-American in the Post-Civil Rights Era* (Albany: State University of New York Press, 1996), 21–22.
3 Myrdal, Gunnar, *An American Dilemma: The Negro Problem and American Democracy* (New York: Harper and Row, 1944 [1962]).
4 Wilson, James Q., *Negro Politics: The Search for Leadership* (Glencoe, IL: Free Press, 1960), chapter 9.
5 Burgess, M., *Negro Leadership in a Southern City* (Chapel Hill: University of North Carolina Press, 1962).
6 Thompson, D., *The Negro Leadership Class* (Englewood Cliffs, NJ: Prentice-Hall, 1963).
7 Burgess, M., *Negro Leadership in a Southern City* (Chapel Hill: University of North Carolina Press, 1962); Matthew, James and Donald Prothro (New York: Harcourt, Brace & World, Inc., 1966); Ladd, E., *Negro Political Leadership* (Ithaca, NY: Cornell University Press, 1966).
8 Thompson, D., *The Negro Leadership Class* (Englewood Cliffs, NJ: Prentice-Hall, 1963).
9 Burgess, M., *Negro Leadership in a Southern City* (Chapel Hill: University of North Carolina Press, 1962).
10 Thompson, D., *The Negro Leadership Class* (Englewood Cliffs, NJ: Prentice-Hall, 1963).
11 Matthew, James and Donald Prothro, *Negroes and New Southern Politics* (New York: Harcourt, Brace & World, Inc., 1966).
12 Burgess, M., *Negro Leadership in a Southern City* (Chapel Hill: University of North Carolina Press, 1962); Thompson, D., *The Negro Leadership Class* (Englewood Cliffs, NJ: Prentice-Hall, 1963).
13 Matthew, James and Donald Prothro, *Negroes and New Southern Politics* (New York: Harcourt, Brace & World, Inc., 1966).
14 McCormick II, Joseph, "How African American Men View Various African American Leadership Types: Findings from the Million Man March," in *Black and Latino/a Politics: Issues in Political Development in the United States*, edited by William Nelson and Jessica Perez-Monforti (Miami, FL: Barnhardt and Ash, 2005), 143–155.
15 McCormick II, J. P., and Charles Jones, "The Conceptualization of Deracialization: Thinking Through the Dilemma," in *Dilemmas in Black Politics: Issues of Leadership and Strategy,* edited by Georgia Persons (New York: Harper Collins, 1993), 66–84.

16 Kilson, Martin, "Problems of Black Politics: Some Progress, Many Difficulties," *Dissent,* 36, no. 4 (1989): 526–534.

17 Chideya, Farai, "The Role of Political Racialization in the Neutralization of the Black Electorate," in *Race and Politics: New Challenges and Responses for Black Activism,* edited by James Jennings (New York: Verso, 1997), chapter 10, 161–173.

18 Marable, Manning, "A New Black Politics." *The Progressive,* 54, no. 8 (1990): 18–23.

19 Holden, Matthew, *The Politics of the Black "Nation"* (New York: Chandler Publishing Company, 1973), chapter 1.

20 Wilson, James Q., *Negro Politics: The Search for Leadership* (Glencoe, IL: Free Press, 1960), chapter 10.

21 Ibid.

22 French, J. and B. Raven, *The Bases of Social Power* (Ann Arbor, MI: Institute for Social Research, 1959).

23 The individuals were chosen primarily based on the availability of data.

24 Results based on 1996 National Black Election Study.

25 Pew Research Center: A Social and Demographic Report, "Optimism about Black Progress Declines: Blacks See Growing Values Gap Between Poor and Middle Class," released November 13, 2007.

26 The racial identity variable was computed using the variables OV1 (what happens to blacks affects me), QW1 (what happens to blacks has a lot to do with me), and QW2 (being black determines how you are treated) in the 1996 National Black Election Study.

27 The racial consciousness variable was computed using the E2C (blacks should always shop in black-owned stores), QK1 (blacks should form their own political party), and E2A (blacks should attend Afro-centric schools) variables in the 1996 National Black Election Study.

28 This conclusion is drawn using a probability set at 10.

29 Kelly, Norman, *The Head Negro in Charge Syndrome, The Dead End of Black Politics: A Controversial Critique of Black Politics and Intellectual Leadership in America* (New York: Nation Books, 2004), 7–8.

30 Ibid.

31 Walters, Ronald and Robert Smith, *African American Leadership* (Albany: State University of New York Press, 1999).

32 Smith, Robert C., *We Have No Leaders: African Americans in the Post-Civil Rights Era* (Albany: State University of New York Press, 1996), chapter 4.

33 Smith, Robert, *We Have No Leaders: African-Americans in the Post-Civil Rights Era.* (Albany: State University of New York Press, 1996), 137.

34 Smith, Robert and Richard Seltze, *African Americans Leadership* (Albany: State University of New York Press, 1999), chapter 4.

35 Smith, Robert and Richard Seltzer, *African American Leadership* (Albany: State University of New York Press, 1999), chapter 4; Kelly, Norman, *The Head Negro in Charge Syndrome, The Dead End of Black Politics: A Controversial Critique of Black Politics and Intellectual Leadership in America* (New York: Nation Books, 2004).

36 Smith, Robert C., *We Have No Leaders: African-Americans in the Post-Civil Rights Era* (Albany: State University of New York Press, 1996), 21–22.

37 Walters, Ronald and Robert C. Smith, *African-American Leadership* (Albany: State University of New York Press, 1999), chapter 4.

38 Covin, David, "Reflections on the Dilemmas of African-American Leadership," in *Dilemmas of Black Politics: Issues of Leadership and Strategy,* edited by Georgia Person (New York: Harper Collins College Publishers, 1993), chapter 2.

39 Barker, Lucius, Mack Jones, and Katherine Tate, *African-Americans and the American Political System,* fifth edition (Englewood Cliffs, NJ: Prentice Hall, 1999).

40 Lawson, Steven, *Running for Freedom: Civil Rights and Black Politics in America Since 1941,* second edition (New York: McGraw Hill, 1997), chapter 5.

41 Walters, Ronald and Robert C. Smith, *African-American Leadership* (Albany: State University of New York Press, 1999), chapter 4.

42 Browning, Rufus, Dale Marshall, and David Tabb, *Protest is Not Enough: The Struggle of Blacks and Hispanics in Urban Politics* (Berkeley: University of California Press, 1984), 242–243.

43 Ibid.

8 BEYOND SOCIOECONOMIC STATUS: OTHER FACTORS INFLUENCING BLACK POLITICS TODAY

1 McCleskey, Clifton, *Political Power and American Democracy* (Pacific Grove, CA: Brooks/ Cole Publishing Co., 1989), chapter 12.

2 Cobb, Roger and Charles Elder, *Participation in American Politics: The Dynamics of Agenda-Building*, second edition (Baltimore, MD: Johns Hopkins University Press, 1983).

3 Bynoe, Yvonne, *Stand and Deliver: Political Activism, Leadership and Hip Hop Culture* (Brooklyn, NY: Soft Skull Press, 2002), 34.

4 Walton, Hanes and Robert Smith, *American Politics and the African American Quest for Universal Freedom* (New York: Longman Press, 2008), chapter 8.

5 Bynoe, Yvonne, *Stand and Deliver: Political Activism, Leadership and Hip Hop Culture* (Brooklyn, NY: Soft Skull Press, 2002), chapter 4.

6 Singer, Alan, Boris Bittker, C. J. Munford, and Charles Ogletree, Jr., *Redress for Historical Injustices in the United States: On Reparations for Slavery, Jim Crow and Their Legacies* (Durham, NC: Duke University Press, 2007), 600.

7 "The National Black Political Agenda," in *The Black Power Movement, Part 1: Amiri Baraka from Black Arts to Black Radicalism*, edited by Komozi Woodard, Randolph Boehm, and Daniel Lewis (Bethesda, MD: University Publications of America, 2000), microfilm, reel 3.

8 Bynoe, Yvonne, *Stand and Deliver: Political Activism, Leadership and Hip Hop Culture* (Brooklyn, NY: Soft Skull Press, 2002), chapter 4.

9 "Barack Obama." 2010. Biography.com. 8 Mar 2010, http://www.biography.com/articles/Barack-Obama-12782369.

10 Congressman Bobby Rush, Biography and Legislative Focus found at http://www.house.gov/rush/bio.shtml.

11 "Barack Obama." 2010. Biography.com. 8 Mar 2010, http://www.biography.com/articles/Barack-Obama-12782369.

12 *2008 Official Presidential General Election Results* General Election Date: 11/04/08, http://www.fec.gov/pubrec/fe2008/2008presgeresults.pdf.

13 "Election Results 2008," *The New York Times*, Wednesday, November 5, 2008 http://elections.nytimes.com/2008/results/president/exit-polls.html.

14 Ibid.

15 Lopez, Mark Hugo and Paul Taylor, "Dissecting the 2008 Electorate: Most Diverse in U.S. History," Pew Research Center, Washington, DC (April 30, 2009).

16 "Blacks Upbeat about Blacks Progress, Prosperity: A Year After Obama Election," Pew Research Center released January 12, 2010. http://Pewresearch.org/pubs/1459/year-after-obama-election-black-public-opinion.

17 Ibid.

18 Newport, Frank, "Little 'Obama Effect' on Views about Race Relations," Gallup, October 29, 2009.

BIBLIOGRAPHY

Adelman, R. M., "Neighborhood Opportunities, Race, and Class: The Black Middle-Class and Segregation," *City and Community*, 3, no.1 (2004): 43–63.

Ali, Omar H., "Black Politics," in *Encyclopedia of African American History, 1986 to the Present: From the Age of Segregation to the Twenty-first Century*, edited by Paul Finkelman (New York: Oxford University Press, 2008).

Allen, Richard, Michael Dawson, and Ronald Brown, "A Schema-Based Approach to Modeling an African-American Racial Belief System," *American Political Science Review*, 83, no.2 (June 1989): 421–441.

Barker, Lucius, Mack Jones, and Katherine Tate, *African-Americans and the American Political System*, fifth edition (Englewood Cliffs, NJ: Prentice Hall, 1999).

Bass, Bernard, "From Transactional to Transformational Leadership: Learning to Share the Vision," *Organizational Dynamics*, 18, no.3 (Winter, 1990): 19–31.

Bass, Bernard, *Stogdill's Handbook of Leadership: A Survey of Theory and Research* (New York: Free Press, 1989).

Bell, Derrick, *Faces at the Bottom of the Well: The Permanence of Racism* (New York: Basic Books, 1992).

Bennett, Stephen Earl, "'Know-Nothings' Revisited Again," *Political Behavior*, 18, no.3 (September: 1996): 213–233.

Bia, Matt, "Is Obama the End of Black Politics?" *The New York Times Magazine* (August 10, 2008).

Billings, Charles, "Racial Identity and the Politics of Place: Collectivized Rights and American Democratic Theory," *International Journal of Contemporary Sociology*, 31, no.2 (October 1994): 297–310.

Billingsley, Andrew, *Black Families in White America* (Englewood Cliffs, NJ: Prentice-Hall, 1968).

Black, Earl and Merle Black, *The Rise of Southern Republicans* (Cambridge, MA: The Belknap Press of Harvard University Press, 2002).

Blackwell, James, *Mainstreaming Outsiders: The Production of Black Professionals* (Dix Hills, NY: General Hall, 1987).

Bositis, David, *Black Elected Officials: A Statistical Summary* (Washington, DC: Joint Center for Political Studies Press, 2001).

Bowser, Benjamin P., *The Black Middle-Class: Social Mobility and Vulnerability* (Boulder, CO: Lynne Rienner Publishers, 2007).

Browning, Rufus, Dale Marshall, and David Tabb, *Protest is Not Enough: The Struggle of Blacks and Hispanics in Urban Politics* (Berkeley: University of California Press, 1984), 242–243.

Bullock, C. and McManus, S. A., "Black and Hispanic Council Representatives: Does Council Size Matter?," *Urban Affairs Quarterly*, 29 (1993): 276–298.

Burgess, M., *Negro Leadership in a Southern City* (Chapel Hill: University of North Carolina Press, 1962).

Bynoe, Yvonne, *Stand and Deliver: Political Activism, Leadership and Hip Hop Culture* (Brooklyn, NY: Soft Skull Press, 2002).

Carmines, Edward G. and James Stimson, *Issue Evolution: Race and the Transformation of American Politics* (Princeton, NJ: Princeton University Press, 1989).

CBS New/Black Entertainment Television (BET) Monthly Poll, ICPSR version. New York: CBS News [producer], July 2004; Ann Arbor, MI: Inter-University Consortium for Political and Social Research [distributor], 2005.

Charles, C. Z., G. Dinwiddie, and D. Massey, "The Continuing Consequences of Segregation: Family Stress and College Academic Performance," *Social Science Quarterly*, 85, no.5 (2004): 1353–1373.

Chideya, Farai, "The Role of Political Racialization in the Neutralization of the Black Electorate," in *Race and Politics: New Challenges and Responses for Black Activism*, edited by James Jennings (New York: Verso, 1997), 161–173.

Chiteji, N. S. and D. Hamilton, "Family Connections and the Black-White Wealth Gap Among Middle-Class Families," *The Review of Black Political Economy*, 30, no.1 (2002): 8–28.

Civil Rights Act of 1964, Public Law 88–352, 78, Statue 241.

Cobb, Roger and Charles Elder, *Participation in American Politics: The Dynamics of Agenda-Building*, second edition (Baltimore, MD: Johns Hopkins University Press, 1983).

Cohen, Cathy, *Democracy Remixed* (New York: Oxford University Press, 2010).

Collins, Sharon, "The Making of the Black Middle-Class," *Social Problems*, 30, no.4 (1983): 369–382.

Covin, David, "Reflections on the Dilemmas of African-American Leadership," in *Dilemmas of Black Politics: Issues of Leadership and Strategy*, edited by Georgia Person (New York: Harper Collins College Publishers, 1993): 17–37.

D'Amico, Ronald and Nan Maxwell, "The Continuing Significance of Race in Minority Male Joblessness," *Social Forces*, 73, no.3 (March 1995): 969–991.

Davis, James A., Tom W. Smith, and Peter V. Marsden, *General Social Surveys, 1972–2006* [CUMULATIVE FILE] [Computer file]. ICPSR04697-v2. Chicago, IL: National Opinion Research Center [producer], 2007. Storrs, CT: Roper Center for Public Opinion Research, University of Connecticut/Ann Arbor, MI: Inter-university Consortium for Political and Social Research [distributors], 2007–09-10. doi:10.3886/ICPSR04697.

Dawson, M. C., "A Black Counterpublic?: Economic Earthquakes, Racial Agenda(s), and Black Politics," *Public Culture*, 7, no.1 (1994): 195–223.

Dawson, Michael, *Behind the Mule: Race and Class in African-American Politics* (Princeton, NJ: Princeton University Press, 1994).

Day-Vines, N. L., J. Patton, and J. Baytops, "Counseling African American Adolescents: The Impact of Race and Middle Class Status," *Professional School Counseling*, 7 (2003): 40–51.

Dorn, Edwin, "Rules of Suffrage and Political Equality," in *Rules and Racial Equality* (New Haven, CT: Yale University Press, 1979).

Dred Scott v. Sandford, 60 U.S. 393, 417, 450–451 (1857).

DuBois, W. E. B., *The Philadelphia Negro: A Social Study* (Philadelphia: University of Pennsylvania Press, 1899/1996).

Durant, Thomas J. and Kathleen Sparrow, "Race and Class Consciousness Among Lower and Middle-class Blacks," *Journal of Black Studies*, 27, no.3 (January 1997): 334 (18).

The Economist (US), "Up from Separatism," 337, no. 7937 (October 21, 1995): 30 (1).

Engstrom, R. F. and M. D. McDonald, "The Elections of Blacks to City Councils: Clarifying The Impact of Electoral Arrangements on the Seats Population Relationship," *American Political Science Review*, 75 (1981): 344–354.

"Fair Housing Act". Sec. 801. [42 U.S.C. 3601].

Fraser, Carly, "Race, Post-Black Politics, and the Democratic Presidential Candidacy of Barack Obama," in *Barack Obama and African American Empowerment: The Rise of Black America's New Leadership*, edited by Manning Marable and Kristin Clarke (New York: Palgrave Macmillan, 2009).

Fraser, Edward and Edward Kick, "The Interpretive Repertoires of Whites on Race-targeted Policies: Claims Making of Reverse Discrimination," *Sociological Perspective*, 43 (Spring 2000): 13–27.

Frazier, E. Franklin, *Black Bourgeoisie: The Rise of a New Middle-class* (Glencoe, IL: Free Press, 1957).

Frazier, E. Franklin, *The Negro in the United States* (New York: MacMillan Company, 1949).

Frederick Douglas Foundation, "2010 Black Republican Candidates," www.frederick-douglasfoundation.com/2010Candidates.html.

Freeman, Lance, "Is Class Becoming a More Important Determinant of Neighborhood Attainment for African-Americans?" *Urban Affairs Review*, 44, no.1 (September 2008): 3–26.

French, J. and B. Raven, *The Bases of Social Power* (Ann Arbor, MI: Institute for Social Research, 1959).

Gates Jr., Henry Louis, "The Two Nations of Black America: The Best of Times and Worst of Times," *Brooking Review*, 16, no. 2 (Spring 1998): 4.

Gilbert, Dennis and Joseph A. Kahls, *The American Class Structure: A New Synthesis* (Belmont, CA: Wadsworth Publishing Company, 1987).

Gilliam, Jr., Franklin D., "Black America: Divided by Class?" *Public Opinion*, 9 (February/March, 1986): 53–57.

Goodman, Walter, "Brown versus Board of Education: Uneven Results 30 Years Later," *New York Times*, May 17, 1984, ProQuest Historical Newspaper, *The New York Times* (1951–2004).

Gordon, Milton, *Assimilation in American Life: The Role of Race, Religion, and National Origins* (New York: Oxford University Press, 1964).

Grant, Moyra, *Key Ideas in Politics* (Cheltenham, UK: Nelson Thornes, 2003).

Gray, Kevin Alexander, *Waiting for Lighting to Strike: The Fundamentals of Black Politics* (Oakland, CA: AK Press, 2008).

Hacker, Andrew, *Two Nations: Black and White, Separate, Hostile, Unequal* (New York: Ballantine Books, 1992).

Hamilton, Charles V., "Political Access, Minority Participation, and The New Normalcy," in *Minority Report*, edited by L. W. Dunbar (New York: Pantheon Books, 1982), 3–25.

Hamilton, Charles V., "Public Policy and Some Political Consequences," in *Public Policy for the Black Community*, edited by Marguerite Ross Barnett and James A. Hefner (New York: Alfred Publishing, Co., 1976).

Handy, K., "Race and Class Consciousness Among Southern Blacks," *Sociological Spectrum*, 4 (1984): 383–403.

Hanks, Lawrence, *The Struggle for Black Political Empowerment in Three Georgia Counties* (Knoxville: University of Tennessee Press, 1987).

Harris, Frederick, "Toward a Pragmatic Black Politics," in *Barack Obama and African American Empowerment: The Rise of Black America's New Leadership*, edited by Manning Marable and Kristen Clarke (New York: Palgrave MacMillan, 2010).

Harry S. Truman Library and Museum, "Desegregation of the Armed Forces: Chronology," http://www.trumanlibrary.org/whistestop/study_collections/desegregation/large/#1947.

Heflin, C. M. and M. Pattillo, "Poverty in the Family: Race, Siblings, and Socioeconomic Heterogeneity," *Social Science Research*, 35, no.4 (2006): 804–822.

Hertz, T., "Rags, Riches and Race: The Intergenerational Economic Mobility of Black and White Families in the U.S." in *Unequal Chances: Family Background and Economic Success*, edited by S. Bowles, H. Gintis, and M. Osborne (New York: Russell Sage Foundation/Princeton, NJ: Princeton University Press, 2005), 165–191.

Hill, Rickey, "The Study of Black Politics: Notes on Rethinking the Paradigm," in *Black Politics and Black Political Behavior: A Linkage Analysis*, edited by Hanes Walton, Jr. (Westport, CT: Praeger, 1994).

Hofstede, Geert H., *Culture's Consequences: Comparing Values, Behaviors, Institutions, and Organizations Across Nations* (Thousand Oaks, CA: Sage Publications, 2001).

Holden, Matthew, *The Politics of the Black "Nation"* (New York: Chandler Publishing Company, 1973).

Hope, J., "The Price They Pay for the Places They Live" in *American Families: Issues in Race and Ethnicity*, edited by C. K. Jacobson (New York: Garland Publishers, 1995), 407–427.

Horton, Carrel and Jessie Carney Smith, *Statistical Record of Black America* (New York: Gale Research Inc., 1990).

Hughes, Michael and Melvin Thomas, "The Continuing Significance of Race Revisited: A Study of Race, Class, and Quality of Life in America, 1972 to 1996," *American Sociological Review*, 63, no.6 (December 1998): 785–795.

Iceland, John, Cicely Sharpe, and Erika Steinmetz, "Class Differences in African-American Residential Patterns in U.S. Metropolitan Areas: 1990–2000," *Social Science Research*, 34 (2005): 252–266.

Inniss, Leslie Baham and Jeralynn Sittig, "Race, Class, and Support for the Welfare State," *Sociological Inquiry*, 66, no.2 (Spring, 1996): 175–196.

Isaacs, J. B., *Economic Mobility of Black and White Families* (Washington, DC: The Pew Charitable Trusts/Brooking Institution, 2007).

Jackson, James S., Vincent L. Hutchings, Ronald Brown, and Cara Wong. *National Politics Study, 2004* [Computer file]. ICPSR 24483-v1. (Ann Arbor, MI: Inter-university Consortium for Political and Social Research [distributor]), 2009-03-23. doi:10.3886/ICPSR 24483.

Jargowshy, P. A., "Take the Money and Run: Economic Segregation in the U.S. Metropolitan Areas," *American Sociological Review*, 61 (1996): 984–998.

Jaynce, Gerald David and Robin Williams, Jr., *A Common Destiny: Blacks and American Society* (Washington, DC: National Academy Press, 1989).

Jennings, James, "Race, Class, and Politics in the Black Community of Boston," *The Review of Black Political Economy*, 11 (Fall 1982): 47–63.

Jones, James M., *Prejudice and Racism*, second edition (New York: The McGraw-Hill Company, 1997).

Jordan, Kenneth A. and Modibo M. Kadlie, "Black Politics During the Era of Presidents Reagan and Bush," in *Black Politics and Black Political Behavior: A Linkage Analysis*, edited by Hanes Walton, Jr. (Westport, CT: Praeger, 1994).

Jynes, Gerald and Robin Williams, *A Common Destiny: Blacks and American Society* (Washington, DC: National Academy Press, 1989).

Kelly, Norman, *Head Negro in Charge Syndrome: The Dead End of Black Politics* (New York: Nation Books, 2004).

Key, V. O., *Southern Politics in State and Nation*, reprint (Knoxville: University of Tennessee Press, 1949).

Kilson, Martin, "Problems of Black Politics: Some Progress, Many Difficulties," *Dissent*, 36, no.4 (1989): 526–534.

Kilson, Martin, "The New Black Political Class," in *Dilemmas of the New Black Middle Class*, edited by Joseph Washington, Jr. ("The edited writings in this volume … were developed for a two-day symposium in the Spring of 1980, sponsored by the University of Pennsylvania's Afro-American Studies Program, entitled 'New Black Middle-Class Prospects'").

King, Kendra, *African-American Politics* (Cambridge, UK: Polity Press, 2010).

Kluegel, James and Eliot Smith, *Beliefs About Inequality* (New York: Aldine de Gruyter, 1986).

Lamis, Alexander, *Southern Politics in the 1990s* (Baton Rouge, Louisiana State University Press, 1999).

Landry, Bart, *Black Working Wives: Pioneers of the American Family Revolution* (Berkeley: University of California Press, 2000).

Lawson, Steven, *Running for Freedom: Civil Rights and Black Politics in America Since 1941* (Oxford, UK: Wiley-Blackwell, 2009).

Lichter, Daniel T., Domenico Parisi, Steven Grice, and Michael Taquino, "Municipal Under Bounding: Annexation and Racial Exclusion in Small Southern Towns," *Rural Sociology*, 72 (2007): 47–69.

Lopez, Mark Hugo and Paul Taylor, "Dissecting the 2008 Electorate: Most diverse in U.S. history," Pew Research Center, Washington, DC (April 30, 2009).

Lublin, David, *The Republican South: Democratization and Partisan Change* (Princeton NJ: Princeton University Press, 2004).

Marable, Manning, "A New Black Politics," *The Progressive*, 54, no.8 (1990): 18–23.

Marable, Manning, *Beyond Black and White: Transforming African-American Politics* (New York: Verso, 1995).

Marable, Manning, "Beyond color-blindness," *The Nation*, 267, no.20 (December 14, 1998): 29 (1).

Marable, Manning, *Race, Reform, and Rebellion: The Second Reconstruction and Beyond in Black America, 1945–2004*, third edition (Jackson: The University Press of Mississippi, 2007).

Marsh, Kris, William Darity, Philip Cohen, Lynne Casper, and Danielle Salters, "The Emerging Black Middle-Class: Single and Living Alone," *Social Forces*, 86, no.2 (December 2007): 735–762.

Massey, Douglas and M. Evers, "The Ecology in Inequality: Minorities and the Concentration of Poverty 1970–1980," *American Journal of Sociology*, 95 (1990): 1153–1188.

Matthew, James and Donald Prothro, "Harcourt, Brace & World, Inc (New York)" in *Negro Political Leadership*, edited by E. Ladd (Ithaca, NY: Cornell University Press, 1966).

Mazumder, Bhashkar, "Upward Intergenerational Economic Mobility in the United States." Economic Mobility Project. An Initiative of the Pew Charitable Trusts (2009).

McAdoo, Harriette P., "Factors Related to Stability in Upwardly Mobile Black Families," *Journal of Marriage and the Family*, 40, no.4 (1978): 762–778.

McBrier, D. B. and G. Wilson, "Going Down? Race and Downward Occupational Mobility for White Collar Workers in the 1990s," *Work and Occupation*, 31, no.3 (August 2004): 283–322.

McCleskey, Clifton, *Political Power and American Democracy* (Pacific Grove, CA: Brooks/Cole Publishing Co., 1989).

McCormick II, Joseph, "How African American Men View Various African American Leadership Types: Findings from the Million Man March," in *Black and Latino/a Politics: Issues in Political Development in the United States*, edited by William Nelson and Jessica Perez-Monforti (Miami, FL: Barnhardt and Ash, 2005), 143–155.

McCormick II, Joseph, and Charles Jones, "The Conceptualization of Deracialization: Thinking through the Dilemma," in *Dilemmas in Black Politics: Issues of Leadership and Strategy*, edited by Georgia Persons (New York: Harper Collins, 1993), 66–84.

Murphy, Reg and Hal Gulliver, *The Southern Strategy* (New York: Charles Scribner's Sons, 1971).

Myrdal, Gunnar, *An American Dilemma: The Negro Problem and American Democracy* (New York: Harper and Row, 1944 (1962)).

National Bureau of Economic Research, Inc., U.S. Census Bureau, Housing and Household Economic Statistics Division, http://www.census.gov/hhes/www/poverty/history/recessn.html.

Newport, Frank, "Blacks as Conservative as Republicans on Some Moral Issues," Gallup. December 3, 2008.

Newport, Frank, "Little "Obama Effect" on Views About Race Relations," Gallup, October 29, 2009.

Oliver, Melvin L. and Thomas M. Shapiro, *Black Wealth/White Wealth: A New Perspective on Racial Inequality* (New York: Routledge Press, 1997).

Parent, Wayne and Paul Stekler, "Black Political Attitudes and Behavior in the 1990s," in *Blacks and the American Political System*, edited by Huey Perry and Wayne Parent (Gainesville: University Press of Florida, 1995), chapter 3.

Park, Robert, *Race and Culture* (New York: The Free Press, 1950).

Park, Robert and Ernest W. Burgess, *Introduction to the Science of Sociology*, first edition (Chicago, IL: University of Chicago Press, 1921).

Pattillo-McCoy, M., *Black Picket Fences: Privilege and Peril in the Black Middle-Class Neighborhood* (Chicago, IL: University of Chicago Press, 1999).

Pattillo-McCoy, M., "The Limits of Out-Migration for the Black Middle-Class," *Journal of Urban Affairs*, 22, no.3 (2000): 225–241.

Pew Research Center's Social and Demographic Trends, "Blacks See Growing Gap Between Poor and Middle Class," Nov. 13, 2007.

Pew Research Center for Social and Demographic Trends, *Oct 2007 Race Survey* (Sept 5–Oct 5, 2007).

Pew Research Center, "Optimism about Black Progress Declines: Blacks See Growing Values Gap Between Poor and Middle Class," A Social and Demographic Report, released November 13, 2007.

Plessey v. Ferguson, 163 U.S. 537; 16 S. Ct. 1138; 41 L. Ed. 256; 1896 U.S.

Pohlmann, Marcus, *Black Politics in Conservative America*, second edition (New York: Addison Wesley Longman, Inc., 1999).

Portes, Alejandro and Min Zhou, "The New Second Generation: Segmented Assimilation and its Variants," *Annals, AAPSS*, 530 (November 1993): 74–96.

Pub L. 88–352, 78 Stat. 241, July 2, 1964.

Reeves, Keith, *Voting Hopes or Fears?: White Voters, Black Candidates and Racial Politics in America* (New York: Oxford University Press, 1997).

Rhodes, Terrel, *Republicans in the South: Voting for the State House, Voting for the White House* (Westport, CT: Praeger Publishers, 2000).

Rustin, Bayard, "From Protest to Politics: The Future of the Civil Rights Movement," *Commentary*, 39, no.2 (1965): 25–31.

Schoenwald, Jonathan, *A Time for Choosing: The Rise of Modern American Conservatism* (New York: Oxford University Press, 2001).

Schuman, Howard, Charlotte Stech, and Lawrence Bobo, *Racial Attitudes in America: Trends and Interpretations* (Cambridge, MA: Harvard University Press, 1997).

Sigelman, Lee and Susan Welch, *Black Americans' Views of Racial Inequality: A Dream Deferred* (Cambridge: Cambridge University Press, 1991).

Singer, Alan, Boris Bittker, C. J. Munford and Charles Ogletree, Jr., *Redress for Historical Injustices in the United States: On Reparations for Slavery, Jim Crow and Their Legacies* (Durham, NC: Duke University Press, 2007).

Smith, J. C. and C. Horton, *Statistical Record of Black America*, fourth edition (Detroit, IL: Gail Research Press, 1997).

Smith, James P. and Finis Welch, "Black Economic Progress after Myrdal," *Journal of Economic Literature*, 27 (1989): 519–564.

Smith, Robert and Richard Seltzer, *African American Leadership* (Albany: State University of New York Press, 1999), Chapter 4.

Smith, Robert., "Black Power and the Transformation from Protest to Politics," *Political Science Quarterly*, 96, no.3 (1981): 431–443.

Smith, Robert., *Racism in the Post-Civil Rights Era* (Albany: State University of New York Press, 1995).

Smith, Sandra and Mignon R. Moore, "Intraracial Diversity and Relations among African-Americans: Closeness among Black Students at a Predominately White University," *American Journal of Sociology*, 16, no.1 (July 2000): 1–38.

Steffensmier, Darrel and Stephen DeMuth, "Ethnicity and Sentencing Outcomes in the U.S. Federal Courts: Who is Punished More Harshly?" *American Sociological Review*, 65, no. 5 (October 2000): 705–729.

Stone, Chuck, "The Negro Vote: Ceteris Paribus," *Black Political Power in America* (New York: The Bobbs-Merrill Company, 1968).

Story, Ronald and Bruce Laurie, *The Rise of Conservatism in America, 1945–2000: A Brief History with Documents* (Boston, MA: Bedford/St. Martins Books, 2007).

Swain, Carol, "Affirmative Action: Legislative History, Judicial Interpretations, Public Consensus," in *American Becoming: Racial Trends and Their Consequence*, Volume 1, edited by Neil J. Smelser, William Julius Wilson, and Faith Mitchell (Washington, DC: National Academy Press, 2001).

Tate, Katherine, *From Protest to Politics: The New Black Voters in American Elections* (New York: Russell Sage Foundation, 1993).

Tate, Katherine, *From Protest to Politics: The New Black Voters in American Elections*, enlarged edition (New York: Russell Sage Foundation, 1994).

Tate, Katherine, *National Black Election Study (Computer File)*. ICPSR version. (Columbus: Ohio State University [producer], 1997; Ann Arbor, MI: Inter-University Consortium for Political and Social Research [distributor], 1998.)

The American National Election Studies (www.electionstudies.org). *The ANES Guide to Public Opinion and Electoral Behavior* (Ann Arbor: University of Michigan, Center for Political Studies [producer and distributor]).

Thernstrom, Stephan, and Abigail Thernstrom, *America in Black and White* (New York: Simon and Schuster, 1997).

Thernstrom, Stephan and Abigail, "We Have Overcome," *The New Republic*, 217, no.15 (October 1997): 23 (5).

Thompson, D., *The Negro Leadership Class* (Englewood, Cliffs, NJ: Prentice-Hall, 1963).

Thompson III., J. Phillip, *Double Trouble: Black Mayors, Black Communities, and the Call for a Deep Democracy* (New York: Oxford University Press, 2005).

Tuch, Steven and Michael Hughes, "White Racial Policy Attitudes." *Social Science Quarterly*, 77, no.4 (1996): 711 (23).

U.S. Census Bureau, *Statistical Abstract of the U. S.: 1986, 1991, and 2001.*

U.S. Census Bureau, *Current Population Reports*, P20–504, P20–524, and P20–542.

U.S. Census Bureau, *Current Population Survey, Annual Social and Economic Supplements.* Poverty and Health Statistics Branch/HHES Division. Table 2. Poverty Status of People by Family Relationship, Race, and Hispanic Origin: 1959–2006.

U.S. Census Bureau, 1990. Census of Population, *General Population Characteristics:* Table 12.

U.S. Census Bureau, *Current Population Survey, Annual Social and Economic Supplements.* Table H-1. Income Limits for Each Fifth and Top 5 Percent of Black Household: 1967 to 2006.

U.S. Census Bureau, *Reported Voting and Registration, by Race, Hispanic Origin, Sex and Age for the U. S., November 2000,* Internet release date, May 2002, and November 2004, Internet release date: May 25, 2005.

U. S. Census Bureau, Table A1. *Reported Voting and Registration, by Race, Hispanic Origin, Sex and Age for Groups: November 1964 to 2008*, Current Population November 2008 and earlier reports: Internet release date: July 2009

"Voting Rights Act of 1965," Pub L. No. 89–110, 79 Stat. 445 (current version at 42 U.S.C. 1971gg-8 2003).

Walters, Ronald and Robert Smith, *African American Leadership* (Albany: State University of New York Press, 1999).

Walton, Hanes, Jr. and Robert Smith, *American Politics and the African American Quest for Universal Freedom* (New York: Longman Press, 2000/2008).

Welch, S., "The Impact of At-large Elections on the Representation of Blacks and Hispanics," *Journal of Politics*, 52 (1990): 1050–1076.

Welch, Susan and Micheal W. Combs, "Intra-racial Differences in Attitudes of Blacks: Class Cleavages or Consensus?" *Phylon*, 46, no.2 (Summer 1985): 91–97.

Welch, Susan and Lorn Foster, "Class and Conservatism in the Black Community," *American Politics Quarterly*, 15, no.4 (October 1987): 445–470.

West, Cornel, *Race Matters* (Boston, MA: Beacon Press, 1993).

Wheary, J., *The Future Middle-Class: African Americans, Latinos and Economic Opportunity* (New York: Demos: A Network of Ideas and Action, 2006).

Williams, David, James Jackson, Tony Brown, Myriam Torres, Tyrone Forman, and Kendrick Brown, "Traditional and Contemporary Prejudice and Urban Whites' Support for Affirmative Action and Government Help.," *Social Problems*, 46 (November 1999): 503–537.

Willie, Charles, "The Inclining Significance of Race," in *Caste and Class Controversy on Race and Poverty: Round Two of the Willie/Wilson Debate*, second edition (New York: General Hall, Inc., 1989).

Wilson, F. H., "Rising Tide or Ebb Tide? Recent Changes in the Black Middle Class in the U.S. 1980–1990," *Research in Race and Ethnic Relations*, 8 (1995): 21–55.

Wilson, George, "Income in Upper-Tier Occupations Among Males over the First Decade of the Work-Career: Is Race Declining in its Significance?" *National Journal of Sociology*, 12, no.1 (Winter 2000): 105–107.

Wilson, George and Ian Sakura-Lemessy, "Earning Over the Early Work Career among Males in the Middle-class: Has Race Declined in its Significance?" *Sociological Perspectives*, 43, no.1 (2000): 159–171.

Wilson, James Q., *Negro Politics: The Search for Leadership* (Glencoe, IL: Free Press, 1960).

Wilson, William Julius, *The Declining Significance of Race: Blacks and Changing Americans Institutions* (Chicago, IL: University of Chicago Press, 1978).

Winant, H., *Racial Conditions: Politics, Theory and Comparisons* (Minneapolis: University of Minnesota Press, 1994).

Yamaguchi, Kazuo, "Black White Differences in Social Mobility in the Past 30 Years: A Latent-class Regression Analysis," *Research in Social Stratification and Mobility*, 27, (2009): 65–78.

Young, I. M., *Justice and the Politics of Difference* (Princeton, NJ: Princeton University Press, 1990).

Zax, J. S., "Election Methods and Black and Hispanic City Council Membership," *Social Science Quarterly*, 71 (1990): 339–355.

INDEX

Note: 'n' after a page number indicates a note; 'f' indicates a figure; 't' indicates a table.